My
Office® 2016

Paul McFedries

que®

800 East 96th Street,
Indianapolis, Indiana 46240 USA

My Office® 2016

Copyright © 2016 by Pearson Education, Inc.

ISBN-13: 978-0-7897-5498-1
ISBN-10: 0-7897-5498-3

Library of Congress Control Number: 2015944950

First Printing: October 2015

Trademarks

Warning and Disclaimer

Special Sales

For information about buying this title in bulk quantities, or for special sales opportunities (which may include electronic versions; custom cover designs; and content particular to your business, training goals, marketing focus, or branding interests), please contact our corporate sales department at corpsales@pearsoned.com or (800) 382-3419.

For government sales inquiries, please contact governmentsales@pearsoned.com.

For questions about sales outside the U.S., please contact international@pearsoned.com.

Editor-in-Chief
Greg Wiegand

Senior Acquisitions Editor
Laura Norman

Development Editor
Brandon Cackowski-Schnell

Managing Editor
Kristy Hart

Senior Project Editor
Lori Lyons

Copy Editor
Geneil Breeze

Indexer
Erika Millen

Proofreader
Kathy Ruiz

Technical Editor
Greg Kettell

Editorial Assistant
Kristen Watterson

Compositor
Kim Scott,
Bumpy Design

Contents at a Glance

Table of Contents

About the Author

Paul McFedries is a Microsoft Office expert and full-time technical writer. Paul has been authoring computer books since 1991 and has more than 85 books to his credit, which combined have sold more than four million copies worldwide. His titles include the Que Publishing books *Formulas and Functions with Microsoft Excel 2016*, *PCs for Grownups*, and *Windows 10 In Depth* (with coauthor Brian Knittel), as well as the Sams Publishing book *Windows 7 Unleashed*. Paul is also the proprietor of Word Spy (www.wordspy.com), a website devoted to *lexpionage*, the sleuthing of new words and phrases that have entered the English language. Please drop by Paul's personal website at www.mcfedries.com or follow Paul on Twitter at twitter.com/wordspy.

Dedication

To Karen

Acknowledgments

If you re-read your work, you can find on re-reading a great deal of repetition can be avoided by re-reading and editing.

—William Safire

In the fast-paced world of computer book writing, where deadlines come whooshing at you at alarming speeds and with dismaying regularity, rereading a manuscript is a luxury reserved only for those who have figured out how to live a 36-hour day. Fortunately, every computer book *does* get reread—not once, not twice, but *many* times. I speak, of course, not of the diligence of this book's author but of the yeoman work done by this book's many and various editors, those sharp-eyed, red-pencil-wielding worthies whose job it is to make a book's author look good. Near the front of the book you find a long list of those hard-working professionals. However, I worked directly with a few folks, and I would like to single them out for extra credit: acquisitions editor Laura Norman, development editors Brandon Cackowski-Schnell and Todd Brakke, project editor Lori Lyons, copy editor Geneil Breeze, Kathy Ruiz, and technical editor Greg Kettell. A heaping helping of thanks to you all!

We Want to Hear from You!

As the reader of this book, you are our most important critic and commentator. We value your opinion and want to know what we're doing right, what we could do better, what areas you'd like to see us publish in, and any other words of wisdom you're willing to pass our way.

We welcome your comments. You can email or write to let us know what you did or didn't like about this book—as well as what we can do to make our books better.

Please note that we cannot help you with technical problems related to the topic of this book.

When you write, please be sure to include this book's title and author as well as your name and email address. We will carefully review your comments and share them with the author and editors who worked on the book.

Email: feedback@quepublishing.com

Mail: Que Publishing
ATTN: Reader Feedback
800 East 96th Street
Indianapolis, IN 46240 USA

Reader Services

Visit our website and register this book at quepublishing.com/register for convenient access to any updates, downloads, or errata that might be available for this book.

Create a new document.

Sign in to your Microsoft account.

Open an existing document.

Create a new document from a template.

In this chapter, you learn about starting the Office 2016 programs, working with documents, and saving your work. Topics include the following:

→ Understanding Office 365 and Office 2016

→ Taking your first steps with Office 2016

→ Creating a new document

→ Preserving your work

→ Working with documents

Getting Started with Office 2016

Most of this book deals with the specific features of six Office 2016 applications—Word, Excel, PowerPoint, Outlook, OneNote, and Access—and a bit later you learn all the most useful and practical techniques that these powerful programs have to offer. However, these programs also have many features in common, and some of these tools and techniques are the most useful and the most important. Sample techniques that fall into these categories include creating documents, saving documents, and duplicating documents.

This chapter takes you through all these techniques, but you begin with an overview of Office 365 and Office 2016 (the Windows version, that is; this book does not cover Office 2016 for Mac).

Understanding Office 365 and Office 2016

We live in a world in which smartphones and tablets garner most of the attention of the technical (and even mainstream) press. This isn't a surprise because technologists and industry insiders have fawned over the latest gadgets for as long as there has been a technology industry. However, gadgets come and go, but one thing has stayed the same over that time: People still need to write, calculate, and present, whether for business or for pleasure.

Microsoft Office is a suite of programs designed to help people do just that. Whether you have a memo to write, a budget to build, a presentation to create, or some notes to jot down, the Office programs have the tools to help you get the job done. Unfortunately, Office is expensive (between $139 and $249, depending on the suite) and difficult to maintain, so most home users have shied away from it.

That is now changing with the introduction of Office 365, which enables everyday folks like you and me to use the Office programs without breaking the bank and without requiring an in-house tech support department.

Learning How Office 365 Works

Office 365 is a subscription-based service that gives you access to the latest Office programs. There are several options for Office 365 subscriptions, but the most popular is Office 365 Home Premium, which offers Word, Excel, PowerPoint, OneNote, Outlook, Publisher, and Access for $10 per month or $99 per year (as of this writing). You're allowed to install these programs on up to five computers, and you can install Office for iPad—a scaled-down version of Office that includes the iPad versions of Word, Excel, PowerPoint, and OneNote—on up to five tablets. Up to five different people can use Office 365, and each person gets 1 TB of storage on OneDrive, Microsoft's online file storage service.

To use Office 365, you (and each person who uses Office 365 in your household) need to have a Microsoft account. This is an email address (it can be one of your existing addresses) that you associate with your Office 365 subscription. By signing in to your account on each computer and tablet where you use Office 365, you get immediate access to your Office 365 settings, customizations, and files. This means, for example, that you can work on a document using a desktop Office program at home, save the document to

OneDrive, and then continue working on the document when you take your notebook or iPad to the local coffee shop.

Try Office 365 Free

If you are not sure whether you want to subscribe to Office 365, you do not have to decide right away. Microsoft offers a free trial that gives you a month to use full-featured versions of each program.

Taking Your First Steps with Office 2016

If you want to use Office 2016 for more than just viewing your documents, you must sign in or create a Microsoft account, and use that account to purchase an Office 365 subscription, if you haven't done so already. This book assumes that you have already downloaded the Office 2016 programs from the Internet and installed them.

Sign In to Your Microsoft Account

Having a Microsoft account means you can save Office documents online in your OneDrive and have your account and application settings follow you from the desktop to the iPad and back. So begin your Office 2016 journey by signing in to your account, if you have one.

1. On your Windows computer (which needs to be connected to the Internet for these steps), open any Office 2016 program. The first time you do this, you see a couple of initial screens that give you an overview; then the sign in dialog box appears.

It's Not All Good

Sharing Usage Data with Microsoft

The initial screen you see when you first start any Office 2016 program asks whether you want to send information to Microsoft. This means sharing data about how you use the Office 2016 applications, as well as statistics generated automatically when an application crashes. This data is anonymous and does not include any personal information, so it's safe to share. However, if you elect to share the data and then later change your mind, you can stop the sharing. To do this, select File, Options; select the Trust Center tab and then select Trust Center Settings. Select the Privacy Options tab and then select to deactivate the Sign Up for the Office Personalized Experience Program check box.

2. Select Sign In. If you need to create an account instead, see the next section, "Create a Microsoft Account."

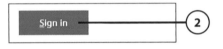

3. Type your Microsoft account email address.

4. Select Next.

5. Type your account password.

6. Select Sign In.

7. Follow the rest of the introductory screen that appears until you see the Office 2016 application you launched in step 1.

Sign in

What email address would you like to use to sign in to Office? (If you already have an account that you use with Office or other Microsoft services, enter it here).

me@here.com ✕

Next

Sign in

Microsoft account What's this?

me@here.com ✕

Password

●●●●●●●●●●●●

Sign in

Create a Microsoft Account

If you don't have a Microsoft account, you need to create one to get the most out of Office 2016. You can use an existing email address for the account or create a new address.

1. On your Windows computer (which needs to be connected to the Internet for these steps), open any Office 2016 program. The first time you do this, you see a couple of initial screens that give you an overview; then the sign in dialog box appears.

2. Select Sign In.

3. Type the email address you want to use (you can change this later if you are creating a new address).

4. Select Next. Microsoft recognizes that your address is not associated with an account.

5. Select Sign Up.

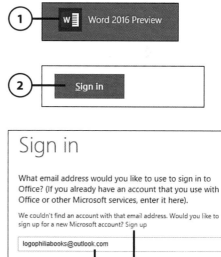

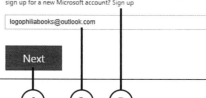

Sign in

What email address would you like to use to sign in to Office? (If you already have an account that you use with Office or other Microsoft services, enter it here).

We couldn't find an account with that email address. Would you like to sign up for a new Microsoft account? Sign up

logophiliabooks@outlook.com

Next

6. Type your first name.

7. Type your last name.

8. Type the email address you want to use.

Creating a New Address

If you don't want to use an existing email address for your Microsoft account, select Or Get a New Email Address, and then specify the address you want.

9. Type the password you want to use.

10. Select your country.

11. Type your ZIP or postal code.

12. Specify your date of birth.

13. Select your gender.

14. Select your phone number country code.

15. Type your phone number.

16. Type the characters your see. This is to prove that you're a real person and not some automated program trying to create the account.

Select here if you want to create a new account.

First name

Paul

Last name

McFedries

Microsoft account name

logophiliabooks@outlook.com

Or get a new email address

Create password

●●●●●●●●●●●●●

8-character minimum; case sensitive

Reenter password

●●●●●●●●●●●●●

Country/region

United States

ZIP code

46290

Birthdate

March | 15 | 1975

Gender

Gender

Male

Help us protect your info

Country code

United States (+1)

Phone number

555-4321

We want to make sure that a real person is creating an account.

Enter the characters you see

New | Audio

ypxwwv

>>>Go Further

YOUR PHONE NUMBER

You need to provide Microsoft with a phone number as a security precaution. If you access your Microsoft account from a new device, Microsoft doesn't know whether it's you trying to access the account or some unauthorized person. To make sure, Microsoft doesn't allow access at first. Instead, it sends a text message to the phone number you provided (or an email message to the address you provided), and you must enter the code from the text message to prove that you're not an intruder.

17. Select Create Account.

Click **Create account** to agree to the Microsoft Services Agreement **and** privacy and cookies statement.

Create account

Sign Out of Your Microsoft Account

If someone else will be using your PC, you might want to sign out of your Microsoft account so that person can't access your online documents and settings.

1. Select File.

2. Select Account.

3. Select Sign Out. The application asks you to confirm.

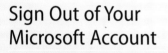

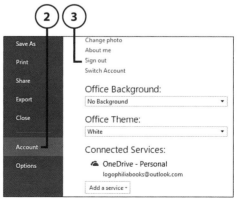

4. Select Yes.

Signing Back In

When you're ready to reconnect to your Microsoft account, select File, select Account, select Sign In, and type your account address. Then select Next, type your account password, and then select Sign In.

Switch Between Office 2016 Applications

Your PC supports multitasking, which means you can have more than one Office 2016 application open at the same time. If you run multiple Office applications, you need to know how to switch between them.

1. Hold down the Alt key and press Tab until the Office application to which you want to switch is selected.

2. Release Alt. Your PC switches to the application. You can also switch to another Office application either by selecting its taskbar button or by selecting any visible part of the application window.

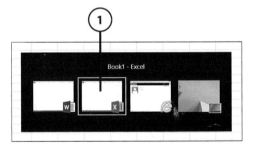

>>>*Go Further*

SWITCHING APPS WITH GESTURES

If you are running Office 2016 on a tablet running Windows 8 or later, you can also switch applications by sliding your finger into the screen from the left edge of the tablet.

Creating a New Document

To perform work in an Office 2016 program, you must first either create a new document or open an existing document. In this section, you learn about creating new documents.

Although OneNote creates a notebook for you to use as soon as you start the program, Word, Excel, and PowerPoint don't create a new document for you automatically. Instead, if you don't need to open an existing document, you must create a new document by hand when you launch these applications. In each case, you can either create a blank document devoid of data and for-matting, or you can create a document from a template, which is a special file that includes prefabricated content and formatting.

>>>*Go Further*

SAVING TIME WITH TEMPLATES

One secret to success in the business world is to let the experts do whatever it is they are good at. Let the salespeople sell, the copywriters write, and the designers design. If you try to do these things yourself, chances are it will take you longer and the results will not be as good.

You can apply the same idea to the Office world. Why spend endless hours tweaking the design and layout of a brochure when a professionally designed brochure is just a few screen clicks or taps away? I am talking about using *templates*, special documents that come with predefined layouts, color schemes, graphics, and text.

Create a Blank Document at Startup

You can create a new, blank document as soon as you start Word, Excel, or PowerPoint.

1. Start the application you want to use.

2. Select the blank option, such as Word's Blank Document icon.

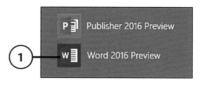

Create a Blank Document After an Office 2016 Application Is Running

If you are already using Word, Excel, or PowerPoint, you can create a new, blank document from within the application.

1. Select File.

Saving a New Document

If the document you're currently working on is new and has never been saved, the application prompts you to save or delete the document. See "Save a New Document" later in this chapter.

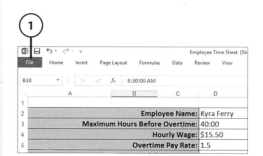

2. Select New to display the New tab.

3. Select the blank option, such as Excel's Blank Workbook icon.

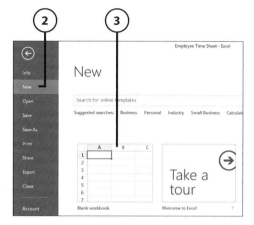

Creating a Document from a Template or Theme

Word and Excel 2016 each come with a few templates that contain preformatted text, images, and other elements that enable you to quickly create great-looking documents such as newsletters, invoices, and budgets. PowerPoint 2016 comes with a few themes, each of which offers preset colors, fonts, and backgrounds for each slide layout.

These were all created by professional designers and most are quite striking. Of course, after you create a document based on a template or theme, you can tweak the layout, design, and text to suit your needs.

1. Select File.

2. Select New to display the New tab.

3. Select a template (in Word or Excel) or a theme (in PowerPoint, which is what's shown here).

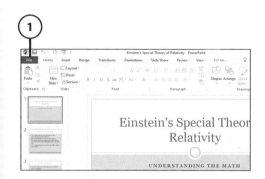

Preserving Your Work

Losing precious data due to a system crash is a constant, nagging worry for PC users. Why is it such a problem? The main reason is that when you work with a document, your PC takes a copy of the document from the hard drive and loads that copy into memory. This makes it much faster to work with the file, but the downside is that all the data loaded into memory is lost when your PC crashes or loses power. This means that if you've made changes to your document, those changes are lost when the memory is wiped.

This is much less of a problem with Office 2016. Yes, the applications still load documents into memory either from the computer's hard drive or from your OneDrive, but the Office 2016 applications have a feature called AutoRecover that automatically saves your data every 10 minutes as you work. The only time you could potentially lose a great deal of work is when you edit a new document that hasn't been saved, or if you perform a great deal of work between automatic saves, so it's important both to save new documents as soon as possible and to save as you work as often as possible.

Save a New Document

To avoid losing work, you should save a new document either immediately, or as soon as you're sure you want to preserve the data you have added to the document.

1. Select File to open the File tab.

2. Select Save As. (You can also select Save.)

3. Select a location, such as OneDrive or your PC.

4. Select a folder within that location. The Save As dialog appears.

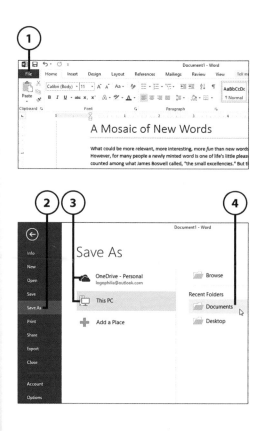

Checking AutoRecover

This is a good time to double-check that the AutoRecover is activated. Select File and then select Options to open the program's Options dialog box. Select the Save tab and then make sure the Save AutoRecover Information Every X Minutes check box is activated. Also, you can use the spin box to set the time interval the program uses to save your work. A shorter interval makes it less likely you'll lose work but might be more taxing on your system.

5. Type a name for the document.

6. Select Save.

>>>*Go Further*

FILE NAMING GUIDELINES

The complete pathname for any document must not exceed 255 characters. The pathname includes not only the filename, but also the location of the document, including the drive letter, colon, folder name (or names), and back-slashes. The filename can include any alphanumeric character, one or more spaces, and any of the following characters:

~ ` @ # $ % ^ & ( ) _ - + = { } [ ] ; , . '

The filename must not include any of the following characters:

* | \ : " < > ?

Create a Duplicate of a Document

One of the best ways to save time and increase your efficiency is to, as the saying goes, avoid reinventing the wheel. With Office 2016, this means that if you need to create a document similar to an existing document, don't build the new document from scratch. Instead, create a copy of the existing document and then modify the copy as needed.

1. Select File.

2. Select Save As.

3. Select the location where you want the duplicate document saved: your OneDrive or your PC.

4. Select the folder that you want to use to store the duplicate document. The Save As dialog box appears.

Safely Saving the Duplicate

To avoid overwriting the existing document, make sure you select a different folder, specify a different filename, or both.

5. Type a name for the copy.

6. Select Save.

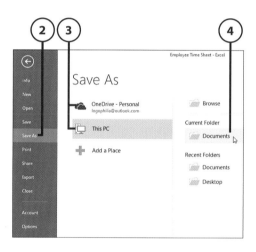

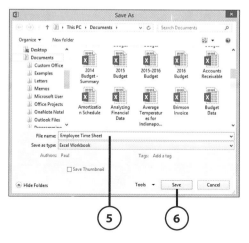

Convert a Document to the Latest Format

Word, Excel, and PowerPoint 2016 can open any document that uses a relatively recent Office file format, which means anything created with Office 97 and later. However, to get the most out of Office 2016, you should use one of the Office Open XML file formats introduced in Office 2007.

1. Open a document that uses an older Office file format.

2. Select File.

3. Select Info.

4. Select Convert. In some Office applications, you see the Save As dialog box.

5. Select Save. The application converts the document to the latest format.

The title bar displays "Compatibility Mode" for documents that use an older file format.

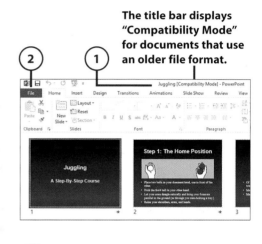

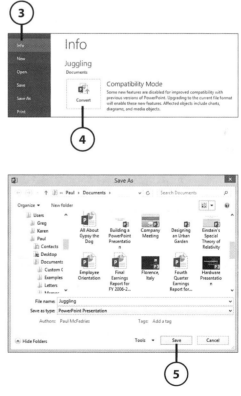

It's Not All Good

Converting Creates a Copy

If you see the Save As dialog box when Office 2016 converts the document to the latest file format, it means the applications creates a copy and leaves the original document untouched. This means it will appear as though you have two documents with the same name. What you actually have is one document (the original) named *something*.doc (to use a Word document as an example) and a second document (the converted copy) named *something*.docx. Office 2016 hides file extensions (the .doc and .docx part of the name), so these two files appear the same, which can be confusing. One way to tell them apart is to examine the icon that appears to the left of each file in the Open dialog. If the icon is the same as the one that appears with the application on the Start screen, then the document uses the latest file format. To avoid this kind of confusion, consider moving the older version of the file to another location.

Working with Documents

You'll spend almost all your Office 2016 time writing, editing, and formatting documents, but you'll also regularly face more mundane document chores, such as opening documents. The rest of this chapter takes you through these day-to-day document tasks.

Open a Document

When you launch an Office 2016 app, the program first displays a window that includes a Recent list, which shows the last few documents that you've worked with in the application. You can reopen a document by selecting it from that list. If you don't see the document you want, you need to use the Open list to select the file.

1. Select File.

2. Select Open to display the Open tab.

Open a Recent Document

If the document is one that you've worked on recently, it might appear on the Recent tab for easy access. Select Recent to see whether the document appears in the list.

3. Select the location where your document resides: your OneDrive or your PC.

4. Select the folder that stores the document. The Open dialog box appears.

5. Select the document.

6. Select Open.

Select Recent to see a list of documents you have recently opened.

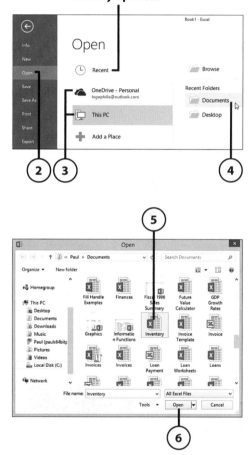

Pin a Document to the Recent Tab

You can make Office 2016 a little more convenient by pinning the documents you use most often to the Recent tab, which ensures they're always no more than three clicks or taps away.

1. Select File.

2. Select Open.

3. Select Recent to display the Recent tab.

4. Select the pin icon next to the document you want to pin.

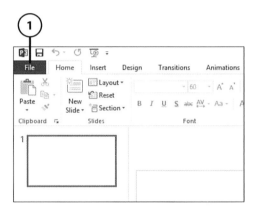

Pinned documents always appear in the Recent tab's Pinned section.

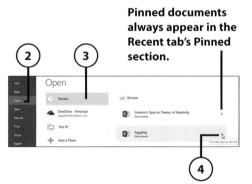

Print a Document

If you prefer to read or edit a document on paper, or you want to file a hard copy, you can print the document.

1. Select File.

2. Select Print to open the Print tab.

Keyboard Shortcut

You can also open the Print tab by pressing Ctrl+P.

3. Select the number of copies you want to print.

4. Select other print settings, as needed.

5. Select Print. Windows prints the document.

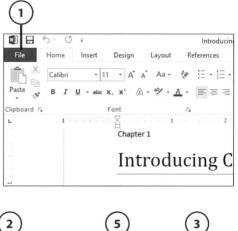

Set the text font and size.

Create bulleted and numbered lists.

Apply styles.

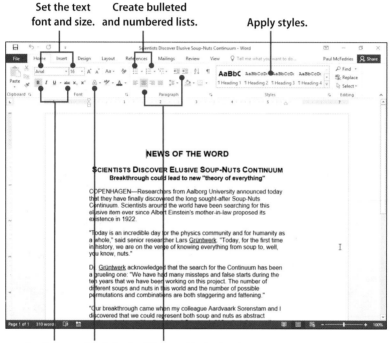

Apply type effects.

Apply text effects.

Align and indent paragraphs.

In this chapter, you learn various ways to format your Office documents, including changing the font, creating bulleted and numbered lists, and applying styles. Topics include the following:

2

→ Setting the typeface, type size, and other font effects

→ Building bulleted and numbered lists

→ Working with indentation and alignment

→ Applying styles to document text

→ Clearing formatting

Formatting Documents

One of the consequences of the domination enjoyed by Microsoft Office in the productivity suite market is that people—particularly businesspeople—now have high expectations. That is, because so many users have access to powerful formatting techniques, people expect the documents they read to have a relatively high level of visual appeal. Send people a plain, unformatted memo and, although they might not throw it away without a glance, they're likely to look down their noses at such a ragtag specimen. So, although you need to always ensure your content is up to snuff (accurate, grammatically correct, and so on), you also need to spend some time making sure that the content looks its best.

When you work with formatting in the Office applications, it helps to remember that there are only three main types of formatting and only two main methods for applying formatting.

Here are the three main types of formatting:

- **Font formatting**—This is also called *character formatting* and it refers to attributes applied to individual characters, including the font (or typeface), type size, text effects (such as bold, italic, and underline), and text color.

- **Paragraph formatting**—This refers to attributes applied to paragraphs as a whole, including indenting, alignment, line spacing, spacing before and after the paragraph, bullets, numbering, background shading, and borders.

- **Document formatting**—This refers to attributes applied to the document as a whole, including margins, headers, footers, columns, page orientation, paper size, columns, line numbers, and hyphenation.

Here are the two main methods for applying font and paragraph formatting in the Office applications:

- **Directly**—With this method, you select individual font and paragraph attributes. If you selected text beforehand, the app applies the formatting to the selection; otherwise, it applies the formatting to the current cursor position.

- **Styles**—A *style* is a predefined collection of formatting options. With this method, when you apply a style to text, the Office application applies all the style's formatting options at once. Also, if you change a formatting option within a style, all the text that uses that style is automatically updated with the new formatting. You learn more about this feature later in this chapter in the "Apply Styles" section.

Selecting Text

Before you can do anything with text in the Office applications—that is, before you can change the font, format paragraphs, apply styles, and so on— you need to tell the app which text you want to work with. You do that by *selecting* the text, which then appears on the screen with a gray background. This applies to text in Word, PowerPoint, and OneNote, as well as to text within an Excel cell. (To learn how to select multiple Excel cells, see "Selecting a Range" in Chapter 7, "Getting More Out of Excel Ranges.")

Select Text with a Mouse

Although you can use a keyboard to select text, in most cases it is easiest to use the mouse.

1. Click to the left of the first word you want to include in the selection. This places the insertion point at the beginning of that word.

2. Drag the mouse to the right. As you drag, the program highlights each letter as the mouse passes over it.

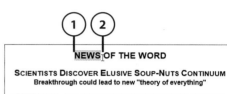

Selecting Text in Excel

Before you can select text in Excel, you must first open the cell for editing by double-clicking the cell. However, if you want to work with the entire cell, you can just click the cell.

Mini Toolbar

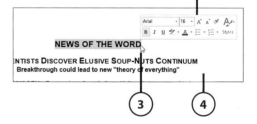

3. When the last character you want to include in the selection is highlighted, release the mouse button. The program displays the Mini Toolbar.

4. When you no longer require the text to be selected, click somewhere else in the document.

Text Selection Tricks

In all the Office applications, you can select a single word by double-clicking that word. In Word, PowerPoint, and OneNote, you can select an entire paragraph by triple-clicking anywhere within that paragraph.

It's Not All Good

Selected Text Is Easily Deleted Text

When you select text—whether just a few characters, a word or two, or one or more paragraphs—the Office applications treat that selection as a single item. That's normally a good thing because it means that when you perform an operation such as applying formatting, the app applies the format to the entire selection. On the downside, it also means that you can easily delete the selection by mistake. If you have text selected when you press a character, the app immediately deletes the selected text and replaces it with that character! So exercise caution around a keyboard while you have text selected. If you do accidentally delete the selected text, immediately click Undo on the Ribbon.

Changing the Font

Windows has turned many otherwise ordinary citizens into avid amateur typographers. Users at cocktail parties the world over debate the relative merits of "serif" versus "sans serif" fonts, expound the virtues of typefaces with names like Calibri and Arial, and throw around font jargon terms such as *ascender*, *feet*, and *points*. (If many, or even all, of these terms are new to you, not to worry: I explain them all in this chapter.)

Okay, so most of us don't take fonts to that extreme. However, we certainly appreciate what they do to jazz up our reports, spreadsheets, and presentations. There's nothing like a well-chosen font to add just the right tone to a document and to make our work stand out from the herd.

I always like to describe fonts as the "architecture" of characters. When you examine a building, certain features and patterns help you identify the building's architectural style. A flying buttress, for example, is usually a telltale sign of a Gothic structure. Fonts, too, are distinguished by a unique set of characteristics. Specifically, four items define the architecture of any character: typeface, type size, type effects, and type color. I discuss all four characteristics in the sections that follow and show you how to apply them using the Office applications.

Understanding Typefaces

A *typeface* is a distinctive design common to any related set of letters, numbers, and symbols. This design gives each character a particular shape and thickness (or *weight*, as it's called in type circles) that's unique to the typeface and difficult to classify. However, four main categories serve to distinguish all typefaces:

- **Serif**—A serif (rhymes with *sheriff*) typeface contains fine cross strokes (called *feet*) at the extremities of each character. These subtle appendages give the typeface a traditional, classy look that's most often used for titles and headings. The Office applications come with several serif typefaces, including Cambria and Times New Roman.

- **Sans serif**—A sans serif typeface doesn't contain cross strokes on the extremities of characters. As a result, sans serif typefaces usually have a cleaner, more modern look that works best for regular text. The default Office typeface for document text, Calibri, is a sans serif typeface.

- **Fixed-width**—A fixed-width typeface—also called a *monospace* typeface—uses the same amount of space for each character, so skinny letters such as *i* and *l* take up as much space as wider letters such as *m* and *w*. This is useful for text such as programming code, but since these fonts tend to look as if they were produced with a typewriter, the resulting text is unattractive for most other uses. Courier New is an example of a fixed-width typeface.

- **Decorative**—Decorative typefaces are usually special designs that are supposed to convey a particular effect. So, for example, if your document needs a fancy, handwritten effect, a font like Snell Roundhand is perfect.

Set the Typeface

When setting the typeface, you can apply it either to existing text or to text that you're about to add to the document.

1. Select the text you want to format. Or if you want to format the next text you type, position the cursor where you want the text to appear.

2. Click the Home tab.

3. Drop down the Font list.

4. Click the typeface you want to use. The program applies the typeface to the selected text.

You can also click the Font list in the Mini Toolbar.

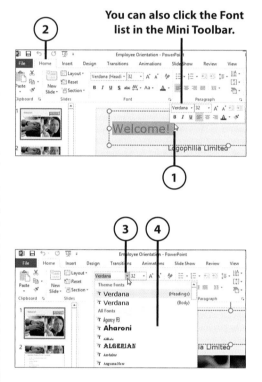

Change the Type Size

You can use type sizes to gain more control over the display of a document. For example, if you want to emphasize a title or heading, you can increase the type size. Similarly, if you want to fit more text into a particular area—such as a worksheet cell or a PowerPoint text box—you can decrease the type size.

You can also click the Font Size list in the Mini Toolbar.

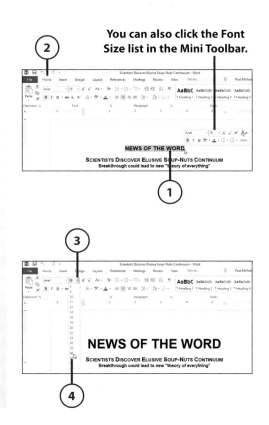

1. Select the text you want to format. Or if you want to format the next text you type, position the cursor where you want the text to appear.

2. Click the Home tab.

3. Drop down the Font Size list.

4. Click the type size you want to use. The Office application applies the type size to the text.

>>>Go Further

UNDERSTANDING TYPE SIZE

The *type size* measures the height of a font. The standard unit of measurement is the *point*, where there are 72 points in one inch. So, for example, the letters in a 24-point font are twice as tall as those in a 12-point font. Technically, type size is measured from the highest point of any letter with an *ascender*, which is the top part of a letter that extends above the letter body (such as the lowercase *f* and *h*), to the lowest point of a letter with a *descender*, which is the bottom part of a letter that extends below the letter baseline (such as the lowercase *g* or *y*). (In case you're wondering, this book is laid out in a 10-point Myriad Pro font.)

Apply Type Effects

The *type effects* of a font refer to extra attributes added to the typeface, such as **bold** and *italic*. Other type effects (often called type *styles*) include underline and ~~strikethrough~~. You normally use these styles to highlight or add emphasis to text.

1. Select the text you want to format. Or if you want to format the next text you type, position the cursor where you want the text to appear.

2. Click the Home tab.

3. Click the icons to select the type effects you want to apply.

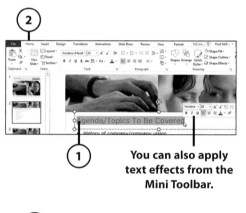

You can also apply text effects from the Mini Toolbar.

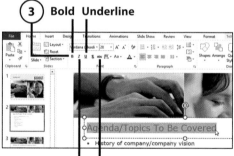

Bold Underline

Italic Strikethrough

Set Text Colors

You can add some visual interest to your documents by changing the color of the document text. In most cases, you want to set the color of just the text. However, in Word and OneNote, you can also highlight sections of a document by applying a color to the text background. As with fonts, the colors you have available in Word, Excel, and PowerPoint depend on the theme applied to the document: Each theme comes with a palette of 60 colors. However, you can also choose a color from the app's palette of 10 standard colors.

1. Select the text you want to format. Or if you want to format the next text you type, position the cursor where you want the text to appear.

2. Click the Home tab.

3. Click the Font Color list.

4. Click the color you want to apply.

5. In Word and OneNote, you can also click the Text Highlight Color list to apply a highlight to the text.

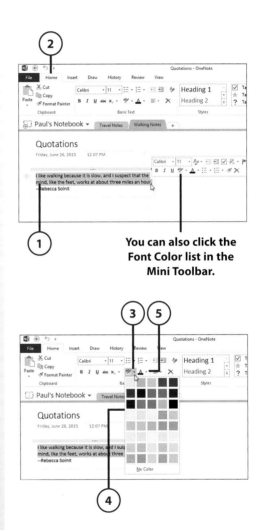

You can also click the Font Color list in the Mini Toolbar.

>>>Go Further

GETTING CREATIVE WITH A CUSTOM COLOR

The 60 colors that appear in the Theme Colors tab and the 10 standard colors that appear on the More Colors tab seem like a large palette, but you might not find the color that's just right for your needs. In that case, you take matters into your own hands and create the color you want. In Word, Excel, and PowerPoint, display the Font Color list, click More Colors, and then click the Custom tab. Use the Colors palette to click the basic color you want to use. In the smaller palette on the right, click and drag the bar to indicate how much gray you want in the custom color. Drag the bar up for a lighter hue (that is, less gray), or drag the bar down for a darker hue (more gray).

Formatting Paragraphs

Word, PowerPoint, and OneNote are simple programs in the sense that it's easy to get started with them: You just create a new document or open an existing document and then start typing. Of course, not all documents consist of basic text. For example, you might require a bulleted or numbered list, or you might need to adjust the indentation or alignment of a paragraph. This section shows you how to perform these tasks in Word, PowerPoint, and OneNote.

Align Paragraphs

You can make a document easier to read by aligning its text horizontally. You can align the text with the left margin (this is the default alignment), with the right margin, or with the center of the document. In Word, you can also justify a paragraph's text, which means the text gets aligned with both the left and right margins.

1. Click inside the paragraph or cell you want to align. If you want to align multiple items, select some or all of the text in each of the paragraphs or select each cell.

2. Click the Home tab.

3. Click the alignment you want to apply.

Applying Alignment

You can apply these alignments to one or more paragraphs in a Word document, to one or more cells in an Excel worksheet, to text in a PowerPoint slide, or to paragraphs in a OneNote page.

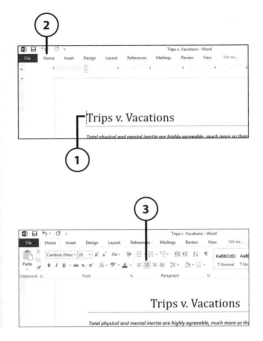

Set the Line Spacing

You can improve the look of your document's slides by adjusting the line spacing, which determines the amount of space between each line in a paragraph. For example, double spacing leaves twice as much space between the lines as the standard single spacing. Increasing the spaces creates more white space in the document, which can make the document easier to read.

You can apply these alignments to one or more paragraphs in a Word document, to one or more cells in an Excel worksheet, to text in a PowerPoint slide, or to paragraphs in a OneNote page.

1. Click inside the paragraph you want to format. If you want to set the spacing for multiple paragraphs, select some or all the text in each of the paragraphs.

2. Click the Home tab.

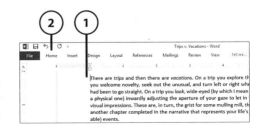

3. Click Line Spacing.

4. Click the line spacing value that you want to apply.

Applying Line Spacing

You can adjust line spacing to one or more paragraphs in a Word document. However, the line spacing feature is not available in Excel, PowerPoint, and OneNote.

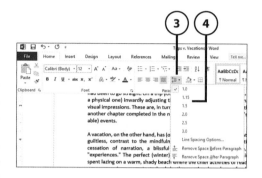

Build a Bulleted List

You can make a list of items more prominent and more readable by formatting those items as a bulleted list. When you do, the app formats the items slightly indented from the regular text, with a small character—called the bullet, which is usually a black dot—in front of each item.

You can either create a bulleted list from scratch or convert an existing list of items to a bulleted list. You also have a choice of several different bullet characters.

1. If you want to convert existing text to a bulleted list, select the text.

Converting Text to a Bulleted List

If you're selecting text to convert to a bulleted list, the text must be a series of items, of any length, each in its own paragraph.

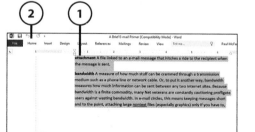

2. Click the Home tab.

3. Click Bullets.

4. Click the bullet style you want to use. If you selected text in advance, the program converts the text to a bulleted list.

5. If you selected text in advance, click at the end of the last item. The insertion point moves to the end of the item.

6. Press Enter. The program creates a new item in the bulleted list.

7. Type the text for the new list item.

8. Repeat steps 6 and 7 until you complete the bulleted list.

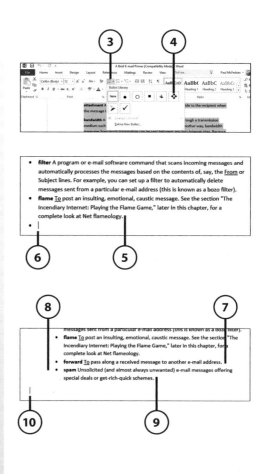

Creating Subbullets

If you want to shift a list item so that it's a subbullet of the item above it, click at the beginning of the item and then press Tab or click Increase Indent. To return the item to its previous level, press Shift+Tab or click Decrease Indent.

9. Click at the end of the last item.

10. Press Return twice to end the bulleted list.

Create a Numbered List

You can make a set of steps or an ordered list more readable and easier to follow by formatting those items as a numbered list. When you do, the app formats the items slightly indented from the regular text, with a number in front of each item. The numbers increase sequentially, usually from 1 to the total number of items in the list.

You can either create a numbered list from scratch or convert an existing list of items to a numbered list. You also have a choice of several different numbering characters.

1. If you want to convert existing text, in this case a bulleted list, to a numbered list, select the text.

Converting Text to a Numbered List

If you're selecting text to convert to a numbered list, the text must be a series of items, of any length, each in its own paragraph.

2. Click the Home tab.

3. Click Numbering.

4. Click the number format you want to use. If you selected text in advance, the app converts the text to a numbered list.

Number Formats

The number formats are available only in Word and PowerPoint. In OneNote, when you click Numbering, the app applies a default numbered list format.

5. If you selected text in advance, click at the end of the last item. The insertion point moves to the end of the item.

6. Press Enter. The app creates a new item in the numbered list.

7. Type the text for the new list item.

8. Repeat steps 6 and 7 until you complete the numbered list.

9. Click at the end of the last item.

10. Press Return twice to end the numbered list. (If you still see the next number in PowerPoint, click Backspace to delete it.)

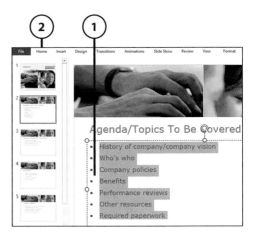

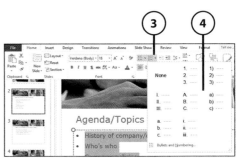

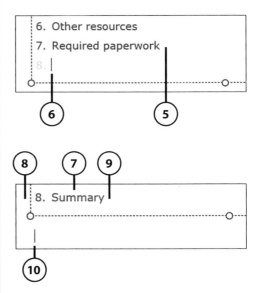

Set the Indentation

You can set off a paragraph from the rest of the text by indenting the paragraph. For example, if a document includes a lengthy quotation, you can indent the quotation to make it stand out. In Word, PowerPoint, and OneNote, you can indent a paragraph from the left.

1. Click inside the paragraph you want to indent. If you want to indent multiple paragraphs, select some or all the text in each of the paragraphs.

2. Click the Home tab.

3. Click Increase Indent. The app shifts the entire paragraph away from the left margin.

4. Repeat step 3 until the paragraph is indented the amount you want. If you indent a paragraph too much, you can shift the text back toward the left margin by clicking Decrease Indent.

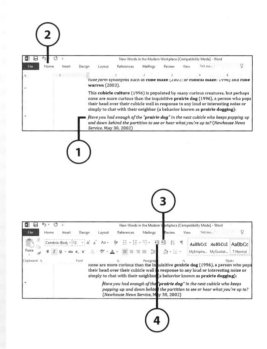

Working with Formatting

Working with text and paragraph formatting can be time-consuming and labor-intensive. It's almost always worth the extra effort to make your Office documents look their best, but that doesn't mean you should waste time performing your formatting chores. The Office applications offer a few handy features that can help reduce the amount of time and effort you expend on your formatting, and the rest of this chapter covers these useful tools.

Apply Styles

You can save time and effort when formatting your documents by taking advantage of the predefined styles available in the Office applications. A *style* is a collection of formatting options, usually including some or all the following: typeface, type size, text color, text effects, and paragraph alignment. When you apply a style to some text, the app applies all the style's formatting at once.

1. Select the text you want to format.

2. Select the Home tab.

3. Open the Styles gallery.

4. Click the style you want to use. The Office app applies the style's formatting to the text.

Applying Styles by App

The Styles gallery is available in Word, PowerPoint, and OneNote. In Excel, click Cell Styles, instead.

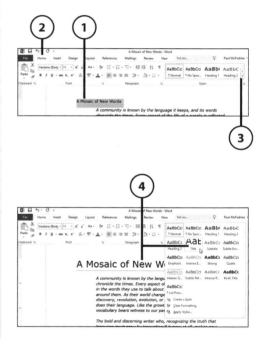

Apply Text Effects

The Office styles apply standard font formatting such as bold, font size, and font color. If you're looking for something with a bit more pizzazz, you can format your words with a text effect, which is a preset style that applies more advanced formatting such as reflections, textures, and 3-D effects.

1. Select the text you want to format.

2. Click the Home tab.

3. Click Text Effects.

4. Click a text effect. Word applies the effect to the selected text.

Text Effects Are Word-Only

The Text Effects feature is available only in Word. In PowerPoint, you can use the Home tab's Text Shadow command to apply a shadow to the selected text.

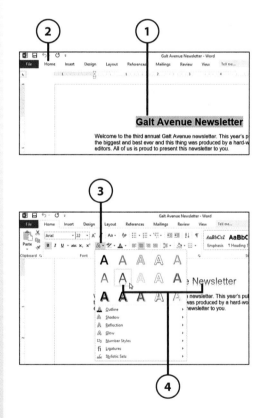

Clear Formatting

If you apply a number of font formats, paragraph options, or styles to some text, you might decide later that you no longer want any of that formatting. Although it's possible to turn off or remove each of the formatting options individually, Word and PowerPoint offer a much easier method: the Clear Formatting command. Selecting this command removes all formatting from the selected text, so this method is much easier than trying to clear the formatting options one by one.

1. Select the text you want to clear.

2. Click the Home tab.

3. Click Clear Formatting. The Office program clears all formatting from the text.

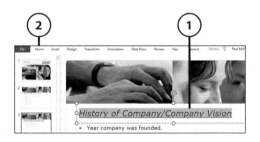

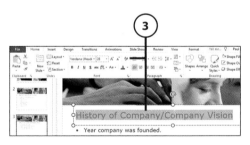

Apply picture styles.

Apply picture effects.

Rotate a graphic.

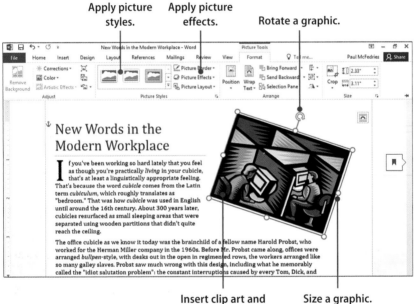

Insert clip art and other images.

Size a graphic.

In this chapter, you learn various techniques for drawing, inserting, and working with graphic objects, such as lines, photos, and clip art. Topics include the following:

→ Drawing lines, rectangles, and circles

→ Inserting photos, clip art, SmartArt graphics, and WordArt images

→ Selecting one or more graphic objects

→ Sizing, moving, and rotating graphic objects

→ Applying styles and effects to graphic objects

Working with Office 2016 Graphics

When most people think about using the Office 2016 applications, they generally think about text—writing sentences and paragraphs in Word, adding formulas and labels in Excel, creating slide titles and bullets in PowerPoint, and so on. It is certainly true that most of the work people do in Office 2016—from papers to purchase orders to presentations—is and should remain text based.

However, if you *only* think text when you think of Office, you're missing out on a whole other dimension. All Office 2016 applications have extensive graphics tools that you can take advantage of to improve the clarity of your work or just to add a bit of pizzazz to liven up an otherwise drab document.

Even better, these graphics tools work the same across applications, so once you learn how to use them, you can apply your knowledge to any program. This chapter shows you how to create, edit, and enhance graphics in the Office 2016 applications.

Working with Shapes

A shape is an object such as a line or rectangle that you draw within your document. You can use shapes to point out key features in a document, enclose text, create flowcharts, and enhance the look of a document. In Office 2016, you can use eight shape types:

- **Lines**—Straight lines, squiggles, free-form polygons, arrows, connectors, and curves

- **Basic shapes**—Rectangles, triangles, circles, boxes, cylinders, hearts, and many more

- **Block arrows**—Two-dimensional arrows of various configurations

- **Equation shapes**—Two-dimensional images for the basic arithmetic symbols, such as plus (+) and equals (=)

- **Flowchart**—The standard shapes used for creating flowcharts

- **Callouts**—Boxes and lines for creating callouts to document features

- **Stars and banners**—Stars, starbursts, scrolls, and more

- **Action buttons (PowerPoint only)**—Buttons such as forward and backward that represent standard slide show actions

Inserting a Line

You can use lines to point out important document information, to create a free-form drawing, or as part of a more complex graphic, such as a company logo.

1. Click the Insert tab. In OneNote, select the Draw tab instead.

2. Click Shapes and then select the shape you want from the Lines section.

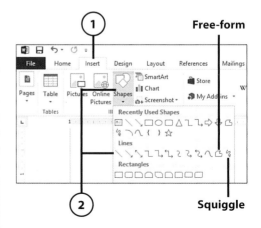

3. Position the crosshair where you want to start drawing the line.

4. Drag to where you want the line to end and then release. If you're drawing a squiggle, drag in the shape of the line you want.

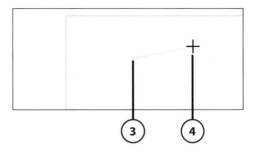

Taming Your Lines

You can restrict straight lines and arrows to horizontal, vertical, and 45-degree angles by holding down the Shift key while you drag the screen.

>>>Go Further

DRAWING A FREE-FORM POLYGON

The Lines section of the Shapes gallery includes a Freeform icon that enables you to draw a free-form polygon, which is really just a series of connected lines that create a closed shape. To draw a free-form polygon, follow steps 1 to 4 to create the first side of the shape. Then, click where you want each subsequent side to end. When you're done, double-click the screen.

Inserting Any Other Shape

You can use the other shapes either on their own—for example, to point out features with callouts or block arrows or to enhance text with stars or banners—or as part of a more complex graphic.

1. Click the Insert tab. In OneNote, select the Draw tab instead.

2. Click Shapes and then select the shape you want to insert.

3. Position the crosshair where you want to start drawing the shape.

4. Drag until the shape has the size and form you want and then release.

Drawing Squares and Circles

You can make your rectangles square, your ellipses circular, and your angled lines 45 degrees, by holding down the Shift key while you drag the screen.

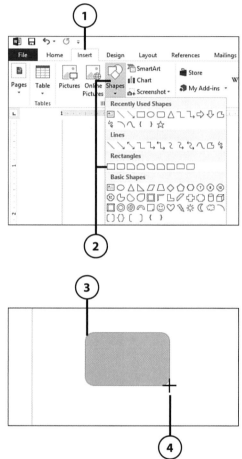

Inserting Images

Although the shape tools that come with the Office 2016 applications are handy for creating simple graphics effects, your document might require something more ambitious or specific. Office 2016 can help here, too, by offering several types of images that you can insert:

- **Picture**—You can enhance the visual appeal and strengthen the message of a document by adding a picture to the file. The Office 2016 applications can work with the most popular picture formats, including BMP, JPEG, TIFF, PNG, and GIF. This means that you can insert almost any photo that you have stored on your computer.

- **Clip art**—This refers to small images or artwork that you can insert into your documents. Office 2016 doesn't come with its own clip art, but it does give you access to online clip art via the Bing Image Search tool.

- **SmartArt**—You use these graphics to help present information in a compact, visual format. A SmartArt graphic is a collection of *nodes*—shapes with some text inside—that enables you to convey information visually. For example, you can use a SmartArt graphic to present a company organization chart, the progression of steps in a workflow, the parts that make up a whole, and much more.

- **Text box**—The graphics you add to your documents will usually consist of images, but sometimes you need to augment those images with text. For example, you might want to add a title and subtitle or insert a label. To add text to an existing image, you draw a text box and then type your text within that box.

- **WordArt**—You can add some pizzazz to your documents by inserting a WordArt image, which is a graphic object that contains text stylized with shadows, outlines, reflections, and other predefined effects. WordArt images enable you to apply sophisticated and fun effects to text with just a few clicks. However, some of the more elaborate WordArt effects can make text difficult to read, so make sure that whatever WordArt image you use does not detract from your document message.

Inserting a Picture

If you have a photo or other image on your computer that you think would add just the right touch, you can insert it into your document.

1. Click the Insert tab.

2. Click Pictures to open the Insert Picture dialog box.

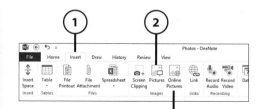

To insert online clip
art, instead, select
Online Pictures.

3. Open the folder that contains the picture you want to insert.

4. Click the picture.

5. Click Insert. The Office 2016 application inserts the picture into the document.

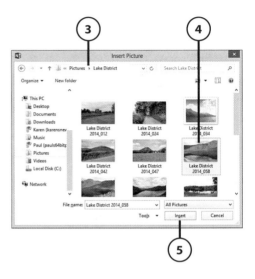

>>>Go Further
LINKING TO THE PICTURE

In Word, Excel, or PowerPoint, you can set up a link between the inserted picture and the original file, so that any changes you make to the original are automatically reflected in the document copy. Follow steps 1 to 4 to select the picture in the Insert Picture dialog box and then open the drop-down menu on the Insert menu.

If you want to keep your document size small, select Link to File to insert the picture as a link to the original file. Use this command when you want edits to the original file to be updated in your document, but you don't want a copy of the picture in the document. Note, however, that if you send the file to someone (say, via email or over a network), that person will not see the image unless he or she has the same image located in the same folder.

Alternatively, select Insert and Link to insert a copy of the picture into the document *and* maintain a link to the original file. Use this command when you want edits to the original file to be updated in your document, but you also want a copy within the document just in case the original is deleted.

Understanding SmartArt Graphics

One of the most impressive of the Office 2016 graphics features is support for the SmartArt format, which is based on the XML (Extensible Markup Language) standard. A SmartArt graphic is a collection of *nodes*—shapes with some text inside—that enable you to convey information visually. You use SmartArt to illustrate concepts in seven main categories:

- **List**—These are concepts that are sequential or that form a progression or a group. Most of these SmartArt graphics consist of shapes arranged in vertical or horizontal lists.

- **Process**—These are concepts that progress from one stage to another, where the overall progress has a beginning and an end. In most of these SmartArt graphics, each stage is represented by a shape and accompanying text, and one-way arrows lead you from one shape to the next.

- **Cycle**—These are concepts that progress from one stage to another in a repeating pattern. In most of these SmartArt graphics, each stage is represented by a shape and accompanying text, and one-way arrows lead you from one shape to the next. The most common structure is a circle, with the last stage leading back to the first stage.

- **Hierarchy**—These are concepts that either show the relative importance of one thing over another or show how one thing is contained within another. These SmartArt graphics look like organization charts.

- **Relationship**—These are concepts that show how two or more items are connected to each other. In most of these SmartArt graphics, each item is represented by a shape and accompanying text, and all the shapes either reside within a larger structure, such as a pyramid, or are positioned relative to one another, such as in a Venn diagram.

- **Matrix**—These are concepts that show the relationship between the entirety of something and its components, organized as quadrants. These SmartArt graphics have one shape that represents the whole and four shapes that represent the component quadrants.

- **Pyramid**—These are concepts with components that are proportional to each other or interconnected in some way. In most of these SmartArt graphics, the component shapes are arranged in a triangle pattern.

Inserting a SmartArt Graphic

To build a SmartArt graphic, you use the Text pane to add text to each node as well as add and delete nodes.

1. Click the Insert tab.

2. Click SmartArt to open the Choose a SmartArt Graphic dialog box.

Locating SmartArt

Depending on the width of your application window, you might need to click Illustrations to see the SmartArt command.

3. Click a SmartArt category.

4. Click the SmartArt style you want to use.

5. Click OK to add the SmartArt graphic to the document.

6. Click a node in the Text pane and then type the text that you want to appear in the node.

7. Repeat step 6 to fill in the other nodes in the SmartArt graphic.

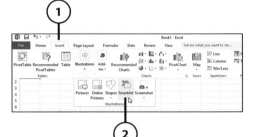

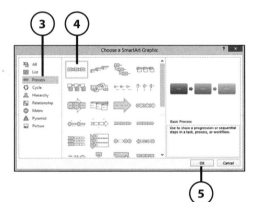

Click Text Pane to toggle the Text pane on and off.

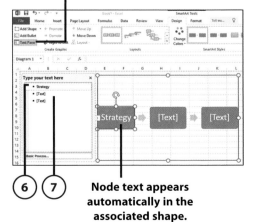

Node text appears automatically in the associated shape.

8. To add a node to the SmartArt graphic, select the existing node you want the new node to come before or after.

9. Click the Design tab.

10. Click Add Shape and then select either Add Shape After or Add Shape Before.

Deleting Nodes

To remove a node from the SmartArt graphic, click and hold (or right-click) the node for a few seconds; then select Cut in the shortcut menu that appears.

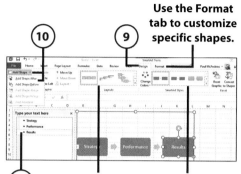

Use the Format tab to customize specific shapes.

Use the Layouts gallery to choose a different layout.

Use the SmartArt Styles gallery to apply a style.

Inserting WordArt

WordArt takes a word or phrase and converts it into a graphic object that applies artistic styles, colors, and shapes to the text. WordArt is therefore useful for newsletter titles, logos, and any time you want text to really stand out from its surroundings.

1. Click the Insert tab.

2. Click WordArt to open the WordArt gallery.

3. Click the WordArt style you want to use. The Office 2016 application adds the WordArt image to the document.

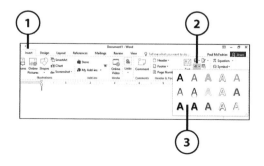

4. Type the text that you want to appear in the WordArt image.

5. Click outside the image to set it.

Use the Shape Styles gallery and commands to customize the image.

Use the WordArt Styles gallery to apply a style.

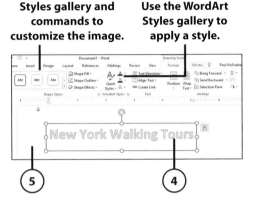

>>>Go Further

ADDING A TEXT BOX

The graphics you add to your documents will usually consist of images, but sometimes you need to augment those images with text. For example, you might want to add a title and subtitle or insert a label. If a WordArt image seems like overkill for this, a better alternative is to draw a text box and then type your text within that box.

To add a text box, select Insert, Text Box, use the mouse to drag until the text box has the size and form you want, and then type your text in the box.

Formatting and Editing Graphic Objects

Inserting a line, shape, picture, or other graphic object is usually only half the battle. To complete your work with the graphic, you usually need to spend a bit of time formatting and editing the object to get it just right. This may include some or all of the following: sizing the graphic; rotating it; moving it; grouping or aligning it with other objects; and formatting the object's fill, lines, and shadow effects. The rest of this chapter provides you with the details of these and other techniques for working with graphic objects.

Selecting Graphic Objects

Every graphic object has an invisible rectangular frame. For a line or rectangle, the frame is the same as the object itself. For all other objects, the frame is a rectangle that completely encloses the shape or image. Before you can format or edit a graphic object, you must select it, which displays selection handles around the frame.

If you just want to work with a single object, you can select it by clicking it. If you need to work with multiple objects, Office 2016 gives you a number of methods, and the one you choose depends on the number of objects and their layout within the document:

- The simplest scenario is when you have just a few objects to select. In this case, hold down the Ctrl key and click each object. If you click an object by accident, keep the Ctrl key held down and click the object again to deselect it.

- To select a few objects, you can "lasso" the objects, as described in the next section.

- To select all the objects in a document, select one and then press Ctrl+A.

Lassoing Graphic Objects

Lassoing graphic objects is done by using the mouse to draw a rectangle around the objects you want to select. Use this technique when the objects you want are located near each other.

1. Click the Home tab.

2. Click Select.

3. Click Select Objects.

Lassoing Objects in Excel

To lasso objects in Excel, select the Home tab, Find & Select, and then click Select Objects.

---

4. Position the mouse pointer at the upper-left corner of the area you want to select.

5. Click and drag to the lower-right corner of the area you want to select. As you drag, the program indicates the selected area with a dashed border.

6. When the selection area completely encloses each object you want to select, release the screen. Excel places selection handles around each object in the selection area.

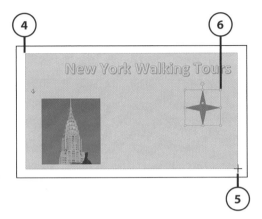

Sizing a Graphic Object

If a graphic is too large or too small for your needs, or if the object's shape is not what you want, you can size the image to change its dimensions or its shape. You might want to size a graphic so that it fits within an open document area.

1. Click the graphic you want to size.

2. To adjust the width of the graphic, drag the left or right handle.

3. To adjust the height of the graphic, drag the top or bottom handle.

4. To adjust the width and height at the same time, drag a corner handle.

Sizing handles appear around the edges of a selected object.

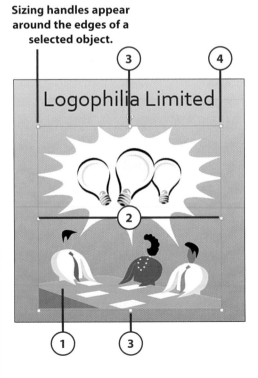

Sizing Multiple Sides

To size the graphic on two sides at once, hold down Ctrl while you drag any corner handle. Similarly, you can size the left and right sides simultaneously by holding down Ctrl while dragging a side handle; you can size the top and bottom sides simultaneously by holding down Ctrl while dragging the top or bottom handle.

Moving a Graphic Object

To ensure that a graphic is ideally placed within a document, you can move the graphic to a new location. For example, you might want to move a graphic so that it does not cover existing document text.

1. Click the graphic you want to move.

2. Place the mouse pointer in the middle of the object. Make sure you don't place the mouse pointer over any of the object's sizing handles.

3. Drag the object to the position you want.

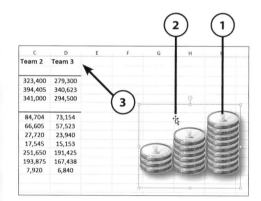

Horizontal or Vertical Moves

To move a graphic object only horizontally or vertically, hold down the Shift key while dragging it.

Rotating a Graphic Object

Most graphic objects get inserted into a document without any rotation: Horizontal borders appear horizontal, and vertical borders appear vertical. A nonrotated image is probably what you want most of the time, but for some occasions an image tilted at a jaunty angle is just the right touch for a document. Many objects come with a rotation handle that you can use to rotate the object clockwise or counterclockwise.

1. Click the graphic you want to rotate.

2. Use the mouse pointer to drag the rotation handle. Drag the handle clockwise to rotate the graphic clockwise; drag the handle counterclockwise to rotate the graphic counterclockwise.

Rotation handle

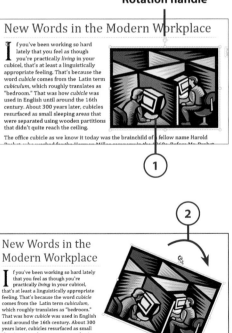

Formatting a Graphic Object

You can enhance your shapes, clip art, photos, WordArt images, and SmartArt graphics by formatting the images. For example, the Office 2016 applications offer more than two dozen picture styles, which are predefined formats that apply various combinations of shadows, reflections, borders, and layouts. Office 2016 also offers a dozen picture effects, which are preset combinations of special effects, such as glows, soft edges, bevels, and 3-D rotations.

1. Click the picture you want to format.

2. Click the Format tab.

3. Click More Picture Styles. The Picture Styles gallery appears.

Picture Style Preview

You can get a preview of what the style's effect will be on your graphic by hovering the mouse pointer over the style.

4. Click the picture style you want to use. The application applies the Quick Style to the picture.

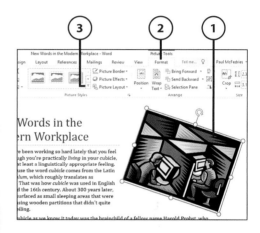

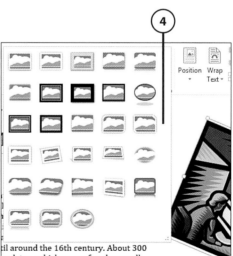

5. Click Picture Effects. If the image is a shape, select Shape Effects instead.

6. Click Preset.

7. Click the effect you want to apply. The application applies the effect to the picture.

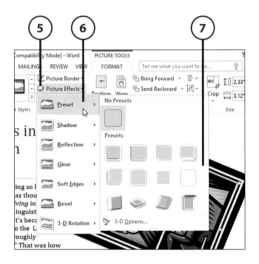

>>>Go Further
MORE EFFECTS

To gain maximum control over your graphic effects, select the object and then select Picture Effects (or Shape Effects). You can then use the six effect categories—Shadow, Reflection, Glow, Soft Edges, Bevel, and 3-D Rotation—to apply specific effects to the image.

It's Not All Good

Reverting to the Original

After playing around with a graphic, you might end up with a bit of a mess. If you don't like the formatting that you've applied to a graphic, you can return the picture to its original look and start over. If you haven't performed any other tasks since applying the formatting, select Undo (or press Ctrl+Z) until the application has removed the formatting. Otherwise, select the Format tab, select Picture Effects (or Shape Effects), select Preset, and then select the icon in the No Presets section. To reverse all the changes made to a picture since you inserted the image, select the picture, select Format, and then select Reset Picture.

Set tabs.   Apply headings.   Find text.

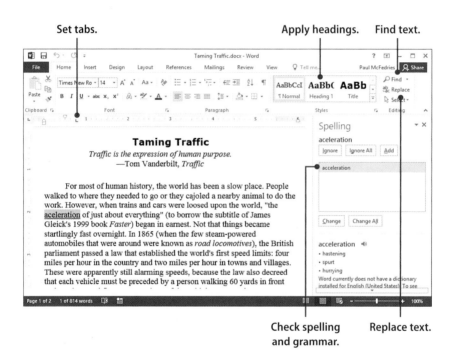

Check spelling   Replace text.
and grammar.

In this chapter, you learn about working with text in Word, including entering and editing text, inserting symbols and tabs, and checking your work for spelling and grammatical mistakes. Topics include the following:

→ Entering and editing Word text

→ Inserting foreign characters and other symbols

→ Adding tabs and headings

→ Finding and replacing document text

→ Checking for spelling and grammar errors

Working with Text in Word

All the Office 2016 applications require at least some written input. From worksheet titles and labels in Excel to slide headings and bullets in PowerPoint to page snippets and lists in OneNote, you always end up working with text in one form or another when you work with Office 2016. However, when you have some *real* writing to do, the Office 2016 tool of choice is, of course, Word and its word processing pedigree. Whether you're firing off a 3-page memo to the troops or putting together a 300-page book, Word can handle any text task you throw at it.

Word is loaded with useful and powerful features that can help you to not only create beautiful documents, but also create those documents in record time. The next few chapters are designed to introduce you to these features and other techniques for getting the most out of Word. This chapter gets you off to a good start by examining a number of handy and powerful techniques for entering and editing text in Word.

Learning Text Basics

Fritterware refers to software programs that contain so many bells and whistles that you can't help but fritter away huge amounts of time trying out different options and features. Word is a big, complex program, so it certainly qualifies as fritterware, particularly when it comes to formatting your work. Even so, you still probably spend the bulk of your Word time entering text, which means you can become immediately more productive if you learn a few techniques for making text entry easier and faster. The next few sections help you do just that.

Enter and Edit Text

You can use your Windows PC's keyboard to enter and edit text in Word.

1. Click at the spot where you want to start entering text. If the document already contains text, click at the spot where you want your next typing to appear.

2. Type your text.

3. To edit text, click at the spot where you want to make your changes, or use the arrow keys to position the insertion point. Then either press Backspace to delete the character to the left of the insertion point, or press Delete to delete the character to the right of the insertion point.

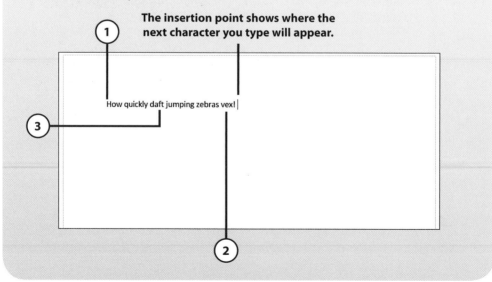

The insertion point shows where the next character you type will appear.

How quickly daft jumping zebras vex!

>>>Go Further
USING CLICK AND TYPE

Most text editors or word processing programs only let you enter text starting at the beginning of a new document or immediately after the end of the text in an existing document. However, Word comes with a feature called Click and Type that enables you to starting entering text anywhere within a document. Just double-click where you want to begin and then start typing.

If you find that Click and Type often causes the insertion point to appear in places where you don't want to start typing, you can turn off this feature. Select File and then select Options to open the Word Options dialog box. Select the Advanced tab and then click to deactivate the Enable Click and Type check box. Select OK to put the new setting into effect.

Enter Text with AutoCorrect

AutoCorrect is a feature that watches what you type and automatically corrects certain mistakes, such as *teh* (instead of *the*) and *woudl* (instead of *would*). If you disagree with a correction, either press Ctrl+Z to undo it or select the correction and then select Change Back To "*text*," where *text* is the uncorrected version of the text.

However, most of us have phrases, sentences, even multiple paragraphs that we add to our documents regularly. Such frequently used bits of text are called *boilerplate*, and having to type them constantly can be both tedious and time wasting. To reduce the drudgery of boilerplate, you can set up AutoCorrect to store the boilerplate and then recall it with a few keystrokes.

1. Select the boilerplate text.
2. Select File.

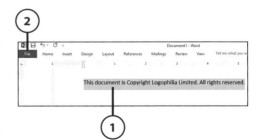

3. Select Options to display the Word Options dialog box.

4. Select Proofing.

5. Select AutoCorrect Options to display the AutoCorrect dialog box.

6. Select the AutoCorrect tab.

7. If the boilerplate is formatted and you want to include that formatting each time you insert the boilerplate, select the Formatted Text option; otherwise, select the Plain Text option.

8. In the Replace text box, type a short abbreviation or code.

9. Select Add.

10. Select OK.

Enter AutoCorrect Text

With your AutoCorrect item now defined, you can enter the full text into any Word document by typing the short abbreviation or code and then either pressing Enter or typing any word-ending symbol such as a comma, period, tab, or hyphen.

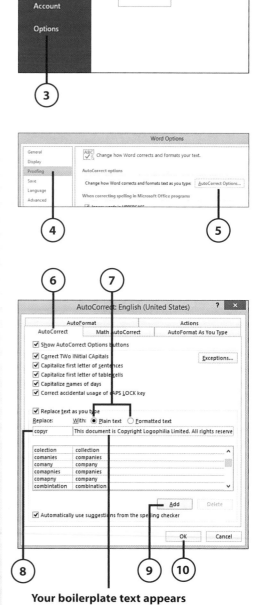

Your boilerplate text appears in the With text box.

Insert Symbols

A Word document does not have to consist solely of those letters, numbers, punctuation marks, and other characters that you can see on your keyboard. In fact, hundreds of other symbols are available to you. These include financial symbols such as €, £, and ¥; business symbols such as ®, ™, and ©; mathematical symbols such as ≤, ∞, and ±; and international characters such as Á, ö, and ç.

1. Position the insertion point where you want the symbol to appear.

2. Select the Insert tab.

3. Select Symbol.

4. If you see the symbol you want to insert, select it. Otherwise, select More Symbols to open the Symbol dialog box.

5. If you want to insert the symbol using a particular font, select the font you want in the Font list.

6. Select the symbol you want to insert.

7. Select Insert. Word inserts the symbol at the insertion point.

Shortcut

You can also double-click the symbol to enter it.

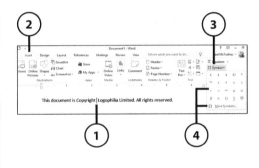

Select this tab to see a list of commonly used symbols.

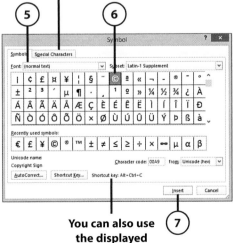

You can also use the displayed shortcut key to insert the symbol.

>>>Go Further

CREATING AN AUTOCORRECT ENTRY FOR A SYMBOL

As you see in the next section, Word has a few predefined AutoCorrect entries for symbols. If you have other symbols that you use more often, you can insert them via the convenience of AutoCorrect.

In the Symbol dialog box, select the symbol you want to work with and then select AutoCorrect. Word displays the AutoCorrect dialog box and shows the symbol in the With text box. In the Replace text box, type the characters you want to use to trigger the correction and then select Add. Word assigns the AutoCorrect entry to the symbol. Select OK to return to the Symbol dialog box and then select Close.

Insert Symbols Using AutoCorrect

Perhaps the easiest and most efficient way to insert a symbol is via Word's AutoCorrect feature because you just need to type the two or three original characters and Word converts them to the symbol automatically. The following table lists Word's predefined AutoCorrect entries for symbols.

Type	To Insert	Description
(c)	©	Copyright symbol
(r)	®	Registered trademark symbol
(tm)	™	Trademark symbol
...	…	Ellipsis
:(	☹	Sad emoticon
:-(	☹	Sad emoticon
:)	☺	Happy emoticon
:-)	☺	Happy emoticon
:|	☺	Indifferent emoticon
:-|	☺	Indifferent emoticon
<--	←	Thin left-pointing arrow

Type	To Insert	Description
<==	⇐	Thick left-pointing arrow
<=>	⇔	Two-sided arrow
==>	⇒	Thick right-pointing arrow
-->	→	Thin right-pointing arrow

Set Tabs

Documents look much better if they're properly indented and if their various parts line up nicely. The best way to do this is to use tabs instead of spaces whenever you need to create some room in a line. Why? Well, a single space can take up different amounts of room, depending on the font and size of the characters you're using. So your document can end up looking pretty ragged if you try to use spaces to indent your text. Tabs, on the other hand, are fastidiously precise: When you press the Tab key, the insertion point moves ahead exactly to the next tab stop, no more, no less.

Tab indicator

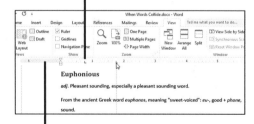

The ruler

1. Place the insertion point inside the paragraph you want to modify. If your version of Word already displays the ruler, skip to step 4.

2. Select the View tab.

3. Select the Ruler check box to display the ruler.

4. Click the ruler at the position where you want the tab to appear.

5. To move a tab, use a mouse to drag the tab left or right along the ruler.

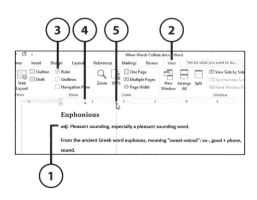

6. To change the tab type, or to modify tabs using a touchscreen, first select the Home tab and then select the Paragraph dialog box launcher.

7. Select Tabs to open the Tabs dialog box.

Mouse Shortcut

If you have a mouse or trackpad, a quicker way to get to the Tabs dialog box is to double-click an existing tab.

8. To change an existing tab, select it.

9. To create a new tab, type its position in the rule and then select Set.

10. Use the options in the Alignment and Leader groups to set the tab type.

11. Select OK.

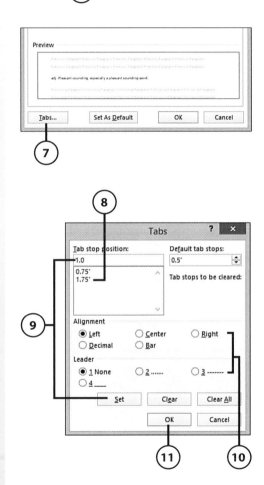

>>>Go Further
WORD'S TAB TYPES

Word has a tab to suit your every need. Here's a summary of the available types:

Left—Text lines up with the tab on the left.

Right—Text lines up with the tab on the right.

Center—Text is centered on the tab.

Decimal—Numbers line up with the tab at their decimal places.

Bar—A vertical line the height of the paragraph is added.

Leader—In this tab type, the tab space for a left, right, center, or decimal tab is filled with a bunch of characters, such as dots.

Enter Headings

Headings are special paragraphs that serve as titles for different sections of a document. You specify headings in Word by applying a heading style, where the Heading 1 style is for the main sections of the document, Heading 2 is for the subsections, Heading 3 is for the sub-subsections, and so on.

1. Place the insertion point any-where inside the paragraph you want to turn into a heading.

2. Select the Home tab.

3. Select the More Styles icon to open the Styles gallery.

If you see the heading style you want, you can select it without opening the gallery.

4. Select the heading style you want to apply.

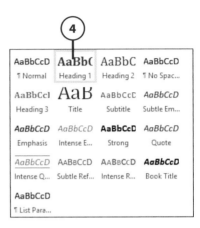

>>>*Go Further*

NAVIGATING WITH THE NAVIGATION PANE

Another benefit of applying headings is that you can use Word's Navigation pane to quickly and easily navigate your document. The Navigation pane has a Headings tab that displays a list of the headings in your document. When you select a heading, Word automatically jumps to that part of the file. The Navigation pane also gives you a quick view of your document's overall structure, so you can often see at a glance whether your document is correctly structured and your headings flow smoothly and logically. To use this feature, select the View tab, select the Navigation Pane check box, and then select Headings in the Navigation pane.

Finding and Replacing Text

We live in a world where the dream of "information at your fingertips" is fast becoming a reality. Search engines such as Google and Bing index online knowledge at a furious clip. And with those search engines at our beck and call full-time, thanks to wireless network connections and portable web surfing devices such as smartphones and tablets, we can call up just about any tidbit of information we need with a minimum of fuss.

This is fine for "googleable" online info, but some of your most useful data probably resides within your own documents. Locating information in a small document is not usually a problem, but when your Word documents grow to tens of pages, locating the text you want becomes a real needle-in-a-haystack exercise. You can make it much easier to locate text in large documents by using Word's Find feature. Word also comes with a powerful Replace feature that enables you to quickly and easily replace multiple instances of a word or phrase with something else.

Find Text

Word's Find feature not only locates a word or phrase, but also offers options for matching uppercase and lower-case letters, finding whole words only, and more.

1. Select the Home tab.

2. Drop down the Find menu.

3. Select Advanced Find to open the Find and Replace dialog box.

4. In the Find What text box, type the text you're looking for.

5. To specify search options, select More to expand the dialog box.

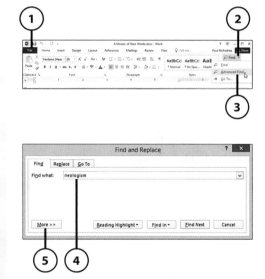

6. Select the Match Case check box to find only those instances that match the uppercase and lowercase letters you specify in the Find What text box. For example, if you type *Bob* as the search text, Find matches *Bob* but not *bob* or *BOB*.

7. Select the Find Whole Words Only check box to find only those instances of the search text that are entire words, not just partial words. For example, if you type *pen* as the search text, Find only matches the word *pen*, not words that contain pen, such as *expenses* and *pencil*.

8. Select the Use Wildcards check box to use wildcard characters in your search text. For example, you can use a question mark (?) to match any character (for example, *c?t* matches *cat*, *cut*, and *incite*, but not *colt* or *cost*) and the asterisk (*) to match any number of characters (for example, *m*t* matches *met*, *meet*, and *demerit*).

9. Select Find Next. Repeat as needed to find the instance of the text that you're looking for.

10. When you're done, select Cancel.

Word highlights the next instance of the text.

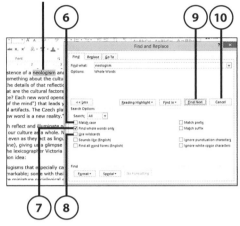

Faster Finds

For simple searches where you're just looking for a bit of text, don't bother with the Find and Replace dialog box. Instead, select the Home tab's Find icon to open the Navigation pane. Type your search term in the text box and Word automatically displays a list of the matching terms in the document.

Replace Text

If you have a number of instances of a word or phrase that require the same edit, performing each edit manually is too time consuming. A much better method is to let Word's Replace feature handle some or all of the edits for you.

1. Select the Home tab.

2. Select Replace to open the Find and Replace dialog box with the Replace tab displayed.

Keyboard Shortcut

You can also open the Find and Replace dialog box with the Replace tab displayed by pressing Ctrl+H.

---

3. Type the text you want to replace in the Find What text box.

4. Type the text you want to use as the replacement in the Replace With text box.

5. If you want to specify search options, you can select More to expand the dialog box. See the previous section "Find Text" for an explanation of the most important search options.

6. Select Find Next. Word highlights the next instance of the Find What text.

7. If you want to replace the high-lighted text, select Replace. Word makes the replacement and then highlights the next instance. Keep selecting this button to continue replacing the text. Alternatively, you can select Replace All to replace every instance of the text in the document.

8. If you come across an instance that you don't want to replace, select Find Next, instead.

9. When you're done, select Cancel.

are notoriously difficult places for the uninitiated to navigate. Each corridor, each
, even each cubicle looks the same as any other, so it doesn't take much for an office
get lost, which has no doubt inspired *cube farm* synonyms such as **cube maze** (200
maze: 1996) and **cube warren** (2002).

Find and Replace

Find   Replace   Go To

Find what: corridor
Options: Search Down, Whole Words

Replace with: hallway

More >>   Replace   Replace All   Find Next   Cancel

7   8   9

>>>Go Further
REPLACING STYLES

One common Word task is to replace an existing style with another style. For example, if you add a new main heading at the top of the document, you might want to change all the existing Heading 1 styles to Heading 2 styles. The Replace feature makes this easy. In the Find and Replace dialog box, select More to see the extra options. Click inside the Find What text box, select Format, select Style, choose the style you want to replace, and then select OK. Click inside the Replace With text box, select Format, select Style, choose the style you want to use as the replacement, and then select OK. Now run the replacement.

It's Not All Good

Replace All with Caution

The Replace All command is the quickest and easiest way to make your replacements, but it's dangerous because you don't see every replacement that Word makes. This is particularly true if you are using search options such as wildcards. Unless you're absolutely certain that you want to replace every instance in your document, use the Replace command instead of Replace All.

Proofing Text

The word *proofing* is short for *proofreading*, and it refers to inspecting a body of writing for errors or inaccuracies. No matter what kind of writing you do, always proof your work before allowing other people to read it. Why? Because one of the easiest ways to lose face in the working world or to lose marks in the academic world is to hand in a piece of writing that contains spelling or grammar mistakes. No matter how professionally organized and formatted your document appears, a simple spelling error or grammatical gaffe will stick out and take your reader's mind off your message. However, mistakes do happen, especially if your document is large. To help you catch these errors, Word offers both spell- and grammar-checking features.

As you type in Word, the spell checker operates in the background and examines your text for errors. When you type a word-separating character (that is, you press the spacebar or Enter or type a period, semicolon, comma, or colon), the checker compares the previous word with its internal dictionary; if it can't find the word in the dictionary, it signals a spelling error by placing a wavy red line under the word.

The grammar checker also operates in the background and scours your text for errors. When you start a new sentence, the grammar checker examines the previous sentence for problems and, if it finds any, it signals a grammatical error by placing a wavy green line under the offending word or phrase.

Handle Spelling and Grammar Errors

You can handle both spelling and grammar errors as you go along, but you can also use the Spelling and Grammar task panes to gain a bit more control over the proofing tools.

1. Select the Review tab.

2. Select Spelling & Grammar. Word displays the Spelling task pane and highlights the first error it finds.

3. Select Change. If you want to correct all instances of the error, select Change All instead.

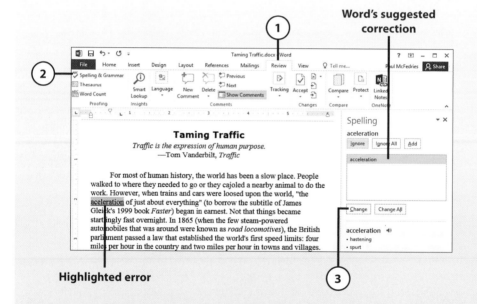

Word's suggested correction

Highlighted error

4. If the spell checker highlights a word that you know is correct, select Ignore. If the word appears multiple times in your document, select Ignore All instead.

Adding Correct Words to the Dictionary

Words such as proper names and technical terms are flagged by the spell checker because they don't appear in its dictionary of acceptable words. If the spell checker keeps flagging a correct word that you use frequently, you can add the word to its dictionary and thus avoid it getting flagged again. The next time the spell checker highlights the word, select Add in the Spelling task pane.

5. If Word flags a grammatical error, you see the Grammar task pane. Select Change to apply the proposed correction. If you believe that your prose is correct, you can select Ignore instead.

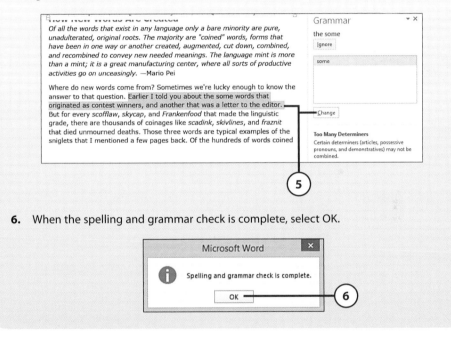

6. When the spelling and grammar check is complete, select OK.

Adding Hyperlinks

A *hyperlink* is a special section of text that, when clicked, opens a website, and we're most familiar with them on web pages. Although web-based hyperlinks have been around for a long time now, it still seems slightly radical that you can insert a hyperlink in a Word document. This useful feature lets you create "active" documents that enable the reader to click text to open the linked website in a web browser.

Insert a Hyperlink

To insert a hyperlink in a Word document, you need to know the web address of the remote site or page. This is most easily accomplished by copying the address from a web browser.

1. In a web browser, use the address box to select the address of the site or page.

2. Right-click the address.

3. Select Copy.

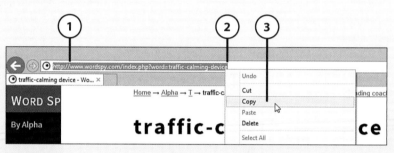

4. In Word, select the text you want to use as the hyperlink.

5. Select the Insert tab.

6. Select Links.

7. Select Hyperlink.

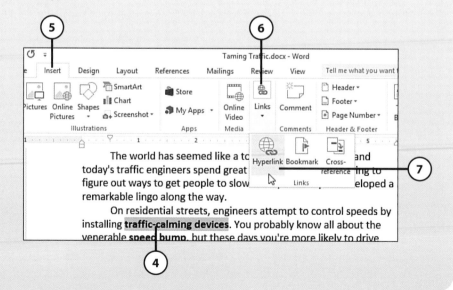

8. Select Existing File or Web Page.

9. Click inside the Address text box.

10. Press Ctrl+V. Word pastes the address.

11. Select OK. Word converts the selected text to a hyperlink.

Removing a Hyperlink

If you no longer require a hyperlink in your Word document, you can remove it. To do this, right-click the hyperlink and then click Remove Hyperlink.

Change the page
orientation.

Display text
in columns.

Contact Name	Company Name	Address	City	Region	Country	Postal Code
Alejandra Camino	Romero y tomillo	Gran Vía, 1	Madrid		Spain	28001
Alexander Feuer	Morgenstern Gesundkost	Heerstr. 22	Leipzig		Germany	04179
Ana Trujillo	Ana Trujillo Emparedados y helados	Avda. de la Constitución 2222	México D.F.		Mexico	05021
Anabela Domingues	Tradição Hipermercados	Av. Inês de Castro, 414	São Paulo	SP	Brazil	05634-030
André Fonseca	Gourmet Lanchonetes	Av. Brasil, 442	Campinas	SP	Brazil	04876-786
Ann Devon	Eastern Connection	35 King George	London		UK	WX3 6FW
Annette Roulet	La maison d'Asie	1 rue Alsace-Lorraine	Toulouse		France	31000
Antonio	Antonio	Mataderos 2312	México D.F.		Mexico	05023

Set the
margins.

Change the
paper size.

Build a table.

In this chapter, you learn about creating tables to hold structured data, adding headers and footers to your documents, and working with page layout options such as margins, page orientation, and paper size. Topics include the following:

→ Inserting a table into a Word document

→ Working with table rows and columns

→ Adding and populating document headers and footers

→ Choosing a page orientation and paper size

→ Setting the page margins

→ Adding footnotes and endnotes

Working with Page Layout and Design in Word

In the previous chapter, you dealt with Word at the "tree" level of words, sentences, and paragraphs. But getting more out of Word also requires that you deal with the program at the "forest" level of pages and documents. This means you need to get familiar with Word's page layout tools.

Page layout refers to how text and paragraphs are laid out on each page, and it involves building tables, adding headers and footers, setting margin sizes, specifying the page orientation, choosing the paper size, and so on. This chapter shows you how to work with these and other page layout features.

Building a Table

Most Word documents consist of text in the form of sentences and paragraphs. However, including lists of items in a document is common, particularly where each item in the list includes two or more details (which means a standard bulleted list won't do the job). For a short list with just a few details, the quickest way to add the list to a document is to type each item on its own line and press Tab between each detail. You could then add tab stops to the ruler (see Chapter 4, "Working with Text in Word") to line up the subitems into columns.

That works for simple items, but to construct a more complex list in Word, you can build a *table*, a rectangular structure with the following characteristics:

- Each item in the list gets its own horizontal rectangle called a *row*.

- Each set of details in the list gets its own vertical rectangle called a *column*.

- The rectangle formed by the intersection of a row and a column is called a *cell*, and you use the table cells to hold the data.

In other words, a Word table is similar to an Excel worksheet or an Access datasheet.

Insert a Table

Although Word gives you no less than a half dozen ways to build a table, you only need to know the most straightforward method.

1. Position the insertion point where you want the table to appear.

2. Select the Insert tab.

3. Select Table.

4. Select Insert Table to display the Insert Table dialog box.

For a small table, you can also click a box that represents the number of rows and columns you want.

For example, click here to insert a table with four columns and three rows.

5. Specify the number of columns you want in your table.

6. Specify the number of rows you want in the table.

7. Select OK. Word inserts the table.

8. Position the insertion point inside a cell and then add the text that you want to store in the cell. Repeat for the other cells in the table.

9. Select the Layout tab.

10. Use the Table Column Width box to set the width of the column.

Displaying the Ruler
If you don't see the ruler, select the View tab and then activate the Ruler check box.

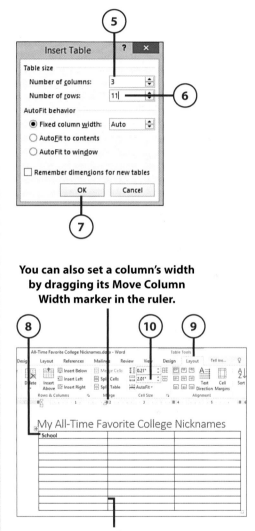

You can also set a column's width by dragging its Move Column Width marker in the ruler.

You can also set a column's width by dragging its right border.

CONVERTING TEXT TO A TABLE

If you already have a list where each column is separated by a tab, comma, or some other consistent character, you can convert that list to a table. To try this out, first select the list. Select the Insert tab, then the Table command, and then Convert Text to Table. Word displays the Convert Text to Table dialog box. Adjust the Number of Columns and Number of Rows values, if necessary. If you separated your columns with a character other than a tab or comma, use the Other text box to type the character. Click OK to convert the list to a table.

Select Table Elements

Before you can change the layout or formatting of a table, you need to select the part of the table you want to work with. Here are the techniques to use:

- **Select a cell**—Select the cell and then select Layout, Select, Select Cell (or triple-click anywhere in the cell).

- **Select two or more adjacent cells**—Select one of the cells and then drag the start and end selection handles to include the other cells.

- **Select a row**—Click any cell in the row and then select Layout, Select, Select Row.

- **Select two or more adjacent rows**—Select at least one cell in each row and then select Layout, Select, Select Row.

- **Select a column**—Click any cell in the column and then select Layout, Select, Select Column.

- **Select two or more adjacent columns**—Select at least one cell in each column and then select Layout, Select, Select Column.

- **Select the entire table**—Click any cell in the table and then select Layout, Select, Select Table.

Format a Table

To change the formatting of the table cells, you select the cells you want to work with and then use Word's standard formatting tools (font, paragraph, and so on). For more table-specific formatting, you can use the Design tab.

1. Click inside the table.

2. Select the Design tab.

3. Select the More button of the Table Styles gallery.

4. Select the style you want to apply to the table.

5. Select Header Row to toggle header formatting on and off for the first row. For example, in some styles the first row is given darker shading, top and bottom borders, and a bold font.

6. Select Total Row to toggle total formatting on and off for the bottom row.

7. Select Banded Rows to toggle alternating formatting for all the rows.

8. Select First Column to toggle special formatting on and off for the first column.

9. Select Last Column to toggle special formatting on and off for the last column.

10. Select Banded Columns to toggle alternating formatting for all the columns.

If you see the style you want to apply, you can select it without opening the Table Styles gallery.

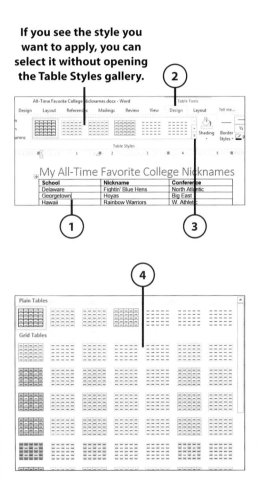

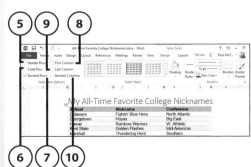

11. Select the cells you want to format and then use the Shading gallery to select a background color.

12. Select the cells you want to format and then use options in the Borders group to select a border style.

Modifying a Table Style

If the predefined table styles aren't quite what you're looking for, you can modify any style to suit your needs. Apply the style that comes closest to what you want, select the More button of the Table Styles gallery, and then select Modify Table Style. In the Modify Style dialog box that appears, use the controls to adjust the style's fonts, colors, borders, and more.

Insert New Rows

There are times when you need to add more data to a table. Word provides several tools that enable you to expand a table. If you're adding new items to the table, you need to add more rows.

1. To add a new row at the end of the table, position the insertion point in the lower-right cell—that is, the last column of the last row—and press Tab.

2. Select the Layout tab.

3. To add a new row above an existing row, position the insertion point inside the existing row and then select Insert Above.

4. To add a new row below an existing row, position the insertion point inside the existing row and then select Insert Below.

>>>Go Further

INSERTING MULTIPLE ROWS

If you want to insert multiple rows, you can insert them all in one operation. To begin, select the same number of existing rows. For example, if you want to insert three rows into your table, select three existing rows. Again, you'll be inserting the new rows either above or below the selection, so select your rows accordingly. Select the Layout tab and then select either Insert Above or Insert Below.

Insert New Columns

If you need to add more details to each item in your table, you need to add more columns.

1. Click inside an existing column.

2. Select the Layout tab.

3. To add a new column to the left of an existing column, select Insert Left.

4. To add a new column to the right of an existing column, select Insert Right.

Inserting Multiple Columns

To insert multiple columns at once, first select the same number of existing columns. For example, if you want to insert two columns into your table, select two existing columns. Select the Layout tab and then select either Insert Left or Insert Right.

My All-Time Favorite College Nicknames

School	Nickname	Conference
Delaware	Fightin' Blue Hens	North Atlantic
Georgetown	Hoyas	Big East
Hawaii	Rainbow Warriors	W. Athletic
Kent State	Golden Flashes	Mid-American
Marshall	Thundering Herd	Southern
Minnesota	Golden Gophers	Big Ten
North Carolina	Tar Heels	ACC
Purdue	Boilermakers	Big Ten
Sam Houston St.	Bear Kats	Southland
South Carolina	Fighting Gamecocks	Southeastern
Southern Illinois	Salukis	Missouri Valley
Texas Christian	Horned Frogs	Southwest
Wake Forest	Demon Deacons	ACC
Western Carolina	Catamounts	Southern
Western Illinois	Leathernecks	Mid-Continent

>>>Go Further
MERGING TABLE CELLS

Although most people use tables to store lists of data, using a table to lay out a page in a particular way is also common. For example, if you are building a Word document that looks like an existing paper form or invoice, you will almost certainly need to use a table to do it. However, on most forms, not all the fields—which will be the cells in the table you create—are the same width: You might have a small field for a person's age, a much wider field for an address, and so on. Changing the row width as you learned in the previous section does not work because you need to change the sizes of individual cells.

The best way to do this is to build your table normally and then merge two or more cells together. For example, if you merge two cells that are side by side in the same row, you end up with a single cell that is twice the width of the other cells. To merge cells, first select the cells. (You can select cells in a single row, a single column, or in multiple rows and columns. However, the selection must be a rectangle of adjacent cells.) Select the Layout tab and then select Merge Cells.

Delete Table Elements

If you no longer need a part of your table—for example, a cell, a row, or a column—you can delete it. You can delete multiple cells, rows, or columns, and, if necessary, you can delete the entire table.

1. Select the table element you want to delete.

Selecting Elements for Deletion

If you want to delete a row or column, you need only click anywhere inside that row or column. If you want to delete multiple rows or columns, you need to select at least one cell in each row or column. If you plan on deleting the entire table, you need only click anywhere inside the table.

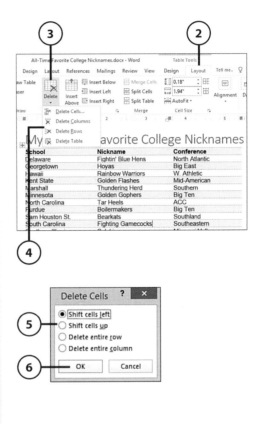

2. Select the Layout tab.

3. Select Delete.

4. Select the command that represents the type of table element you want to delete. If you select the Delete Cells command, the Delete Cells dialog box opens.

5. Select whether you want to shift the remaining cells to the left or up, or if you would rather delete the entire row or column.

6. Select OK.

Working with Headers and Footers

A *header* is a section that appears at the top of each page between the top margin and the first line of text. Any text, graphics, or properties you insert in any header appear at the top of every page in the document. Typical header contents include the document title and the date the document was created or modified.

A *footer* is a section that appears at the bottom of each page between the bottom margin and the last line of text. As with a header, anything you insert in any footer appears at the bottom of every page in the document. Typical footer contents include the page number and document filename.

Here are your choices for adding content to a header or footer:

- **Text**—You can type any text, such as a brief document description, a note to the reader, or your company name.

- **Page numbers**—You can insert just the page number, the phrase Page *X* (where *X* is the current page number), or Page *X* of *Y* (where *X* is the current page number and *Y* is the total number of pages in the document).

- **The current date and time**—You can display the current date, time, or both the date and time using various formats. You can also configure the date and time to update automatically each time you open the document.

- **Document information**—You can insert a number of document properties, including Author, Comments, Status, Subject, and Title.

- **A field**—Choose Design, Document Info, Field, and then use the Field dialog box to insert the field code.

- **Picture or clip art**—You can insert a photo or other image from your computer or you can grab a piece of online clip art.

Adding a Header

You can create a header from scratch by inserting a blank header (with one or three columns) or you can select a predefined header template.

1. Select the Insert tab.

2. Select Header.

3. Select the type of header you want to add. Word inserts the header and displays the Header & Footer Tools tab.

4. If you want to include a page number in your header, select Page Number.

5. Select Top of Page.

6. Select a page number style from the gallery.

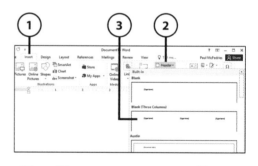

>>>Go Further

CREATING A UNIQUE FIRST-PAGE HEADER

By default, once you define the content for one header, Word displays the same content in every header in the document. However, many situations arise in which this default behavior is not what you want. One common situation is when you want to use a different header in the first page of a document. For example, many texts use *no* header on the first page. Another example is when you want to insert document instructions or notes in the first header, but you do not want that text repeated on every page.

For these kinds of situations, you can tell Word that you want the first page's header to be different from the headers and footers in the rest of the document. You set this up by selecting the Different First Page check box. Word changes the label of the first page header to First Page Header.

---

7. If you want to include the date or time (or both) in your header, select Date & Time to open the Date and Time dialog box.

8. Select the format you want to use.

Updating the Date and Time Automatically

If you want Word to update the displayed date and time automatically each time you open the document, select the Update Automatically check box (in the Date and Time dialog box).

---

9. Select OK.

10. If you want to include a document property in your header, select Document Info.

11. Select Document Property.

12. Select the property you want to add.

13. If you want to include an image from your computer, select Pictures. See "Inserting a Picture" in Chapter 3, "Working with Office 2016 Graphics."

14. If you want to include clip art, select Online Pictures.

15. To add text, position the insertion point within the header and then type your text.

16. Select Close Header and Footer.

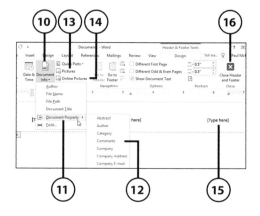

>>>Go Further

CREATING UNIQUE ODD AND EVEN PAGE HEADERS

Many documents require different layouts for the header on odd and even pages. A good example is the book you are holding. Notice that the even page header has the page number on the far left, followed by the chapter number and chapter title, while the odd page header has the name of the current section followed by the page number on the far right.

To handle this type of situation, you can configure your document with different odd and even page headers and footers by selecting the Different Odd & Even Pages check box (on the Options drop-down list). Word changes the labels of the page headers to Even Page Header and Odd Page Header.

Adding a Footer

You can create a footer from scratch by inserting a blank footer or you can select a predefined footer template.

1. Select the Insert tab.

2. Select Footer.

3. Select the type of footer you want to add.

4. If you want to include a page number in your footer, select Page Number.

5. Select Bottom of Page.

6. Select a page number style from the gallery.

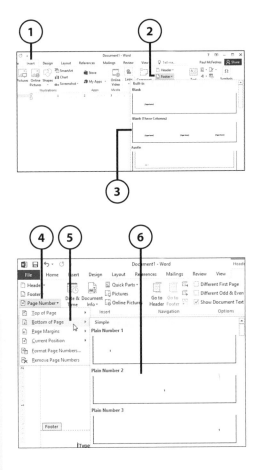

7. If you want to include the date or time (or both) in your footer, select Date & Time to open the Date and Time dialog box.

8. Select the format you want to use.

9. Select OK.

10. If you want to include a document property in your footer, select Document Info.

11. Select Document Property.

12. Select the property you want to add.

13. If you want to include an image from your computer, select Pictures. See "Inserting a Picture" in Chapter 3.

14. If you want to include clip art, select Online Pictures.

15. To add text, position the insertion point within the footer and then type your text.

16. To switch to the header, select Go to Header. Once you're in the header, you can switch back to the footer by selecting Go to Footer.

17. Select Close Header and Footer.

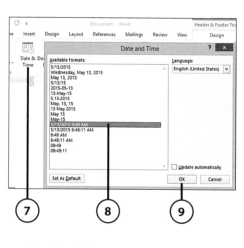

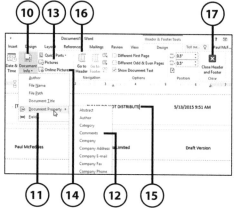

Changing the Page Setup

Word's options and features for setting up pages are legion, but few of us use them with any regularity. That's a shame because Word's page setup tools are often useful and easy to use, once you get to know them. The next few sections take you through the most useful of Word's page setup features.

Setting the Margins

One of the most common page layout changes is to adjust the *margins*, the blank space to the left and right, as well as above and below the document text (including the header and footer). The standard margins are one inch on all sides. Decreasing the margins fits more text on each page (which is useful when printing a long document), but it can also make the printout look cluttered and uninviting. If you increase the margins, you get less text on each page, but the added whitespace can make the document look more appealing.

You can set specific margin sizes for the Top, Bottom, Left, and Right margins, and you can also specify where you want Word to apply the new margins: to the whole document or from the insertion point forward.

1. Select the Layout tab.

2. Select Margins.

3. Select Custom Margins. Word opens the Page Setup dialog box and displays the Margins tab.

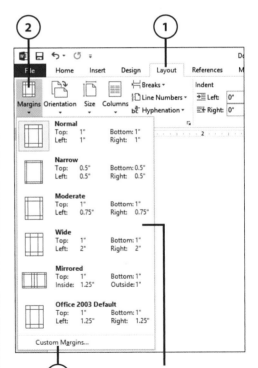

If you see the margin size option you want to use, you can select it without opening the Page Setup dialog box.

4. Use the Top spin box to set the top margin.

5. Use the Bottom spin box to set the bottom margin.

6. Use the Left spin box to set the left margin.

7. Use the Right spin box to set the right margin.

Adding a Gutter

You can also set the size and position of the *gutter*, which is extra whitespace added (usually) to the inside margin to handle document binding. In the Margins tab of the Page Setup dialog box, use the Gutter spin box to set the size of the gutter, and use the Gutter Position list to select whether you want the gutter in the left margin or the top margin.

8. Use the Apply To list to select whether you want your new margins applied to the whole document or only from the insertion point forward.

9. Select OK.

Changing the Page Orientation

By default, page text runs across the short side of the page, and down the long side. This is called the *portrait orientation*. Alternatively, you can configure the text to run across the long side of the page and down the short side, which is called *landscape orientation*.

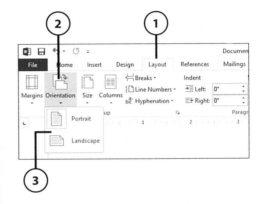

1. Select the Layout tab.

2. Select Orientation.

3. Select the page orientation you want to use.

>>>Go Further

LANDSCAPE VERSUS PORTRAIT

You would use the landscape orientation mostly when you have text or an image that is too wide to fit across the page in portrait orientation. If you're using letter-size paper and your margins are set to 0.75 inches, you have only seven inches of usable space across the page. Wide images, a table with many columns, or a long line of programming code are just a few of the situations where this width might not be enough. If you switch to landscape, however, the usable space grows to 9.5 inches, a substantial increase.

Changing the Paper Size

Word assumes that you will be printing your documents on standard letter-size paper, which is 8.5 inches by 11 inches. If you plan to use a different paper size, you need to let Word know what you will be using so that it can print the document correctly.

1. Select the Layout tab.

2. Select Size.

3. Select More Paper Sizes. Word opens the Page Setup dialog box and displays the Paper tab.

4. Select a paper size.

5. If you need to set a custom paper width, use the Width spin box.

6. If you need to set a custom paper height, use the Height spin box.

7. Use the Apply To list to select whether you want your new paper size applied to the whole document or only from the insertion point forward.

8. Select OK.

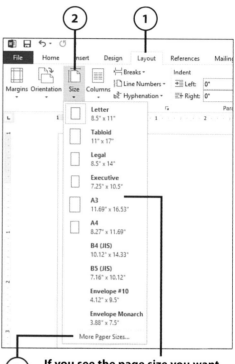

If you see the page size you want to use, you can select it without opening the Page Setup dialog box.

>>>Go Further
PRINTING ON THE EDGE

Getting the proper printout isn't the only reason for configuring Word to use a different page size. An old trick is to tell Word you are using a larger paper size than you actually are. Word then prints the page as if you're using the larger size, which with some experimentation means you can get Word to print right to (or pretty close to) the edge of a regular sheet of paper or an envelope.

Add a Page Break

If you have a paragraph that must begin at the top of a page, you can ensure that happens by inserting a *page break* just before that paragraph.

1. Click at the beginning of the paragraph that you want to appear on a new page.

2. Select the Insert tab.

3. Select Pages.

4. Select Page Break.

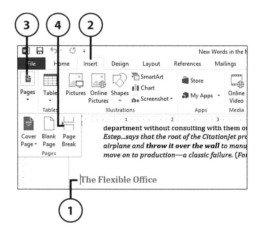

Understanding Sections

In Word-related training sessions and question-and-answer periods, some of the most common complaints and queries center on using multiple page layouts in a single document:

- How can I have different headers (or footers) for different parts of a document?

- I have a long table on one page. How can I set up that one page with landscape orientation?

- Can I switch from a two-column layout to a three-column layout for part of a document?

Most people end up splitting a single document into multiple documents to accomplish these and similar tasks. However, you do not have to break up your document just because you want to break up the page layout. The secret to doing this is the *section*, a document part that stores page layout options such as the following:

- Margins

- Page size and page orientation

- Headers and footers

- Columns

- Line numbering

- Footnotes and endnotes

Add a Section Break

When you create a document, Word gives it a single section that comprises the entire document. However, you are free to create multiple sections within a single document, and you can then apply separate page layout formatting to each section. The transition from one section to another is called a *section break*.

1. Click where you want the new section to begin.

2. Select the Layout tab.

3. Select Breaks.

4. Select a section break.

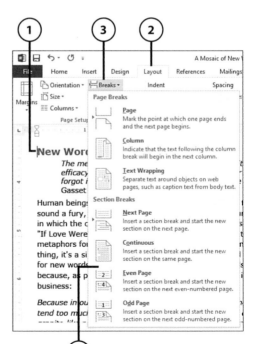

>>>Go Further

WORD'S SECTION BREAKS

Word offers four types of section breaks:

- **Next Page**—Starts a new section on a new page
- **Continuous**—Starts a new section at the insertion point (does not add a page break)
- **Even Page**—Starts a new section on the next even numbered page
- **Odd Page**—Starts a new section on the next odd numbered page

Display Text in Columns

If you put together a brochure, newsletter, or any document where you want to mimic the layout of a newspaper or magazine, you probably want your text to appear in two or more columns. When you use columns, as the text in the first column reaches the bottom of the page, it continues at the top of the next column. It's only when the text reaches the bottom of the last column that it continues on the next page.

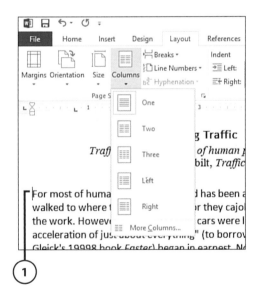

1. Click where you want to convert the text to columns.

Positioning the Insertion Point for Columns

If your document has only one section and you want to use columns for the entire document, position the insertion point anywhere within the document. If your document has multiple sections and you want to use columns for a single section, position the insertion point anywhere within that section. If your document has multiple sections and you want to use columns for the entire document, select the entire document.

---

2. Select the Layout tab.

3. Select Columns.

4. Select More Columns. Word opens the Columns dialog box.

5. Select the number of columns.

6. Use these spin boxes to set the width of each column.

Applying Unequal Column Widths

By default, Word assumes you want each column to be the same width. To set unique widths for each column, you must first deactivate the Equal Column Width check box.

7. Use these spin boxes to set the spacing between each column.

8. Use the Apply To list to select whether you want your new column settings applied to the whole document or only from the insertion point forward.

9. Select OK.

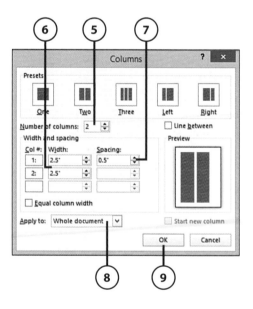

If you see the column preset you want to use, you can select it without opening the Columns dialog box.

>>>*Go Further*

WORD'S COLUMN PRESETS

Word offers five column presets:

- **One**—Reverts the text to a single column
- **Two**—Splits the text into two columns of the same width
- **Three**—Splits the text into three columns of the same width
- **Left**—Splits the text into two columns, with a narrow column on the left and a wide column on the right
- **Right**—Splits the text into two columns, with a narrow column on the right and a wide column on the left

Adding Footnotes and Endnotes

A *footnote* is a short note at the bottom of a page that provides extra information about something mentioned in the regular text on that page. Word indicates a footnote with a *reference mark*, a number or other symbol that appears as a superscript in both the regular text and in a special footnote box at the bottom of the page. An *endnote* is similar, except that is appears at the end of the document.

Word makes working with footnotes and endnotes a breeze. Not only are they easy to insert, but Word also keeps track of the reference marks and updates the numbers (or whatever) automatically no matter where you insert new notes in the document.

Insert a Footnote or Endnote

A default footnote appears at the bottom of the current page and uses Arabic numerals (1, 2, 3, and so on) as the reference marks. A default endnote appears at the end of the document and uses lowercase Roman numerals (i, ii, iii, and so on) as the reference marks.

1. Position the insertion point where you want the footnote or endnote reference mark to appear.

2. Select the References tab.

3. Select Insert Footnote. If you prefer to insert an endnote, select the Insert Endnote command, instead.

Keyboard Shortcut

You can also insert a footnote by pressing Ctrl+Alt+F. If you want to insert an endnote instead, press Ctrl+Alt+D.

4. Type your note text.

5. To navigate footnotes or endnotes, select Next Footnote and then select whether you want to see the next or previous footnote or endnote.

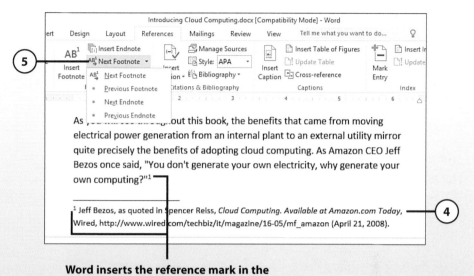

**Word inserts the reference mark in the
text and in the note area.**

>>>Go Further
CREATING CUSTOM FOOTNOTES
AND ENDNOTES

If Word's default footnotes and endnotes are not what you need, the program has plenty of options you can wield to customize your notes. For example, you can position the footnote area below the last line of the page instead of at the bottom of the page; for the reference marks, you can use Arabic numerals, uppercase or lowercase letters, uppercase or lowercase Roman numerals, or symbols such as the following: *, †, ‡, §. In fact, you can use any symbol available in the Symbol dialog box; you can start the reference marks at a specific number, letter, or symbol; and you can have the reference marks restart with each page or each section.

To create a custom footnote or endnote that uses some or all of these options, position the insertion point where you want the reference mark to appear, select the References tab, and then select the dialog box launcher in the lower-right corner of the Footnotes tab. Word displays the Footnote and Endnote dialog box. Select your options and then select Insert.

Build a table.

Create formulas.

Add functions to formulas.

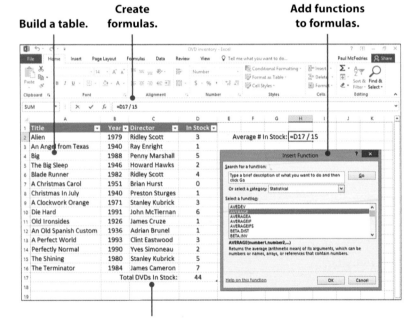

Enter data.

In this chapter, you learn about entering data into an Excel worksheet, building formulas, working with functions, and storing data in tables. Topics include the following:

→ Entering numbers, text, dates, and times

→ Editing cell data

→ Building formulas to add calculations to a worksheet

→ Creating and working with Excel tables

Entering Excel Data

If you've never used a spreadsheet before, Excel may seem intimidating, and getting it to do anything useful may seem daunting. However, a spreadsheet is really just a fancy electronic version of a numeric scratch pad. With the latter, you write down a few numbers and then use elementary school techniques to calculate a result. At its most basic level, an Excel worksheet is much the same: You type one or more values and then you create a formula that calculates a result.

The first part of this basic Excel method is entering your worksheet data, and that's what this chapter is all about. You learn the best ways to get your data into the worksheet, some tips and tricks for easier data entry, how to build formulas, and how to use tables to make your data easier to read and understand.

Understanding Worksheet Cells and Data

A worksheet is a rectangular arrangement of rows and columns. The rows are numbered, where the topmost row is 1, the row below it is 2, and so on all the way to 1,048,576. (Although, as you can imagine, worksheets that use more than a million rows are rare!) The columns are labeled with letters, where A is the leftmost column, the next column is B, and so on. After column Z come columns AA, AB, and so on, all the way up to XFD; that's 16,384 columns in all.

The intersection of each row and column is called a *cell*, and each cell has a unique address that combines its column letter (or letters) and row number. For example, the upper-left cell in a worksheet is at the intersection of column A and row 1, so its address is A1. When you click a cell, it becomes the *active cell*—which Excel designates by surrounding the cell with a heavy border and by displaying a small square in the lower-right corner—and its address appears in the Name box, which is located just above column A.

You use these worksheet cells to enter your data, which you learn more about in the next few sections. For now, you should know that worksheet cells can hold four kinds of data:

- **Numbers**—These entries can be dollar values, weights, interest rates, or any other numerical quantity.

- **Text**—These entries are usually labels, such as *August Sales* or *Territory*, that make a worksheet easier to read, but they can also be text/number combinations for items such as phone numbers and account codes.

- **Dates and times**—These entries are specific dates (such as 8/23/2016), specific times (such as 9:05 a.m.), or combinations of the two. You mostly use dates (and, to a lesser extent, times) in tables and lists to record when something took place, although Excel also lets you calculate with dates and times.

- **Formulas**—These are calculations involving two or more values, such as 2*5 or A1+A2+A3. See the "Working with Formulas and Functions" section later in this chapter.

Working with Numbers

Worksheets are all about numbers. You add them together, subtract them, take their average, or perform any number of mathematical operations on them. Excel recognizes that you're entering a number if you start the entry with a decimal point (.), a plus sign (+), a minus sign (-), or a dollar sign ($). Here are some other rules for entering numbers:

- You can enter percentages by following the number with a percent sign (%). Excel stores the number as a decimal. For example, the entry **15%** is stored as 0.15.

- You can use scientific notation when entering numbers. For example, to enter the number 3,879,000,000, you could enter **3.879E+09**.

- You can also use parentheses to indicate a negative number. If you make an entry such as **(125)**, Excel assumes you mean negative 125.

- You can enter commas to separate thousands, but you have to make sure that each comma appears in the appropriate place. Excel interprets an entry such as **12,34** as text.

- If you want to enter a fraction, you need to type an integer, a space, and then the fraction (**5 1/8**, for example). This is true even if you're entering only the fractional part; in this case, you need to type a zero, a space, and then the fraction or else Excel interprets the entry as a date. For example, **0 1/8** is the fraction one-eighth, but **1/8** is January 8.

Working with Text

In Excel, text entries can include any combination of letters, symbols, and numbers. Although text is sometimes used as data, you'll find that you mostly use text to describe the contents of your worksheets. This is important because even a modest-sized spreadsheet can become a confusing jumble of numbers without some kind of guideline to keep things straight. There is no practical limit on the length of text entries (they can be up to 32,767 characters long!), but in general, you shouldn't use anything too fancy or elaborate; a simple phrase such as *Monthly Expenses* or *Payment Date* will usually suffice.

Working with Dates and Times

Excel uses *serial numbers* to represent specific dates and times. To get a date serial number, Excel uses December 31, 1899, as an arbitrary starting point and counts the number of days that have passed since then. For example, the date serial number for January 1, 1900, is 1; for January 2, 1900, it is 2; and so on. Table 6.1 displays some examples of date serial numbers.

Table 6.1   Examples of Date Serial Numbers

Serial Number	Date
366	December 31, 1900
16229	June 6, 1944
42735	December 31, 2016

To get a time serial number, Excel expresses time as a decimal fraction of the 24-hour day to get a number between 0 and 1. The starting point, midnight, is given the value 0, so noon—halfway through the day—has a serial number of 0.5. Table 6.2 displays some examples of time serial numbers.

Table 6.2   Examples of Time Serial Numbers

Serial Number	Time
0.25	6:00:00 AM
0.375	9:00:00 AM
0.70833	5:00:00 PM
.99999	11:59:59 PM

You can combine the two types of serial numbers. For example, 42735.5 represents noon on December 31, 2016.

The advantage of using serial numbers in this way is that it makes calculations involving dates and times easy. A date or time is really just a number, so any mathematical operation you can perform on a number you can also perform on a date. This is invaluable for worksheets that track delivery times, monitor accounts receivable or accounts payable aging, calculate invoice discount dates, and so on.

Although it's true that the serial numbers make it easier for the computer to manipulate dates and times, it's not the best format for humans to comprehend. For example, the number 25,404.95555 is meaningless, but the moment it represents (July 20, 1969, at 10:56 p.m. EDT) is one of the great moments in history (the *Apollo 11* moon landing). Fortunately, Excel takes care of the conversion between these formats so that you never have to worry about it.

To enter a date or time, use any of the formats outlined in Table 6.3. Note that no matter which format you use, Excel still stores the date or time as a serial number. Also, you're not stuck with the format you use when you enter the date or time—you're free to change the format any time.

Table 6.3   Excel Date and Time Formats

Format	Example
m/d	8/23
m/d/yy	8/23/16
d-mmm	23-Aug (Excel assumes the current year)
d-mmm-yy	23-Aug-16
mmm-yy	Aug-16 (Excel assumes the first day of the month)
mmmm-yy	August-16
mmmm d, yyyy	August 23, 2016
dddd, mmmm d, yyyy	Monday, August 23, 2016
h:mm AM/PM	3:10 PM
h:mm:ss AM/PM	3:10:45 PM
h:mm	15:10
h:mm:ss	15:10:45
mm:ss.0	10:45.7
m/d/yy h:mm AM/PM	8/23/16 3:10 PM
m/d/yy h:mm	8/23/16 15:10

Entering and Editing Data

A spreadsheet is only as useful—and as accurate—as the data it contains. Even a small mistake can render your results meaningless. So the first rule of good spreadsheet style is to enter and edit your data carefully.

Enter Cell Data

If you're new to spreadsheet work, you'll no doubt be pleased to hear that entering data into a worksheet cell is straightforward.

1. Select the cell you want to use to enter your data. The easiest way to do this is to click the cell, but you can also use the arrow keys to navigate to the cell you want.

2. Type your data. Excel automatically opens the cell for editing and places your typing inside the cell.

3. When your entry is complete, press Enter. Excel moves the active cell to the cell below. If you don't want the active cell to move after you confirm your entry, click the Enter button, instead.

The Enter button **As you type, your characters also appear inside the Formula bar.**

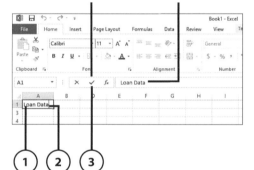

Confirming Data Entry with the Arrow Keys

You can also confirm your entry by pressing any of the arrow keys or by selecting another cell. The active cell moves either in the direction of the arrow or to the cell you selected. This feature is handy if you have, say, a lengthy row of data to type in. By pressing (in this case) the right arrow key to confirm each entry, you automatically move the active cell along the row.

Edit Cell Data

If you make a mistake when entering data or you have to update the contents of a cell, you need to edit the cell to get the correct value. If you want to replace the entire cell contents, follow the steps in the previous section. This section shows you how to make changes to a cell's existing content.

1. Double-click the cell. The insertion point appears inside the cell.

Keyboard Shortcut

You can also open the active cell for editing by pressing F2.

---

2. Click (or use the left and right arrow keys) to position the insertion point where you want to make your changes.

3. Edit the contents of the cell.

4. Confirm your changes by pressing Enter or clicking the Enter button. To cancel the edit without confirming your changes, press Esc or click the Cancel button.

Insertion point

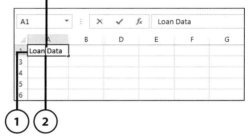

Cancel button

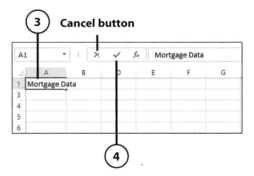

Working with Formulas and Functions

Any worksheet is merely a collection of numbers and text until you define some kind of relationship between the various entries. You do this by creating *formulas* that perform calculations and produce results. This section takes you through some formula basics and then shows you how to build your own formulas.

Excel divides formulas into three main groups: arithmetic, comparison, and text. Each group has its own set of operators, and you use each group in different ways.

Let's start with *arithmetic formulas*, which are by far the most common type of formula. They combine numbers, cell addresses, and function results with mathematic operators to perform calculations. Table 6.4 summarizes the mathematic operators used in arithmetic formulas.

Table 6.4   The Arithmetic Operators

Operator	Name	Example	Result
+	Addition	=10+5	15
-	Subtraction	=10-5	5
-	Negation	=-10	-10
*	Multiplication	=10*5	50
/	Division	=10/5	2
%	Percentage	=10%	.1
^	Exponentiation	=10^5	100,000

Most of the operators in Table 6.4 are straightforward, but the exponentiation operator may require further explanation. The formula $=x^y$ means that the value x is raised to the power y. For example, $=3^2$ produces the result 9 (that is, 3*3=9). Similarly, $=2^4$ produces 16 (that is, 2*2*2*2=16).

A *comparison formula* is a statement that compares two or more numbers, text strings, cell contents, or function results. If the statement is true, the result of the formula is given the logical value TRUE (which is equivalent to 1). If the statement is false, the formula returns the logical value FALSE (which is equivalent to 0). Table 6.5 summarizes the operators you can use in comparison formulas.

Table 6.5   Comparison Formula Operators

Operator	Name	Example	Result
=	Equal to	=10=5	FALSE
>	Greater than	=10>5	TRUE
<	Less than	=10<5	FALSE
>=	Greater than or equal to	="a">="b"	FALSE
<=	Less than or equal to	="a"<="b"	TRUE
<>	Not equal to	="a"<>"b"	TRUE

There are many uses for comparison formulas. For example, you could determine whether to pay a salesperson a bonus by using a comparison formula to compare the person's actual sales with a predetermined quota. If the sales are greater than the quota, the salesperson is awarded the bonus. Another example is credit collection. If the amount a customer owes is, say, more than 150 days past due, you might send the receivable to a collection agency.

Build a Formula

Building a formula is much like entering data into a cell, with the exception that all Excel formulas must begin with an equal sign (=).

1. Select the cell you want to use for the formula.

2. Type an equal sign (=). Excel opens the cell for editing and enters the equal sign.

3. Enter a value, cell reference, range, range name, or function name.

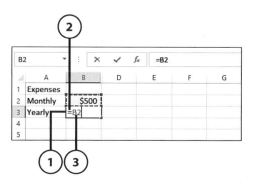

Clicking to Enter a Cell Address

When entering a cell reference in a formula, you could just type in the cell address, but it's often faster and more accurate to let Excel do the work by clicking the cell. The address appears automatically in the formula at the insertion point.

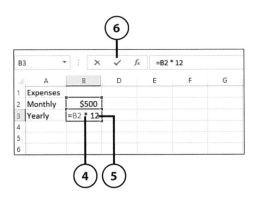

4. Enter an operator (such as + or *).

5. Repeat steps 3 and 4 until the formula is complete.

6. Press Enter or click the Enter button to accept the formula.

>>>Go Further
CONTROLLING THE ORDER OF CALCULATION

When you use the operators listed earlier in Tables 6.4 and 6.5, be aware that Excel processes the operators not only from left to right, but also by giving some operators precedence over others. For example, Excel always performs multiplication and division before it performs addition and subtraction. In some cases, you might need to control the order of calculation so that, say, Excel performs an addition operation before it performs a multiplication. To do this, enclose the operation you want performed first in parentheses. Excel always calculates expressions enclosed in parentheses first, so you can use this technique to force Excel to calculate your formulas in whatever order you require.

Understanding Functions

Consider the following scenario: You want to deposit a certain amount in an investment that earns a particular rate of interest over a particular number of years. Assuming you start at 0, how much will the investment be worth at the end of the term? Given a present value (represented by *pv*), a regular payment (*pmt*), an annual interest rate (*rate*), and some number of years (*nper*), here's the formula that calculates the future value of the investment:

```
pv(1 + rate) ^ nper + pmt * (((1 + rate) ^ nper) - 1) / rate
```

That's a *really* complex formula, but this complexity wouldn't be a big deal if this formula were obscure or rarely used. However, calculating the future value of an investment is one of the most common Excel chores (it is, for example, the central calculation in most retirement planning models). Having to type such a formula once is bad enough, but it is one you may need dozens of times. Clearly, entering such a formula by hand so many times is both time consuming and prone to errors.

Fortunately, Excel offers a solution: a worksheet function called `FV()` (Future Value), which reduces the earlier formula to the following:

```
fv(rate, nper, pmt, pv)
```

Not only is this formula much simpler to use and faster to type, you also don't have to memorize anything other than the function name because, as you soon see, Excel shows you the full function syntax (that is, the list of arguments and the order in which they appear) as you type it.

In general, a *function* is a predefined formula that calculates a result based on one or more *arguments*, which are the function's input values (such as `rate` and `nper` in the `FV()` example). Note that most functions have at least one argument, and that for functions with two or more arguments, in most cases some of those arguments are required (that is, Excel returns an error if the arguments are not present) and some are optional.

Functions not only simplify complex mathematical formulas, but they also enable you to perform powerful calculations such as statistical correlation, the number of workdays between two dates, and square roots.

Add a Function Directly to a Cell

The quickest way to include a function in a formula is to type the function and its arguments directly into the cell.

1. Enter your formula up to the point where you want to include the function.

2. Begin typing the function name. As you type, Excel displays a list of function names that begin with what you have typed so far.

3. Click a function name to select it and see its description.

4. To add the selected function name to the formula, double-click it (or press Tab). Excel adds the function name and a left parenthesis—(.

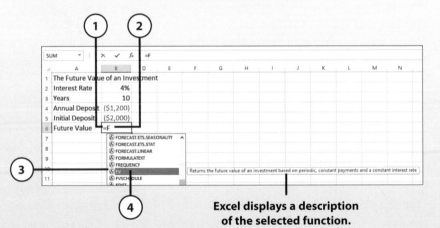

Excel displays a description of the selected function.

5. If you're typing the function name by hand, be sure to add the left parenthesis after the name. Excel now displays a ScreenTip with the function syntax.

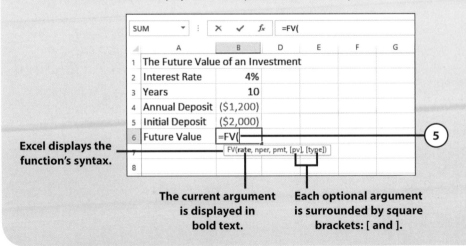

Excel displays the function's syntax.

The current argument is displayed in bold text.

Each optional argument is surrounded by square brackets: [and].

6. Enter the required arguments, separated by commas. If you also need to use any of the optional arguments, enter them separated by commas.

7. Type the right parenthesis: **)**.

8. Press Enter or click the Enter button. Excel enters the formula and displays the formula result in the cell.

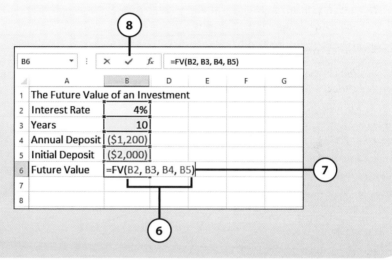

Add a Function Using the Function Wizard

Excel's pop-up function list and syntax ScreenTips are so useful that typing functions by hand is almost always the fastest way to incorporate functions into your formulas. However, if you're not sure which function you need, or if you want to see the function results before committing the function to the formula, you need to turn to Excel's Function Wizard.

1. Enter your formula up to the point where you want to include the function.

2. Select the Formulas tab.

3. Select Insert Function. You can also click the Insert Function button beside the Formula bar. The Insert Function dialog box opens.

4. In the Or Select a Category list, select the category that contains your function. If you are not sure which category to choose, select All.

The Most Recently Used List

Excel maintains a list of the last 10 functions you have used. If the function you want is one that you used recently, click Most Recently Used in the list of categories, and then use the Select a Function list to click the function if it appears.

Select AutoSum to quickly add the SUM() function.

You can also use these lists to select the function you want.

3

2

	A	B	D	E	F	G
1	The Future Value of an Investment					
2	Interest Rate	4%				
3	Years	10				
4	Annual Deposit	($1,200)				
5	Initial Deposit	($2,000)				
6	Future Value	=				
7						

The Insert Function button

5. In the Select a Function list, select the function you want to use.

6. Select OK. Excel displays the Function Arguments dialog box.

5

4

7. Enter the values or cell references you want to use for each argument. If you want to use a cell reference, note that you can enter it by tapping the cell.

8. Select OK. Excel inserts the function into the formula.

Required arguments are shown in bold type. (7)

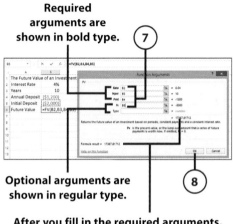

Optional arguments are shown in regular type. (8)

After you fill in the required arguments, Excel displays the result of the function and the result of the cell formula.

Building a Table

Excel's forte is spreadsheet work, of course, but its row-and-column layout also makes it a natural database manager. In Excel, a *table* is a collection of related information with an organizational structure that makes it easy to find or extract data from its contents. Specifically, a table is a collection of cells that has the following properties:

- **Field**—A single type of information, such as a name, an address, or a phone number. In Excel tables, each column is a field.

- **Field value**—A single item in a field. In an Excel table, the field values are the individual cells.

- **Field name**—A unique name you assign to every table field (worksheet column). These names are always found in the first row of the table.

- **Record**—A collection of associated field values. In Excel tables, each row is a record.

Convert Cells to a Table

Excel has a number of commands that enable you to work efficiently with table data. To take advantage of these commands, you must convert your data from normal cells to a table.

Make sure you have your field names in the top row.

1. Select any cell within the group of cells that you want to convert to a table.

2. Select the Insert tab.

3. Select Table. Excel displays the Create Table dialog box.

4. If your range has column headers in the top row (as it should), make sure the My Table Has Headers check box is selected.

5. Select OK. Excel converts the cells to a table.

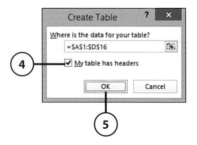

Select Table Elements

Before you can change the layout or formatting of a table, you need to select the part of the table you want to work with. Here are the techniques to use:

- **Select a cell**—Click the cell.

- **Select two or more adjacent cells**—Select one of the cells and then click and drag to include the other cells.

- **Select a row**—Right-click a cell in the row, click Select, and then click Table Row.

- **Select two or more adjacent rows**—Select at least one cell in each row, right-click the selection, click Select, and then click Table Row.

- **Select a column**—Right-click a cell in the column, click Select, and then click either Entire Table Column (to include the header) or Table Column Data (to exclude the header).

- **Select two or more adjacent columns**—Select at least one cell in each column, right-click any cell in the selection, click Select, and then click either Entire Table Column (to include the headers) or Table Column Data (to exclude the headers).

Format a Table

To change the formatting of the table cells, you select the cells you want to work with and then use Excel's standard formatting tools (font, paragraph, and so on). For more table-specific formatting, you can use the Design tab.

1. Click inside the table.

2. Select the Design tab.

3. Select Quick Styles. Excel opens the Table Quick Styles gallery.

4. Select the style you want to apply to the table.

5. Select Header Row to toggle header formatting on and off for the first row. For example, in some styles the first row is given darker shading, top and bottom borders, and a bold font.

6. Select Total Row to toggle the Total row (which shows the totals for the table's rightmost column) and that row's total formatting on and off.

7. Select Banded Rows to toggle alternating formatting for all the rows.

8. Select First Column to toggle special formatting on and off for the first column.

9. Select Last Column to toggle special formatting on and off for the last column.

10. Select Banded Columns to toggle alternating formatting for all the columns.

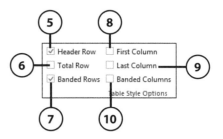

Creating a Custom Table Style

If the predefined table styles aren't quite what you're looking for, you can create a custom style to suit your needs. Select Quick Styles to open the Table Quick Styles gallery, and then select New Table Style. In the New Table Style dialog box that opens, select a table element, select Format, and then use the controls to adjust the style's fonts, colors, borders, and more. Repeat for each table element you want to format, and then select OK.

Add New Rows and Columns

When it's time to add more data to your table, Excel provides several tools that enable you to expand the table. If you're adding new items to the table, you need to add more rows; if you're adding more details to each item, you need to add more columns.

1. To add a new row at the end of the table, select the lower-right cell—that is, the last column of the last row—and press Tab.

2. Select the Home tab.

3. To add a new row above an existing row, position the active cell inside the existing row, select Insert, and then select Insert Table Rows Above.

4. To add a new column to the left of an existing column, position the active cell inside the existing column, select Insert, and then select Insert Table Columns to the Left.

Adding Multiple Rows or Columns

If you want to insert multiple rows or columns, you can insert them all in one operation by first selecting the same number of existing rows or columns. For example, if you select two rows and then select Insert Table Rows Above, Excel inserts two rows above the selected rows.

Delete Rows and Columns

If you find you no longer need a part of your table —for example, a row or a column—you can delete it. You can also delete multiple rows or columns.

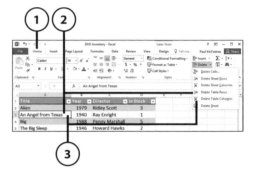

1. Select the Home tab.

2. To delete a row, position the active cell inside the row, select Delete, and then select Delete Table Rows.

3. To delete a column, position the active cell inside the column, select Delete, and then select Delete Table Columns.

Selecting Elements for Deletion

If you want to delete a row or column, you need only select anywhere inside that row or column. If you want to delete multiple rows or columns, you need to select at least one cell in each row or column.

Sort a Table

One of the advantages of using a table is that you can rearrange the records so that they're sorted alphabetically or numerically. Sorting enables you to view the data in order by customer name, account number, part number, or any other field.

Excel offers two kinds of sorts:

- **Ascending**—This type of sort arranges the items in a field from smallest to largest if the field is numeric, from A to Z if the field is text, and from oldest to newest if the field contains date or time data.

- **Descending**—This sort type arranges the items in a field from largest to smallest if the field contains numbers, from Z to A if the field contains text, and from newest to oldest if the field contains dates or times.

1. Select the Filter and Sort button (the drop-down arrow that appears beside the field header) for the field you want to use for the sort.

2. To sort a text field in ascending order, select Sort A to Z. If the field has numeric values, select Sort Smallest to Largest; if the field has date or time values, select Sort Oldest to Newest.

3. To sort a text field in descending order, select Sort Z to A. If the field has numeric values, select Sort Largest to Smallest; if the field has date or time values, select Sort Newest to Oldest.

To indicate that a field is sorted, Excel adds an arrow to the field's Filter and Sort button (up for ascending; down for descending).

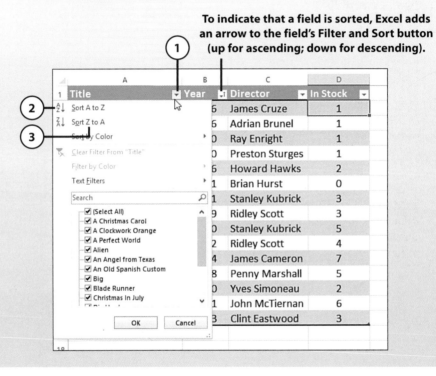

Filter a Table

One of the biggest problems with large tables is that it's often hard to find and extract the data you need. Sorting can help, but in the end, you're still working with the entire table. You need a way to define the data that you want to work with and then have Excel display only those records onscreen. This is called *filtering* your data, and Excel's Filter feature makes filtering out subsets of your data as easy as selecting check boxes from the *filter list*, a collection of the unique values in the field. When you deselect an item's check box, Excel temporarily hides all the table records that include that item in the field.

1. Select the Filter and Sort button for the field you want to use for the filter. Excel displays the field's filter list.

2. Deselect the check box for each item that you want to hide in the table.

3. Select OK.

To indicate that a field is filtered, Excel adds a funnel icon to the field's Filter and Sort button.

Quick filter

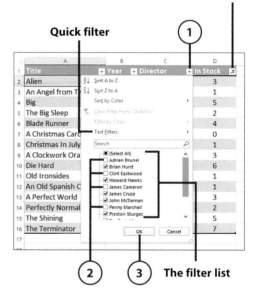

The filter list

>>>Go Further

FILTERING USING QUICK FILTERS

Besides allowing you to filter a table using a filter list, Excel also offers a set of *quick filters* that enable you to apply specific criteria. The quick filters you see depend on the data type of the field, but in each case, you access them by clicking a field's Filter and Sort button and then clicking one of the following commands:

- **Number Filters**—This command appears when you're working with a numeric field. It displays a submenu of filters, including Equals, Does Not Equal, Greater Than, Greater Than Or Equal To, Less Than, Less Than Or Equal To, Between, Top 10, Above Average, and Below Average.

- **Date Filters**—This command appears when you're working with a date field. It displays a submenu of filters, including Equals, Before, After, Between, Tomorrow, Today, Next Week, This Month, and Last Year.

- **Text Filters**—This command appears when you're working with a text field. It displays a submenu of filters, including Equals, Does Not Equal, Begins With, Ends With, Contains, and Does Not Contain.

In some cases, the quick filter doesn't require any input from you. For example, Above Average filters a table to show just the records that have a field value above the average for the field. However, most of the quick filters require some kind of input from you to complete the filter criteria. For example, Greater Than filters your table to show just the records that have a field value above some value that you specify.

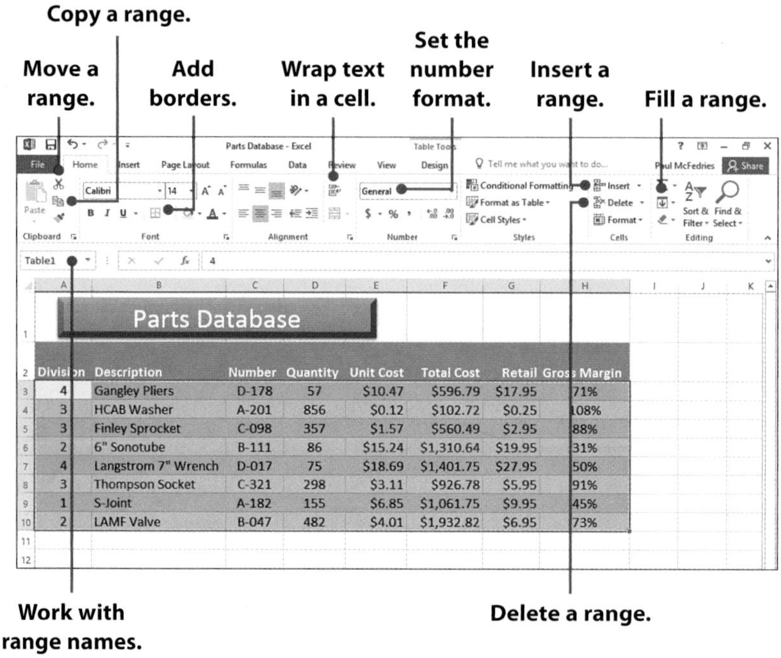

Copy a range.

Move a range.   **Add borders.**   **Wrap text in a cell.**   **Set the number format.**   **Insert a range.**   **Fill a range.**

Division	Description	Number	Quantity	Unit Cost	Total Cost	Retail	Gross Margin
4	Gangley Pliers	D-178	57	$10.47	$596.79	$17.95	71%
3	HCAB Washer	A-201	856	$0.12	$102.72	$0.25	108%
3	Finley Sprocket	C-098	357	$1.57	$560.49	$2.95	88%
2	6" Sonotube	B-111	86	$15.24	$1,310.64	$19.95	31%
4	Langstrom 7" Wrench	D-017	75	$18.69	$1,401.75	$27.95	50%
3	Thompson Socket	C-321	298	$3.11	$926.78	$5.95	91%
1	S-Joint	A-182	155	$6.85	$1,061.75	$9.95	45%
2	LAMF Valve	B-047	482	$4.01	$1,932.82	$6.95	73%

Work with range names.

Delete a range.

In this chapter, you learn about various techniques for working with Excel ranges, including selecting, filling, copying, moving, deleting, naming, and formatting ranges. Topics include the following:

→ Selecting ranges

→ Automatically filling a range with data

→ Copying, moving, inserting, and deleting ranges

→ Working with named ranges

→ Applying formatting to a range

Getting More Out of Excel Ranges

For small worksheets, working with individual cells doesn't usually present a problem. However, as your worksheets get larger, you'll find that performing operations cell by cell wastes both time and energy. To overcome this, Excel lets you work with multiple cells in a single operation. You can then move, copy, delete, or format the cells as a group.

A group of related cells is called a *range*. A range can be as small as a single cell and as large as an entire spreadsheet. Most ranges are rectangular groups of adjacent cells. Rectangular ranges, like individual cells, have an address, and this address is given in terms of *range coordinates*. Range coordinates have the form *UL:LR* where *UL* is the address of the cell in the upper-left corner of the range and *LR* is the address of the cell in the lower-right corner of the range (for example, A1:C5 and D7:G15).

This chapter shows you how to select ranges in Excel, and then how to work with ranges by filling them with data, copying and moving them, inserting and deleting them, applying names to them, and formatting them.

Selecting a Range

Ranges speed up your work by enabling you to perform operations or define functions on many cells at once instead of one at a time. For example, suppose you wanted to copy a large section of a worksheet to another file. If you worked on individual cells, you might have to perform the copy procedure dozens of times. However, by creating a range that covers the entire section, you could do it with a single copy command.

Similarly, suppose you wanted to know the average of a column of numbers running from B1 to B50. You could enter all 50 numbers as arguments in Excel's AVERAGE() function, but typing AVERAGE(B1:B50) is decidedly quicker.

Select a Range with a Mouse

If you're using Excel on a PC, the easiest way to select a range is by using the mouse.

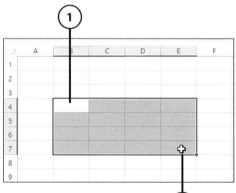

1. Click the first cell in the range you want to select. This is usually the cell in the upper-left corner of the range.

2. Drag the mouse to select the rest of the range. If the initial cell is the upper-left corner of the range, drag the mouse down and to the right until the range you want to work with is selected.

Selecting Entire Rows or Columns

To select an entire row, click the row's heading. To select multiple rows, click and drag up or down along the row headings. To select an entire column, click the column's heading. To select multiple columns, click and drag left or right along the column headings.

Select a Range on a Touchscreen

If you're using Excel on a touchscreen PC, you can use gestures to select a range.

1. Tap the first cell in the range you want to select. This is usually the cell in the upper-left corner of the range.

2. Tap and drag the end selection handle down (if you want to include multiple rows in the range) or to the right (to include multiple columns). As you drag the handle, Excel selects the cells.

Selecting Entire Rows or Columns

To select an entire row, tap the row's heading. If you want to select multiple rows, tap and drag the selection handles left or right. To select an entire column, tap the column's heading. If you want to select multiple columns, tap and drag the selection handles up or down.

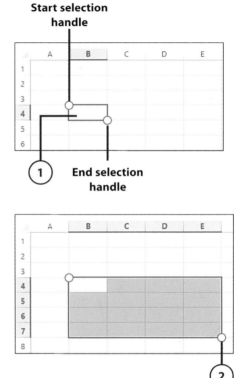

Start selection handle

End selection handle

Working with Excel Ranges

Once you've selected a range, you need to do something with it. What can you do with a range? Well, perhaps a better question would be what *can't* you do with a range? Most Excel tasks you perform involve ranges in some form or another. The next few sections, though, show you only some of the most common range chores, including filling, copying, moving, inserting, and deleting ranges.

Fill a Range with a Specific Value

You might occasionally need to fill a range with a particular value. For example, you might want to populate a range with a number for testing purposes, or you might need a value repeated across a range. Rather than type the value in by hand for each cell, you can use Excel's Fill tool to fill the range quickly.

1. Type the value you want to repeat.

2. Select the range you want to fill, including the initial cell.

3. Select the Home tab.

4. Select Fill.

5. Select the appropriate command from the submenu that appears. For example, if you're filling a range down from the initial cell, select the Down command.

Keyboard Shortcut
Press Ctrl+D to select Home, Fill, Down; press Ctrl+R to select Home, Fill, Right. You can also select the range you want to fill, type the value or formula, and then press Ctrl+Enter.

Fill a Range with a Series of Values

Worksheets often use text series (such as January, February, March; or Sunday, Monday, Tuesday) and numeric series (such as 1, 3, 5; or 2014, 2015, 2016). Instead of entering these series by hand, you can use Excel's Series feature to create them automatically.

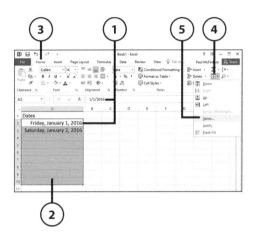

1. Select the first cell you want to use for the series and enter the starting value. If you want to create a series out of a particular pattern (such as 2, 4, 6, and so on), fill in enough cells to define the pattern.

2. Select the entire range you want to fill.

3. Select Home.

4. Select Fill.

5. Select Series. Excel displays the Series dialog box.

6. If you selected a column, select the Columns option; otherwise, select the Rows option.

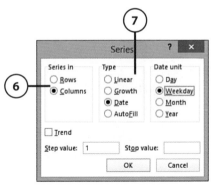

7. Use the Type group to select the type of series you want. Select the Date option if you're filling a series of dates. To fill in the range based on the pattern of the initial cell values you entered, select the AutoFill option. Use the Linear option to calculate the next series value by adding the step value (see step 9) to the preceding value in the series.

8. If you chose a Date series, select an option that specifies how you want the dates incremented: by Day, Weekday, Month, or Year.

9. If you chose a Linear or Date series type, enter a number in the Step Value box. Excel uses this number to increment each value in the series.

10. To place a limit on the series, enter the appropriate number in the Stop Value box.

11. Click OK. Excel fills in the series and returns you to the worksheet.

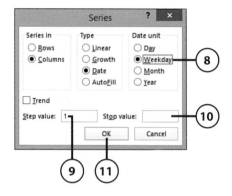

>>>Go Further

USING AUTOFILL

For many series, you can fill the range directly on the worksheet. Begin by entering two or more values—enough to define the range pattern—and then select those values. Move the mouse pointer to the bottom-right corner of the selection (the pointer changes to a cross), and then drag the corner down to the end of the range you want to fill. When you release the mouse, Excel fills the range based on the pattern established by the initial values.

Make a Copy of a Range

The quickest way to become productive with Excel is to avoid reinventing your worksheets. If you have a formula that works, or a piece of formatting that you've put a lot of effort into, don't start from scratch if you need something similar. Instead, make a copy and then adjust the copy as necessary. Note that Excel automatically adjusts formula references in the copied cells.

1. Select the range you want to copy.

2. Select the Home tab.

3. Select Copy. Excel copies the contents of the range to the Clipboard and displays a dashed border around the range.

Keyboard Shortcut

You can also run the Copy command by pressing Ctrl+C.

---

4. Select the upper-left cell of the destination range.

5. Select the Home tab.

6. Select the top half of the Paste button. Excel pastes a copy of the range from the Clipboard to your destination.

Keyboard Shortcut

You can also run the Paste command by pressing Ctrl+V.

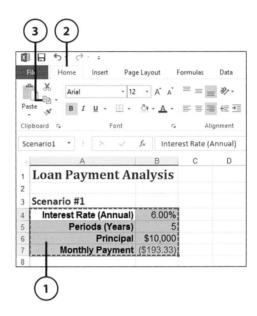

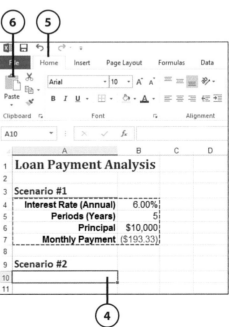

It's Not All Good

Don't Overwrite Existing Cells

Before copying a range to another area, look at the destination area and make sure you won't be overwriting any nonblank cells. Remember that you can use the Undo command if you accidentally destroy some data. If you want to insert the range among some existing cells without overwriting existing data, see the "Insert a Range" section later in this chapter.

Move a Range

If a range is in the wrong section of a worksheet, you can move the range to the sheet area that you prefer.

1. Select the range you want to move.

2. Select the Home tab.

3. Select Cut. Excel places the contents of the range on the Clipboard and displays a dashed border around the range.

Keyboard Shortcut

You can also run the Cutd command by pressing Ctrl+X.

4. Select the upper-left cell of the destination range.

5. Select the Home tab.

6. Select the top half of the Paste button. Excel pastes the range data from the Clipboard to the destination and deletes the original text.

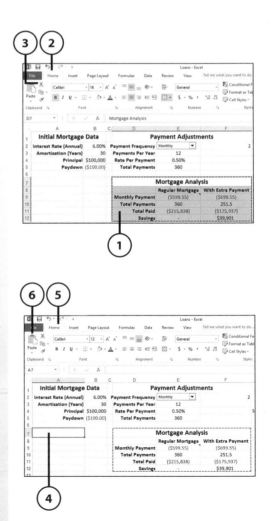

Insert a Range

When you begin a worksheet, you use up rows and columns sequentially as you add data and formulas. Invariably, however, you'll need to go back and add in some values or labels that you forgot or that you need for another part of the worksheet. When this happens, you need to insert ranges into your spreadsheet to make room for your new information.

1. Select the range where you want the new range to appear. If you're inserting a horizontal range, select the cells above which you want the new range to appear. If you're inserting a vertical range, select the cells to the left of which you want the new range to appear.

2. Select the Home tab.

3. Drop down the Insert menu.

4. Select Insert Cells. The Insert dialog box opens.

5. Select the option that fits how you want Excel to adjust the existing cells to accommodate your inserted range. For example, if you're inserting a horizontal range, select Shift Cells Down to make horizontal room for your new range. Similarly, if you're inserting a vertical range, select Shift Cells Right to make vertical room for your new range.

6. Select OK. Excel inserts the range and shifts the existing cells accordingly.

Select Insert Sheet Rows to insert an entire row.

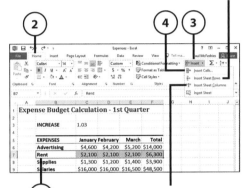

Select Insert Sheet Columns to insert an entire column.

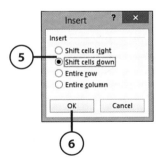

Delete a Range

When you're building a worksheet, you often have to remove old or unnecessary data, and that requires you to delete ranges. It's often easiest to delete an entire row or column, but in some worksheets, you may need to delete only a single cell or a range of cells so as not to disturb the arrangement of surrounding data.

1. Select the range you want to delete.

2. Select the Home tab.

3. Drop down the Delete menu.

4. Select Delete Cells. The Delete dialog box opens.

5. Select the option that fits how you want Excel to adjust the existing cells to accommodate your deleted range. For example, if you're deleting a horizontal range, select Shift Cells Up to close the horizontal gap in your range. Similarly, if you're deleting a vertical range, select Shift Cells Left to close the vertical gap in your range.

6. Select OK. Excel inserts the range and shifts the existing cells accordingly.

Select Delete Sheet Rows to delete an entire row.

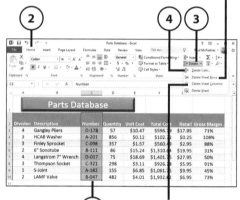

Select Delete Sheet Columns to delete an entire column.

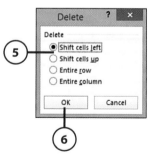

Working with Range Names

Working with multiple cells as a range is much easier than working with the cells individually, but range coordinates are not very intuitive. For example, if you see a formula that uses the function AVERAGE(A1:A25), knowing what the range A1:A25 represents is impossible unless you look at the range itself.

You can make ranges more intuitive using *range names*, which are labels that you assign to a single cell or to a range of cells. With a name defined, you can use it in place of the range coordinates. For example, assigning the name ClassMarks to a range such as A1:A25 immediately clarifies the purpose of a function such as AVERAGE(ClassMarks).

Excel also makes range names easy to work with by automatically adjusting the coordinates associated with a range name if you move the range or if you insert or delete rows or columns within the range.

Range names are generally flexible, but you need to follow a few restrictions and guidelines:

- The range name can be no longer than 255 characters.

- The range name must begin with either a letter or the underscore character (_). For the rest of the name, you can use any combination of characters, numbers, or symbols, except spaces. For multiple-word names, separate the words by using the underscore character or by mixing case (for example, August_Expenses or AugustExpenses). Excel doesn't distinguish between uppercase and lowercase letters in range names.

- Don't use cell addresses (such as Q1) or any of the operator symbols (such as +, –, *, /, <, >, and &) because they could cause confusion if you use the name in a formula.

- Keep your names as short as possible to reduce typing, but long enough that the name retains some of its meaning. NetProfit16 is faster to type than Net_Profit_For_Fiscal_Year_2016, and it's certainly clearer than the more cryptic NetPft16.

The Name box to the left of Excel's Formula bar usually just shows you the address of the active cell. However, the Name box also comes with two extra features that are useful when you are working with range names: After you define a name, it appears in the Name box whenever you select the range; the Name box contains a list of the defined names. To select a named range quickly, drop down the list and click the name you want.

Name a Range

The Name box is also the quickest way to define a range name.

1. Select the range you want to name.

2. Click inside the Name box to display the insertion point.

3. Type the name you want to use.

4. Press Enter. Excel defines the new name automatically.

>>>Go Further

NAMING A RANGE USING WORKSHEET TEXT

If you have a few ranges to name—for example, a series of rows or columns—you can speed things up by using the worksheet text adjacent to each range as the range name. To try this, first select the range of cells you want to name, including the appropriate text cells that you want to use as the range names. Select the Formulas tab and then select Create from Selection. Excel displays the Create Names from Selection dialog box, and Excel guesses where the text for the range name is located and activates the appropriate check box (such as Top Row or Left Column). If this isn't the check box you want, deselect it and then select the appropriate one. Click OK.

Formatting a Range

Your worksheets must produce the correct answers, of course, so most of your Excel time should be spent on getting your data and formulas entered accurately. However, you also need to spend some time formatting your work, particularly if other people will be viewing or working with the spreadsheet. Labels, data, and formula results that have been augmented with fonts, borders, alignments, numeric formats, and other formatting are almost always easier to read and understand than unformatted sheets.

Learning About Data Formats

One of the best ways to improve the readability of worksheets is to display data in a format that is logical, consistent, and straightforward. Formatting currency amounts with leading dollar signs, percentages with trailing percent signs, and large numbers with commas are a few of the ways you can improve your spreadsheet style.

When you enter numbers in a worksheet, Excel removes any leading or trailing zeros. For example, if you enter 0123.4500, Excel displays 123.45. The exception to this rule occurs when you enter a number that's wider than the cell. In this case, Excel usually expands the width of the column to fit the number. However, in some cases, Excel tailors the number to fit the cell by rounding off some decimal places. For example, the number 123.45678 might be displayed as 123.4568. Note that, in this case, the number is changed for display purposes only; Excel still retains the original number internally.

When you create a worksheet, each cell uses this format, known as the general number format, by default. If you want your numbers to appear differently, you can choose from among Excel's six categories of numeric formats:

- **Number**—The Number format has three components: the number of decimal places (0–30), whether the thousands separator (,) is used, and how negative numbers are displayed. For negative numbers, you can display the number in four ways: with a leading minus sign; in red; surrounded by parentheses; or in red surrounded by parentheses.

- **Currency**—The Currency format is similar to the Number format, except that the thousands separator is always used and the number appears with a leading dollar sign ($).

- **Accounting**—The Accounting format is the same as the Currency format, except Excel displays the dollar sign ($) flush left in the cell. All negative entries are displayed surrounded by parentheses.

- **Percentage**—The Percentage format displays the number multiplied by 100, with a percent sign (%) to the right of the number. For example, .506 is displayed as 50.6%. You can display 0–30 decimal places.

- **Fraction**—The Fraction format enables you to express decimal quantities as fractions.

- **Scientific**—The Scientific format displays the most significant number to the left of the decimal, 2–30 decimal places to the right of the decimal, and then the exponent. So, 123000 is displayed as 1.23E+05.

The quickest way to format numbers is to specify the format as you enter your data. For example, if you begin a dollar amount with a dollar sign ($), Excel automatically formats the number as Currency. Similarly, if you type a percent sign (%) after a number, Excel automatically formats the number as Percentage. Here are a few more examples of this technique. Note that you can enter a negative value using either the minus sign (-) or parentheses.

Number Entered	Number Displayed	Format Used
$1234.567	$1,234.57	Currency
($1234.5)	($1,234.50)	Currency
10%	10%	Percentage
123E+02	1.23E+04	Scientific
5 3/4	5 3/4	Fraction
0 3/4	3/4	Fraction
3/4	4-Mar	Date

Entering a Simple Fraction

Excel interprets a simple fraction such as 3/4 as a date (March 4, in this case). Always include a leading zero, followed by a space, if you want to enter a simple fraction from the Formula bar.

If you include dates or times in your worksheets, you need to make sure that they're presented in a readable, unambiguous format. For example, most people would interpret the date 8/5/16 as August 5, 2016. However, in some countries, this date would mean May 8, 2016. Similarly, if you use the time 2:45, do you mean a.m. or p.m.? To avoid these kinds of problems, you can use Excel's built-in date and time formats, listed in Table 7.1.

Table 7.1   Excel's Date and Time Formats

Format	Display
m/d	8/3
m/d/yy	8/3/16
mm/dd/yy	08/03/16
d-mmm	3-Aug
d-mmm-yy	3-Aug-16
dd-mmm-yy	03-Aug-16
mmm-yy	Aug-16
mmmm-yy	August-16
mmmm d, yyyy	August 3, 2016
dddd, mmmm d, yyyy	Wednesday, August 3, 2016
h:mm AM/PM	3:10 PM
h:mm:ss AM/PM	3:10:45 PM
h:mm	15:10
h:mm:ss	15:10:45
mm:ss.0	10:45.7
[h]:[mm]:[ss]	25:61:61
m/d/yy h:mm AM/PM	8/23/16 3:10 PM
m/d/yy h:mm	8/23/16 15:10

You use the same methods to select date and time formats that you used for numeric formats. In particular, you can specify the date and time format as you input your data. For example, entering **Jan-16** automatically formats the cell with the mmm-yy format. You also have the following commands available:

- **Short Date**—Choose this command to display a date using the mm/dd/yyyy format.

- **Long Date**—Choose this command to display a date using the dddd, mmmm d, yyyy.

- **Time**—Choose this command to display a time using the hh:mm:ss AM/PM format.

Apply a Numeric or Date Format

Specifying the numeric format as you enter a number is fast and efficient because Excel guesses the format you want to use. Unfortunately, Excel sometimes guesses wrong (for example, interpreting a simple fraction as a date). In any case, you don't have access to all the available formats (for example, displaying negative dollar amounts in red). To overcome these limitations, you can select your numeric formats from a list.

1. Select the cell or range of cells to which you want to apply the new format.

2. Select the Home tab.

3. Drop down the Number Format list. Excel displays its built-in formats.

4. Select the format you want to use. Excel applies the numeric format to the cell or range.

Customizing Numeric Formats

To get a bit more control over the numeric formats, drop down the Number Format list and then select More Number Formats. The Number tab of the Format Cells dialog box enables you to specify the number of decimal places, the currency symbol, and more.

Control the Number of Decimal Places

You can make your numeric values easier to read and interpret by adjusting the number of decimal places that Excel displays. For example, you might want to ensure that all dollar-and-cent values show two decimal places, while dollar-only values show no decimal places. You can either decrease or increase the number of decimal places that Excel displays.

1. Select the range you want to format.

2. Select the Home tab.

3. In the Number group, select the Decrease Decimal button. Excel decreases the number of decimal places by one.

4. To increase the number of decimal places instead, select the Increase Decimal button.

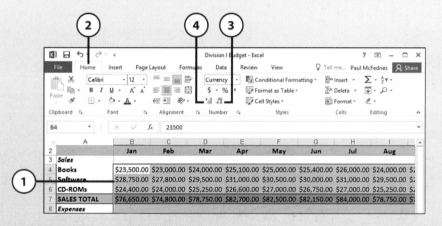

Handling Multiple Numbers of Decimal Places

How does Excel handle situations in which the selected range has values that display different numbers of decimal places? In this case, Excel uses the value that has the most displayed decimal places as the basis for formatting all the values. For example, if the selected range has values that display zero, one, two, or four decimal places, Excel uses the value with four decimal places as the basis. If you click Decrease Decimal, Excel displays every value with three decimal places; if you click Increase Decimal, Excel displays every value with five decimal places.

Resize Columns

You can use column width adjustments to improve the appearance of your worksheet in a number of different ways. For example, if you're faced with a truncated text entry or a number that Excel shows as ######, you can enlarge the column so the entry can appear in full.

1. Select at least one cell in each column you want to resize.

2. Select the Home tab.

3. Select Format.

4. Select Column Width. Excel displays the Column Width dialog box.

5. In the Column Width text box, type the width you want.

6. Select OK. Excel sets the column width and returns you to the worksheet.

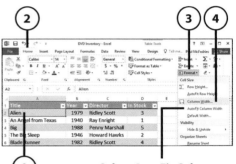

Select AutoFit Column Width to have Excel fit the column to its widest item.

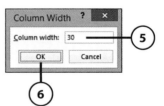

Resizing a Column with a Mouse

It's often faster to resize a column using the mouse. Move the mouse pointer to the column header area and position the pointer at the right edge of the column you want to resize. The mouse pointer changes to a two-headed horizontal arrow with a vertical bar in the middle. Either drag the edge of the column right (to increase the width) or left (to decrease the width), or double-click to automatically size the column to its widest entry.

Resize Rows

Although Excel normally adjusts row heights automatically to accommodate the tallest font in a row, you can make your own height adjustments to give your worksheet more breathing room or to reduce the amount of space taken up by unused rows.

1. Select at least one cell in each row you want to resize.

2. Select the Home tab.

3. Select Format.

4. Select Row Height. Excel displays the Row Height dialog box.

5. In the Row Height text box, type the height you want.

6. Select OK. Excel sets the row height and returns you to the worksheet.

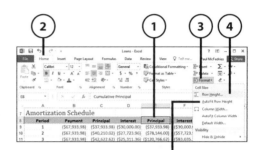

Select AutoFit Row Height to have Excel fit the row to its tallest item.

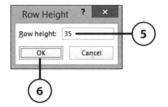

Resizing a Row with a Mouse

To adjust the row height with a mouse, move the mouse pointer to the row header area and position the pointer at the bottom edge of the row you want to resize. The mouse pointer changes to a two-headed vertical arrow with a horizontal bar in the middle. Either drag the edge of the row up (to increase the height) or down (to decrease the height), or double-click to automatically size the row to its tallest entry.

Add Borders

Excel lets you place borders of patterns around your worksheet cells or ranges. This is useful for enclosing different parts of the worksheet, defining data entry areas, and separating headings from data. You can also use borders to make a range easier to read. For example, if a range has totals on the bottom row, you can add a border above the totals.

1. Select the range you want to format.

2. Select the Home tab.

3. Select Borders. Excel displays a list of border types.

4. Select the border type you want to use. Excel applies the border to the range.

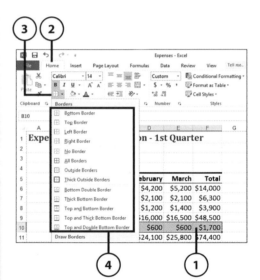

Wrap Text Within a Cell

If you type more text in a cell than can fit horizontally, Excel either displays the text over the next cell if that cell is empty or displays only part of the text if the next cell contains data. To prevent Excel from showing only truncated cell data, you can format the cell to wrap text within the cell. Excel then increases the height of the row to ensure that all the text is displayed.

1. Select the range you want to format.

2. Click the Home tab.

3. In the Alignment group, click Wrap Text. Excel wraps the text as needed within each cell in the range and then increases the height of the row to ensure that all the text is displayed.

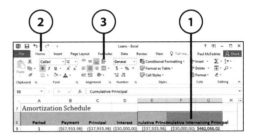

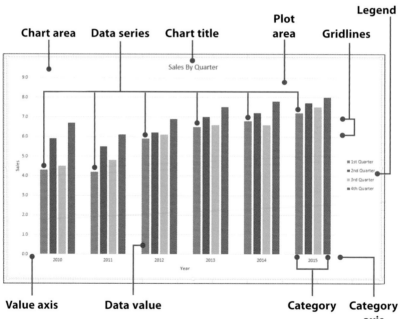

Chart area   **Data series**   **Chart title**   **Plot area**   **Gridlines**   **Legend**

Sales By Quarter

■ 1st Quarter
■ 2nd Quarter
■ 3rd Quarter
■ 4th Quarter

Sales

Year

2010   2011   2012   2013   2014   2015

Value axis   **Data value**   **Category**   **Category axis**

In this chapter, you learn about creating, customizing, and formatting charts to help visualize your Excel data. Topics include the following:

→ Converting Excel data into a chart

→ Working with Excel's different chart types

→ Moving, resizing, and changing the layout of a chart

→ Selecting and formatting chart elements

→ Adding chart titles, a legend, and data labels

Visualizing Excel Data with Charts

One of the best ways to analyze your worksheet data—or get your point across to other people—is to display your data visually in a chart. Excel gives you tremendous flexibility when creating charts: It enables you to place charts in separate documents or directly on the worksheet itself. Not only that, but you have dozens of different chart formats to choose from, and if none of Excel's built-in formats is just right, you can further customize these charts to suit your needs.

Creating a Chart

When plotting your worksheet data, you have two basic options: You can create an embedded chart that sits on top of your worksheet and can be moved, sized, and formatted; or you can create a separate chart sheet. Whether you choose to embed your charts or store them in separate sheets, the charts are linked with the worksheet data. Any changes you make to the data are automatically updated in the chart.

Before getting to the specifics of creating a chart, you should familiarize yourself with some basic chart terminology:

- **Category**—A grouping of data values on the category horizontal axis.

- **Category axis**—The axis (usually the x-axis) that contains the category groupings.

- **Chart area**—The area on which the chart is drawn.

- **Data marker**—A symbol that represents a specific data value. The symbol used depends on the chart type. In a column chart, for example, each column is a marker.

- **Data series**—A collection of related data values. Normally, the marker for each value in a series has the same pattern.

- **Data value**—A single piece of data. Also called a *data point*.

- **Gridlines**—Optional horizontal and vertical extensions of the axis tick marks. These make data values easier to read.

- **Legend**—A guide that shows the colors, patterns, and symbols used by the markers for each data series.

- **Plot area**—The area bounded by the category and value axes. It contains the data points and gridlines.

- **Tick mark**—A small line that intersects the category axis or the value axis. It marks divisions in the chart's categories or scales.

- **Value axis**—The axis (usually the y-axis) that contains the data values.

Create an Embedded Chart

An *embedded* chart is one that appears on the same worksheet as the data that it's based on. Creating an embedded chart is by far the easiest way to build a chart in Excel because the basic technique requires just a few steps.

1. Select the range you want to plot, including the row and column labels if there are any. Make sure that no blank rows are between the column labels and the data.

2. Select Insert.

3. In the Charts group, drop down the list for the chart type you want. Excel displays a gallery of chart types.

4. Select a chart type. Excel embeds the chart.

If you're not sure which chart type to use, select Recommended Charts.

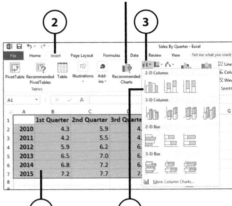

Create a Chart in a Separate Sheet

If you don't want a chart taking up space in a worksheet, or if you want to print a chart on its own, you can create a separate chart sheet.

1. Select the range you want to plot, including the row and column labels if there are any. Make sure that no blank rows are between the column labels and the data.

2. Right-click the tab of the worksheet before which you want the chart sheet to appear.

3. Select Insert. Excel displays the Insert dialog box.

4. Select Chart.

5. Select OK. Excel creates the chart sheet and adds a default chart.

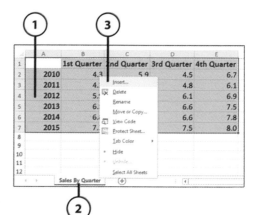

Keyboard Shortcut

To insert a chart in a separate sheet using the keyboard, select the data you want to chart and then press F11.

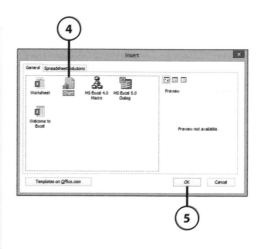

Working with Charts

Once you've created a chart, Excel offers various tools for working with the chart, including changing the chart type, moving and resizing the chart, and changing the chart layout. The next few sections provide the details.

Understanding Excel's Chart Types

To help you choose the chart type that best presents your data, the following list provides brief descriptions of all of Excel's chart types:

- **Area chart**—An *area chart* shows the relative contributions over time that each data series makes to the whole picture. The smaller the area a data series takes up, the smaller its contribution to the whole.

- **Bar chart**—A *bar chart* compares distinct items or shows single items at distinct intervals. A bar chart is laid out with categories along the vertical axis and values along the horizontal axis. This format lends itself to competitive comparisons because categories appear to be "ahead" or "behind."

- **Bubble chart**—A *bubble chart* is similar to an XY chart, except that it uses three data series, and in the third series the individual plot points are displayed as bubbles (the larger the value, the larger the bubble).

- **Box & Whisker chart**—Visualizes several statistical values for the data in each category, including the average, range, minimum, and maximum.

- **Column chart**—Like a bar chart, a *column chart* compares distinct items or shows single items at distinct intervals. However, a column chart is laid out with categories along the horizontal axis and values along the vertical axis (as are most Excel charts). This format is best suited for comparing items over time. Excel offers various column chart formats, including *stacked columns*. A stacked column chart is similar to an area chart; series values are stacked on top of each other to show the relative contributions of each series. Although an area chart is useful for showing the flow of the relative contributions over time, a stacked column chart is better for showing the contributions at discrete intervals.

- **Doughnut chart**—A *doughnut chart*, like a pie chart, shows the proportion of the whole that is contributed by each value in a data series. The advantage of a doughnut chart, however, is that you can plot multiple data series. (A pie chart can handle only a single series.)

- **Histogram**—Groups the category values into ranges, called *bins*, and shows the frequency with which the data values fall within each bin.

- **Line chart**—A *line chart* shows how a data series changes over time. The category (x) axis usually represents a progression of even increments (such as days or months), and the series points are plotted on the value (y) axis. Excel offers several stock chart formats, including an Open, High, Low, Close chart (also called a *candlestick chart*), which is useful for plotting stock-market prices.

- **Pie chart**—A *pie chart* shows the proportion of the whole that is contributed by each value in a single data series. The whole is represented as a circle (the "pie"), and each value is displayed as a proportional "slice" of the circle.

- **Radar chart**—A *radar chart* makes comparisons within a data series and between data series relative to a center point. Each category is shown with a value axis extending from the center point. To understand this concept, think of a radar screen in an airport control tower. The tower itself is the central point, and the radar radiates a beam (a value axis). When the radar makes contact with a plane, a blip appears onscreen. In a radar chart, this data point is shown with a data marker.

- **Sunburst chart**—Displays hierarchical data as a series of concentric circles, with the top level as the innermost circle and each circle divided proportionally according to the data values within that level.

- **Treemap chart**—For hierarchical data, shows a large rectangle for each item in the top level, and then divides each rectangle proportionally based on the value of each item in the next level.

- **Waterfall chart**—Shows a running total as category values are added (positive values) or subtracted (negative values).

- **XY (scatter) chart**—An *XY chart* (also called a scatter chart) shows the relationship between numeric values in two different data series. It also can plot a series of data pairs in x,y coordinate. An XY chart is a variation of the line chart in which the category axis is replaced by a second value axis. You can use XY charts for plotting items such as survey data, mathematical functions, and experimental results.

- **3-D charts**—In addition to the various 2-D chart types presented so far, Excel also offers 3-D charts. Because they're striking, 3-D charts are suitable for presentations, flyers, and newsletters. (If you need a chart to help with data analysis, or if you just need a quick chart to help you visualize your data, you're probably better off with the simpler 2-D charts.) Most of the 3-D charts are just the 2-D versions with an enhanced 3-D effect. However, some 3-D charts enable you to look at your data in new ways. For example, some 3-D area chart types enable you to show separate area plots for each data series (something a 2-D area chart can't do). In this variation, the emphasis isn't on the relative contribution of each series to the whole; rather, it's on the relative differences among the series.

Change the Chart Type

If you feel that the current chart type is not showing your data in the best way, you can change the chart type. This enables you to experiment not only with the 10 different chart types offered by Excel, but also with its nearly 100 chart type configurations.

1. Select the chart.

2. Select the Design tab.

3. Select Change Chart Type. The Change Chart Type dialog box opens.

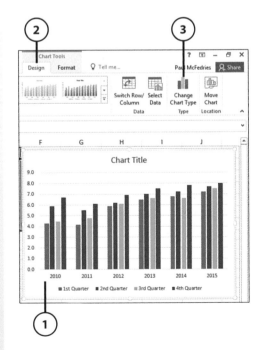

4. Select the chart type you want to use. Excel displays the chart type configurations.

5. Select the general configuration you want to use.

6. Select the specific configuration you want to use.

7. Select OK.

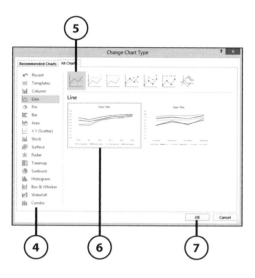

>>>Go Further
CREATING A CHART TEMPLATE

Once you've changed the chart type, as described in this section, and performed other chart-related chores such as applying titles, adding labels, and choosing a layout (described later in this chapter), you might want to repeat the same settings on another chart. Rather than repeating the same procedures on the second chart, you can make your life easier by saving the original chart as a chart template. This enables you to then build the second chart (and any subsequent charts) based on this template. To save the chart as a template, right-click the chart's plot area or background and then select Save as Template. Type a name for the template and then select Save. To reuse the template, follow steps 1 to 3 in this section, select Templates, select your template, and then select OK.

Move a Chart

You can move a chart to another part of the worksheet. This is useful if the chart is blocking the worksheet data or if you want the chart to appear in a particular part of the worksheet.

1. Click the chart to select it.

2. Click and drag an empty section of the chart to the location you want. As you drag, Excel moves the chart.

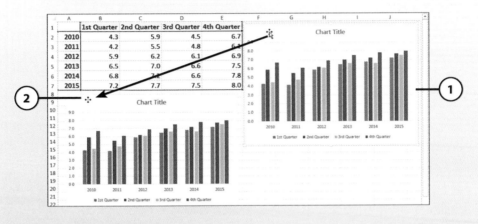

Dragging an Edge

If you drag a chart object such as the plot area or the chart title, you'll only move that object, not the entire chart. If you're having trouble finding a place to drag, try dragging any edge of the chart. However, try to avoid dragging any of the selection handles (see the next section), or you'll just resize the chart.

>>>Go Further

MOVING A CHART TO A SEPARATE SHEET

In the "Create a Chart in a Separate Sheet" section, earlier in this chapter, you learned how to create a new chart in a separate sheet. If your chart already exists on a worksheet, you can move it to a new sheet. Click the chart, select the Design tab, and then select Move Chart to open the Move Chart dialog box. Select the New Sheet option, use the New Sheet text box to type a name for the new sheet, and then select OK.

Resize a Chart

You can resize a chart. For example, if you find that the chart is difficult to read, making the chart bigger often solves the problem. Similarly, if the chart takes up too much space on the worksheet, you can make it smaller.

1. Click the chart. Excel displays a border around the chart, which includes selection handles on the corners and sides.

2. Click and drag a selection handle until the chart is the size you want. When you release the screen, Excel resizes the chart.

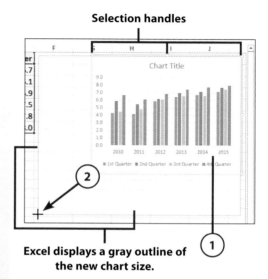

Selection handles

Excel displays a gray outline of the new chart size.

Change the Chart Layout and Style

You can quickly format your chart by applying a different chart layout. The chart layout includes elements such as the titles, data labels, legend, and gridlines. The Quick Layouts feature in Excel enables you to apply these elements in different combinations in just a few steps. You can also apply a chart style, which governs the formatting applied to the chart background, data markers, gridlines, and more.

1. Click the chart.

2. Select the Design tab.

3. Select Quick Layout.

4. Select the layout you want to use.

5. Select the More button in the Chart Styles section. Excel displays the Chart Styles gallery.

6. Select the style you want to apply.

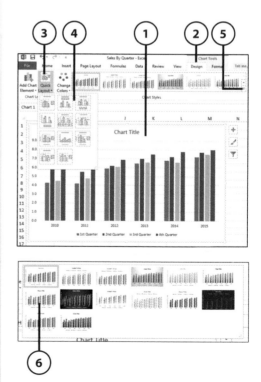

Working with Chart Elements

An Excel chart is composed of elements such as axes, data markers, gridlines, and text, each with its own formatting options. In the rest of this chapter, you learn how to work with several of these elements, including titles, legends, and data markers.

Select Chart Elements

Before you can format a chart element, you need to select it.

1. Click the chart.
2. Select the Format tab.
3. Drop down the Chart Elements list to display a list of all the elements in the current chart.
4. Select the element you want to work with.

Selecting Chart Elements Directly
You can also select many chart elements directly by clicking them.

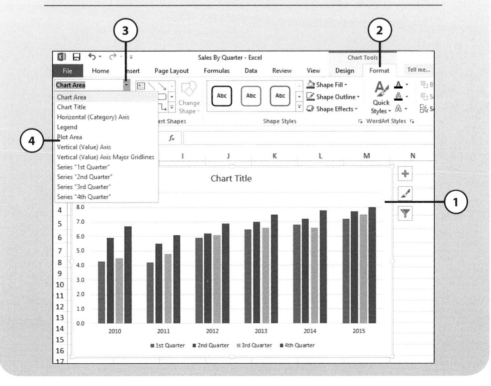

Format Chart Elements

If you want to format a particular chart element, the Format tab offers several options for most chart elements. However, the bulk of your element formatting chores will take place in the Format task pane, the layout of which depends on the selected element.

1. Select the chart element you want to format.

2. Select the Format tab.

3. Select Format Selection. Excel displays the Format task pane.

4. Select the Options tab to work with the element's settings.

5. Select the Size & Properties tab to control the size of the element and set the element's properties.

6. Select the Effects tab to control element formatting such as shadows, glow effects, soft edges, and 3-D effects.

7. Select the Fill & Line tab to control formatting such as the element's background color and the color and style of its borders.

Format Task Pane Tabs

Not all chart elements display all the tabs mentioned here.

You can use the options in the Shape Styles group to apply formatting to most chart elements.

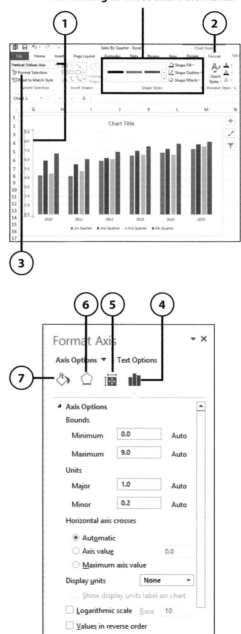

Add Titles

Excel enables you to add four kinds of titles: the *chart title* is the overall chart title, and you use it to provide a brief description that puts the chart into context; the *category (X) axis title* appears below the category axis, and you use it to provide a brief description of the category items; the *value (Y) axis title* appears to the left of the value axis, and you use it to provide a brief description of the value items; and the *value (Z) axis title* appears beside the z-axis in a 3-D chart, and you use it to provide a brief description of the z-axis items.

1. Click the chart.

2. Select the Design tab.

3. Select Add Chart Element.

4. Select Chart Title.

5. Select Above Chart. Excel adds the title box.

6. Type the title.

7. Select Add Chart Element.

8. Select Axis Titles.

9. Select Primary Horizontal. Excel adds the title box.

10. Type the title.

11. Select Add Chart Element.

12. Select Axis Titles.

13. Select Primary Vertical. Excel adds the title box.

14. Type the title.

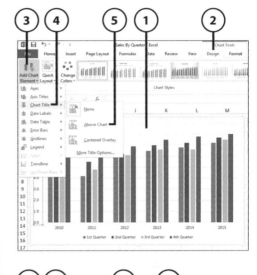

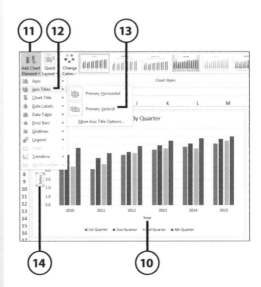

Add a Chart Legend

If your chart includes multiple data series, you should add a legend to explain the series markers. Doing so makes your chart more readable and makes it easier for others to distinguish each series.

1. Click the chart.

2. Select the Design tab.

3. Select Add Chart Element.

4. Select Legend.

5. Select the position you want to use for the legend. Excel adds the legend.

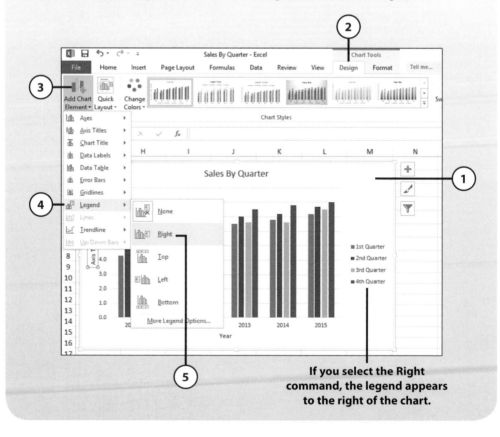

If you select the Right command, the legend appears to the right of the chart.

Add Data Marker Labels

You can make your chart easier to read by adding data labels. A *data label* is a small text box that appears in or near a data marker and displays the value of that data point.

1. Click the chart.

2. Select the Design tab.

3. Select Add Chart Element.

4. Select Data Labels.

5. Select the position you want to use for the data labels. Excel adds the labels to the chart.

Data Label Positions

The data label position options you see depend on the chart type. For example, with a column chart you can place the data labels within or above each column, and for a line chart you can place the labels to the left or right, or above or below, the data marker.

If you select the Outside End command, the data labels appear above the markers on a column chart.

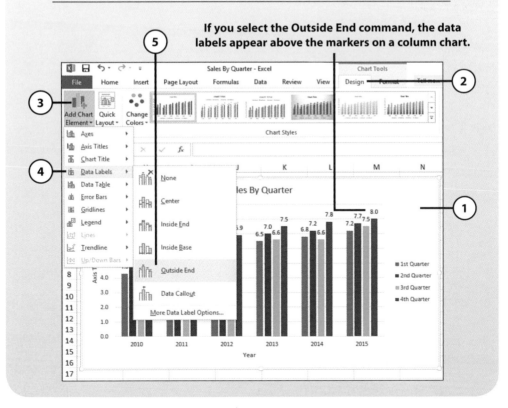

Add new slides.

Insert a slide title.

Add a chart.

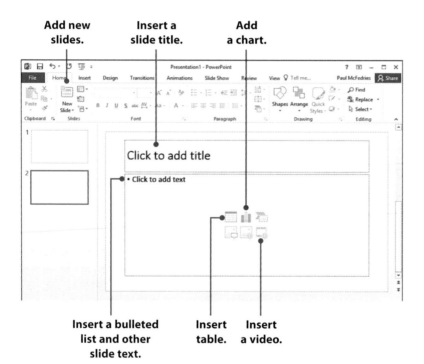

Insert a bulleted list and other slide text.

Insert table.

Insert a video.

In this chapter, you learn the basics of building a PowerPoint presentation, from inserting slides to adding text, graphics, charts, and other content. Topics include the following:

→ Inserting and duplicating slides

→ Adding slide content, such as text, graphics, charts, and tables

→ Working with slide layouts

→ Adding presentation notes to a slide

→ Understanding and using the Slide Master

Building a PowerPoint Presentation

It's probably not a stretch to claim that, in terms of market share, PowerPoint is the most dominant software program in the world. A few years ago, Microsoft said that PowerPoint had 95% of the presentation graphics market, but it wouldn't surprise me if that number were even higher today. And with many of our kids learning and using PowerPoint in school, this dominance is poised to continue into the foreseeable future. In short, we live in a PowerPoint world.

So learning how to get along in this world is important, and that is what this chapter and the next can help you do. The focus is on a PowerPoint "middle way" that avoids the two most common PowerPoint faults: drab, lifeless presentations that are ineffective because they bore the audience to tears and *PowerPointlessness*—those overly fancy formats, transitions, sounds, and other effects that have no discernible purpose, use, or benefit. With the middle way, you learn how to create attractive presentations that offer visual interest without sacrificing clarity.

Adding a Slide to the Presentation

The heart and soul of any presentation is the collection of slides that comprise the bulk of its content and that serve as both the focal point and the organizing structure of the talk. The slides are the bridge between the audience—who, for the most part, has no idea what you're going to talk about—and yourself—who knows exactly what you want to say (presumably!). Building an effective presentation consists mostly of creating and organizing slides, which in turn involves four things:

- The content—the text and graphics—presented on each slide

- The organization of the content presented on each slide

- The formatting applied to each slide: fonts, colors, background, and so on

- The placement of the slides within the context of the entire presentation

The bulk of this chapter takes you through various PowerPoint techniques that support these four design ideas.

Understanding Slide Layouts

Before we get to the specifics of adding a slide, you should understand that all slides contain some combination of the following three elements:

- **Title**—This is a text box that you normally use to add a title for the slide.

- **Text**—This is a text box that you normally use to add text to the slide, which is usually a collection of bullets.

- **Content**—This is a container into which you add any type of content supported by PowerPoint: text, a picture, or a SmartArt graphic. In some cases, PowerPoint displays placeholders for specific types of content. For example, a Picture placeholder can contain only a picture.

In each case, the new slide contains one or more *placeholders*, and your job is to fill in a placeholder with text or a content object. Each slide uses some combination of Title, Text, and Content placeholders, and the arrangement of these placeholders on a slide is called the *slide layout*. PowerPoint offers nine layouts:

- **Title Slide**—A slide with two text boxes: a larger one for the overall presentation title and a smaller one for the subtitle

- **Title and Content**—A slide with a Title placeholder and a Content placeholder

- **Section Header**—A slide with two Text placeholders: one for the description and one for the title of a new presentation section

- **Two Content**—A slide with a Title placeholder above two Content placeholders placed side by side

- **Comparison**—A slide with a Title placeholder, two Content placeholders placed side by side, and two Text placeholders (one above each Content placeholder)

- **Title Only**—A slide with just a Title placeholder

- **Blank**—A slide with no placeholders

- **Content with Caption**—A Content placeholder with two Text placeholders to the left of it: one for the content title and the other for the content description

- **Picture with Caption**—A Picture placeholder with two Text placeholders beneath it: one for the picture title and the other for the picture description

Insert a New Slide

Inserting a new slide into your presentation is a straightforward matter of deciding what content you want on the slide and then deciding which slide layout would best display that content. Note that you can always change the slide layout later on (see "Change the Layout of a Slide" later in this chapter).

1. In the slide sorter, select the slide after which you want the new slide to appear.

2. Select the Home tab.

3. Select the bottom half of the New Slide button.

4. Select the slide layout you want to use. PowerPoint inserts the new slide.

Keyboard Shortcut

You can quickly add a slide that uses the Title and Content layout by pressing Ctrl+M.

You can click here to add a slide that uses the Title and Content layout.

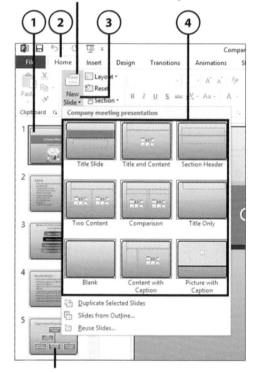

The slide sorter

Duplicate a Slide

If you have a slide in the current presentation that has similar content and formatting to what you want for a new slide, you can save yourself a great deal of time by inserting a duplicate of that slide and then adjusting the copy as needed.

1. In the slide sorter, select the slide you want to duplicate.

2. Select the Home tab.

3. Select the bottom half of the New Slide button.

4. Select Duplicate Selected Slides. PowerPoint creates a copy of the slide and inserts the copy below the selected slide.

Duplicating Via Copy-and-Paste

A quicker way to duplicate a slide is to select it, select the Home tab, select Copy (or press Ctrl+C) to copy it, and then select Paste (or press Ctrl+V) to paste the copy. If you want the copy to appear in a particular place within the presentation, select the slide after which you want the copy to appear and then select Paste (or press Ctrl+V).

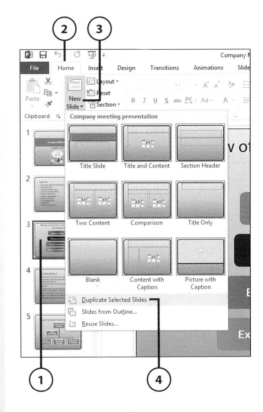

>>>Go Further

REUSING A SLIDE FROM ANOTHER PRESENTATION

One of the secrets of PowerPoint productivity is to avoid redoing work you have performed in the past. If you have a slide with boilerplate legal disclaimer text, why re-create it in each presentation? If you create an organization chart slide and your organization has not changed, you don't need to build the chart from scratch every time you want to add it to a presentation.

In this section, you saw how to duplicate a slide from the current presentation. However, the far more common scenario is that the slide you want to reuse exists in another presentation. Select the Home tab, select New Slide, and then select Reuse Slides to open the Reuse Slides task pane. If this is the first time you've displayed the Reuse Slides pane in the current PowerPoint session, select the Open a PowerPoint File link; otherwise, pull down the Browse list, select Browse File, select the presentation you want to use, and then select Open. PowerPoint adds the presentation's slides to the Reuse Slides task pane. If you want the formatting of the original slide to appear in the new slide, select the Keep Source Formatting check box to activate it. Select the slide you want to reuse to insert it into the presentation.

Adding Data to a Slide

After you have added one or more slides, the next step is to fill in the placeholders. The next few sections take you through some of the details. For now, you should know that the Content placeholder contains six icons grouped together in the middle of the box. These icons represent the six main types of content you can add to the placeholder, and clicking each icon launches the process of inserting that content type. In the sections that follow, I ignore the picture-related icons because I already covered adding graphics in Chapter 3, "Working with Office 2016 Graphics."

Add Text

With a Title or Text placeholder, select inside the placeholder to enable editing and then type your text. In a Text placeholder, PowerPoint assumes that you'll be adding bullet points, so the Bullets format is on by default. PowerPoint supports four standard *list levels*, which determine where a bullet appears in the list hierarchy:

- **Level 1**—This is the main level. It uses a solid, round bullet and appears flush with the left side of the placeholder.

- **Level 2**—This is the next level in the hierarchy. It uses a slightly smaller bullet and appears indented by one tab stop from the left side of the placeholder.

- **Level 3**—This is the next level in the hierarchy. It uses an even smaller bullet and appears indented by two tab stops from the left side of the placeholder.

- **Level 4**—This is the final level in the hierarchy. It uses the smallest bullet and appears indented by three tab stops from the left side of the placeholder.

You can actually create higher and higher levels, but the bullet remains the same size and PowerPoint simply indents the bullets farther from the left. The next section illustrates what these levels look like.

Create a Bulleted List

Populating a Text placeholder with a bulleted list will likely be your most common PowerPoint chore.

1. Click inside a Text placeholder to open it for editing. PowerPoint displays the first bullet.

2. Type the text for the list item.

3. Press Enter. PowerPoint adds a bullet for the next item in the list.

If you prefer to enter just regular text, select Home and then Bullets to turn off the bulleted list format.

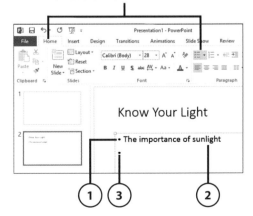

4. Repeat steps 2 and 3 to add more items to the list.

5. To increase the list level of the current item, select the Home tab and then select Increase List Level.

6. To decrease the list level of the current item, select the Home tab and then select Decrease List Level.

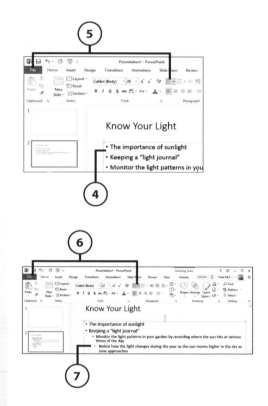

Keyboard Shortcut

To change the list level via the keyboard, place the insertion point at the beginning of an item and then press either Tab to increase the list level, or Shift+Tab to decrease the list level.

7. Repeat steps 2 through 6 until your list is complete.

>>>Go Further

CONVERTING REGULAR TEXT TO A BULLETED LIST

What if a slide already includes regular text that you want to display as a bulleted list? Select the entire list, select the Home tab, and then select the Bullets icon in the Ribbon. PowerPoint converts the text into a bulleted list.

Add a Video

Earlier in this chapter (see "Understanding Slide Layouts"), I described PowerPoint slide layouts and said you need a Content placeholder to insert a picture into a slide. Five layouts come with Content placeholders: Title and Content, Two Content, Comparison, Content with Caption, and Picture with Caption. Before you can insert a video into a presentation, you must first add a slide that uses one of these five layouts.

1. Select a slide that contains a Content placeholder.

2. In the Content placeholder, select the Insert Video icon. PowerPoint displays the Insert Video dialog box.

3. Select From a File. PowerPoint displays the Insert Video dialog box.

4. Select the location of the video.

5. Select the video file you want to insert.

6. Select Insert. PowerPoint inserts the video into the placeholder.

7. Drag the video's selection handles to set the size of the video.

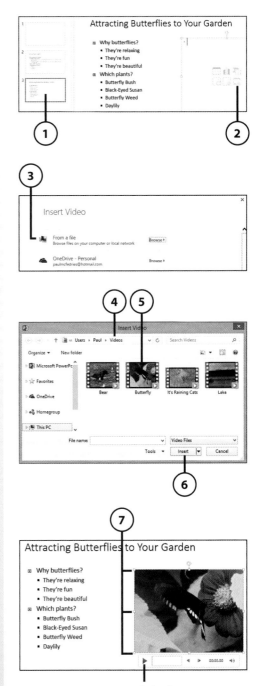

You can click Play to preview your video.

>>>Go Further

EMBEDDING AN ONLINE VIDEO

If you have an online video you want to use, you can insert a special code that embeds the video into your slide. All online video sites—including YouTube—offer with each video a special code called the *video embed code*, as well as a mechanism for copying that code. Once you've copied the embed code for the video you want, select a slide that contains a Content placeholder and then select the Insert Video icon to open the Insert Video dialog box. Click inside the From a Video Embed Code text box, paste the copied code, and then click the Insert arrow.

Add a Chart

If you have numeric results to present, one surefire way to make your audience's eyes glaze over is show them a slide crammed with numbers. Most slide shows present the "big picture," and nothing translates numeric values into a digestible big-picture format better than a chart. PowerPoint uses Excel charts, which means that adding a chart to a PowerPoint slide is not that much different from creating a chart in Excel, which I explain in detail in Chapter 8, "Visualizing Excel Data with Charts."

1. Select a slide that contains a Content placeholder.

2. In the Content placeholder, select the Insert Chart icon. PowerPoint displays the Insert Chart dialog box.

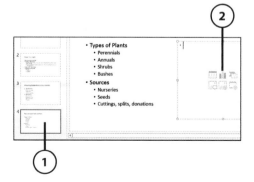

3. Select the chart type you want to use.

4. Select OK. PowerPoint launches Excel, adds sample data to a worksheet, inserts a chart into the slide, and displays the Excel content in a new window.

5. Adjust the worksheet labels and values as needed.

6. When you are done, select Close.

7. Click the chart title and then type the title you want to use.

8. To change the chart data, select Design, Edit Data, Edit Data.

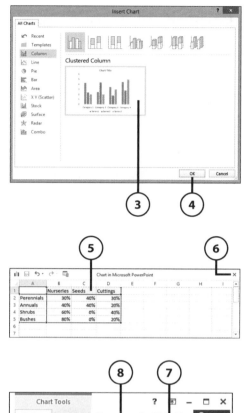

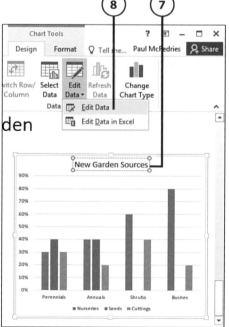

Add a Table

If you want to present data that would look best in a row-and-column format, use a table. Note that a PowerPoint table is nearly identical to a Word table, so see the section "Building a Table" in Chapter 5, "Working with Page Layout and Design in Word," for more table details.

1. Select a slide that contains a Content placeholder.

2. In the Content placeholder, select the Insert Table icon. PowerPoint displays the Insert Table dialog box.

3. Specify the number of columns you want in your table.

4. Specify the number of rows you want in your table.

5. Select OK. PowerPoint inserts the table into the slide.

6. Type your column headings.

7. Type your table data.

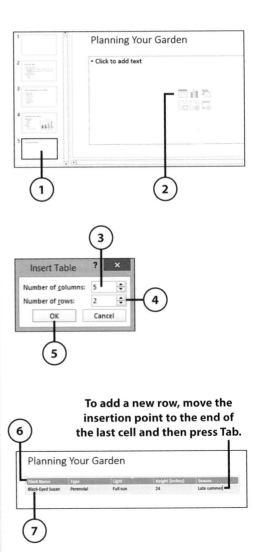

To add a new row, move the insertion point to the end of the last cell and then press Tab.

Working with Slides

Now that your presentation is populated with a few slides and your slides have some content on them, it's time to learn a few useful techniques for working with your slides. The rest of this chapter shows you how to select and rearrange slides, change the slide layout, hide a slide, add slide notes, and work with the Slide Master.

Select Slides

To work with slides, you must first select one or more. Here are the techniques you can use in the slide sorter:

- To select a single slide, click it.

- To select multiple, consecutive slides, click the first slide, hold down Shift, and then click the last slide.

- To select multiple, nonconsecutive slides, click the first slide, hold down Ctrl, and click each of the other slides.

- To select all the slides, select any slide and then press Ctrl+A. You can also choose Home, Select, Select All.

Rearrange Slides

PowerPoint gives you two different methods for changing the order of slides in a presentation:

- In the slide sorter, select the slide you want to move, select the Home tab, and then select Cut (or press Ctrl+X). Select the slide after which you want the moved slide to appear, and then select Paste (or press Ctrl+V).

- In the slide sorter, click and drag the slide and drop it below the slide after which you want it to appear.

Change the Layout of a Slide

If the original layout you applied to a slide is not what you want, you can change it.

1. Select the slide or slides you want to change.

2. Select the Home tab.

3. Select Layout. PowerPoint displays a gallery of slide layouts.

4. Select the layout you want to use. PowerPoint applies the new layout to the selected slides.

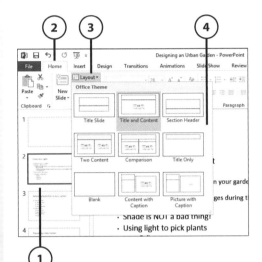

No Content Is Lost

It's okay to select a slide layout that has fewer placeholders than the current slide layout. In this case, Excel retains the data, but it now appears in the slide as a separate object rather than in its own placeholder.

Hide a Slide

In some presentations, there may be slides you don't want to show:

- You might have a short version and a long version of a presentation.

- You might want to omit certain slides, depending on whether you are presenting to managers, salespeople, or engineers.

- You might have "internal" and "external" versions; that is, you might have one version for people who work at your company and a different version for people from outside the company.

You could accommodate these different scenarios by creating copies of a presentation and then removing slides as appropriate. However, this process takes a great deal of work, wastes disk space, and is inefficient when one slide changes and you have to make the same change in every version of the presentation that includes the slide.

A much better solution is to use a single presentation but mark the slides you don't want to show as *hidden*. PowerPoint skips hidden slides when you present the show.

1. In the slide sorter, select the slide you want to hide.

2. Select the Slide Show tab.

3. Select Hide Slide. PowerPoint displays a faded version of the slide thumbnail and adds a strikethrough to the slide number.

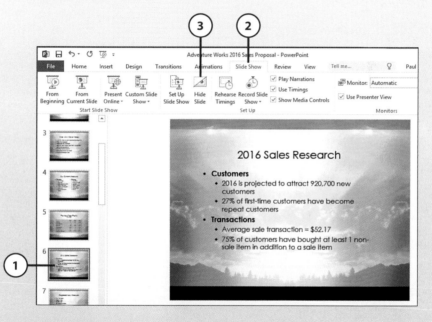

Unhiding a Slide

To unhide a slide, select it, select Slide Show, and then select Hide Slide. You can also right-click the slide in the slide sorter and then click Hide Slide to turn off that command.

>>>*Go Further*

DELETING A SLIDE

If you have a slide that you no longer need, you should delete it from your presentation to reduce the size of the presentation, reduce clutter in the slide sorter, and prevent the slide from appearing when you present the show. To delete a slide, right-click on the slide in the slide sorter, and then click Delete Slide.

Add Notes to a Slide

When determining the content of a presentation, you keep the actual amount of information on a slide to a minimum—just the high-level points to provide the framework for the topics you want to present. How, then, do you keep track of the details you want to cover for each slide? You add notes to the presentation. When you run through the presentation in PowerPoint's Reading View mode, you (or any other viewer) can display the notes.

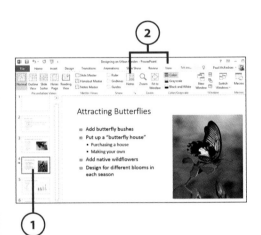

1. Select the slide you want to work with.

2. If you don't see the Notes page (the section with the Click to Add Notes text) below the slide, select the View tab and then select Notes.

3. Click anywhere inside the Notes page below the slide. PowerPoint converts the section to a text box.

4. Type your notes.

5. Click outside the Notes page to close it for editing.

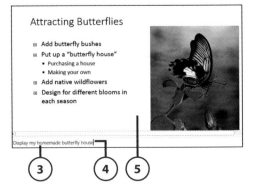

Making Room for Notes

If you want more room to type in the Notes page, PowerPoint provides a couple of choices. First, you can click and drag the separator bar at the top of the Notes page. Drag the bar up until the Notes page is the size you want, and then release the bar. This gives you less room for the slide, but you can also return the Notes page to its original size after you have added your notes. The second way to get a larger Notes area is to select the View tab and then select Notes Page. This changes the view to display the full Notes Page text box.

>>>Go Further

USING SLIDE NOTES

Here are some suggested ways you can use notes:

- As additional details for the audience.

- As a student guide. If you use a presentation as your primary teaching medium, you can put additional information on notes pages for your learners.

- As an instructor's guide. Again, if you teach from your presentation, you might have points you want to make, or other information associated with a particular slide. Add this information as notes, and you have your instructor's guide, perfectly in sync with the information you're giving your learners.

- As your presentation notes.

- As additional detailed handouts for your audience.

The first two points here apply to both offline presentations (where you present in front of an audience) and online presentations (where audience members run the show themselves), but the last three apply only to offline presentations.

Understanding the Slide Master

One of PowerPoint's templates might be just right for your presentation. If so, great! Your presentation's design will be one less thing to worry about on your way to an effective presentation. Often, however, a template is just right except for the background color, title alignment, or font. Or perhaps you need the company's logo to appear on each slide. Using the template as a starting point, you can make changes to the overall presentation so that it's just right for your needs.

However, what if your presentation already has a number of slides? It will probably require a great deal of work to change the background, alignment, or font on every slide. Fortunately, PowerPoint offers a much easier way: the Slide Master, which is available for every presentation. The Slide Master acts as a kind of "design center" for your presentation. The Slide Master's typefaces, type sizes, bullet styles, colors, alignment options, line spacing, and more are used on each slide in your presentation. Not only that, but any object you add to the Slide Master—a piece of clip art, a company logo, and so on—also appears in the same position on each slide.

The beauty of the Slide Master is that any change you make to this one slide, PowerPoint propagates to all the slides in your presentation. Need to change the background color? Just change the background color of the Slide Master. Prefer a different type size for top-level items? Change the type size for the top-level item shown on the Slide Master. You can also make separate adjustments to the masters of the seven standard layouts (Title Slide, Title and Content, and so on).

Work with the Slide Master

Before you can work with the Slide Master, you must first switch to it.

1. Select the View tab.

2. Select Slide Master. PowerPoint switches to Slide Master view.

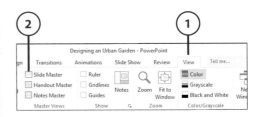

3. Select the Slide Master and then make your changes to the Slide Master formatting.

Formatting the Slide Master

Whether you're working with the Slide Master or a layout master, you can format the text, background, bullets, and colors as if you were working in a regular slide.

4. To apply a theme to the masters, select Slide Master, Themes and then select a theme.

5. Select the layout master you want to work with.

6. Select a placeholder.

7. To size a placeholder, click and drag the selection handles.

8. To move a placeholder, click and drag the placeholder border (being careful to not drag a selection handle).

The Slide Master applies to every slide.

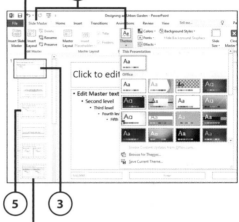

The rest of the items are the masters for the standard slide layouts.

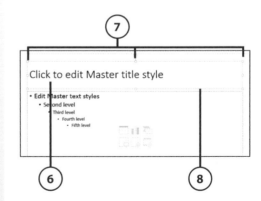

9. To add a placeholder to the layout master, select Slide Master, Insert Placeholder, and then select the placeholder type you want.

10. To toggle the title on and off for the layout master, select the Title check box.

11. To display an object—such as clip art or a text box—on the layout, select the Insert tab and then insert the object into the master.

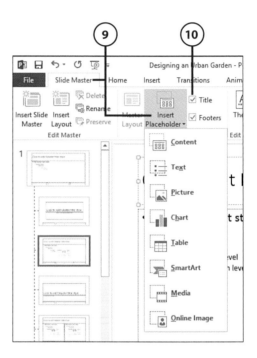

>>>Go Further

ADDING A CUSTOM LAYOUT

To add a custom layout to the Slide Master, select the Slide Master tab and then select Insert Layout. To supply a name to the new custom layout, select it, select Slide Master, Rename; then use the Rename Layout dialog box to type a new name and select Rename. Use the Slide Master, Insert Placeholder command to add placeholders to the new layout.

12. Select the Slide Master tab.

13. Select Close Master View.

Start the slide show.

Add transitions between slides.

Animate slide objects.

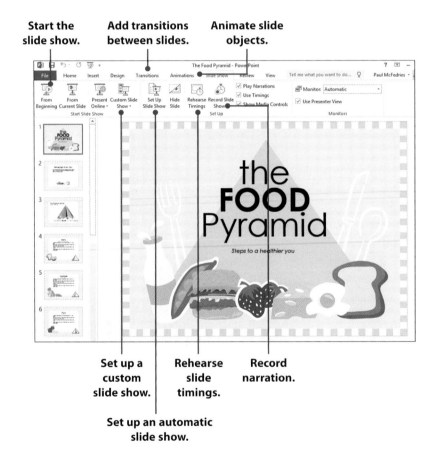

Set up a custom slide show.

Rehearse slide timings.

Record narration.

Set up an automatic slide show.

In this chapter, you learn how to work with PowerPoint slide shows, including how to set up slide animations, work out slide timings, record narration, and run the slide show. Topics include the following:

→ Adding transitions to your slides

→ Working with predefined and custom animations

→ Rehearsing the timing of each slide

→ Recording narration for a slide or entire presentation

→ Starting and navigating a slide show

Working with PowerPoint Slide Shows

In Chapter 9, "Building a PowerPoint Presentation," I mentioned that your goal when creating your slides should be to achieve a balance between eye candy and content. That is, although you need to tweak your slide fonts, colors, and effects to a certain extent to add visual interest, you do not want to go so far that your message is lost.

The same idea applies to the slide show as a whole, particularly if you want to add some dynamism to the presentation with slide transitions and object animations. These are fine additions to any presentation, but going overboard and therefore overwhelming your content is easy to do. This chapter gives you the details and techniques that can help you create the dynamic and interesting slide shows that audiences crave, but always remember that the message is the most important thing in any presentation.

Defining Slide Animations

Many years ago, someone defined *fritterware* as any software program that offers so many options and settings that you could fritter away hours at a time tweaking and playing with the program. PowerPoint's animation features certainly put it into the fritterware category because whiling away entire afternoons playing with transitions, entrance effects, motion paths, and other animation features is not hard. So consider yourself warned that the information in the next few sections might have adverse effects on your productivity.

Animation Guidelines

Before you learn how to apply slide transitions and object animations, it's worth taking a bit of time now to run through a few guidelines for making the best use of slide show animations:

- **Enhance your content**—The goal of any animation should always be to enhance your presentation, either to emphasize a slide object or to keep up your audience's interest. Resist the temptation to add effects just because you think they are cool or fun, because chances are most of your audience won't see them that way.

- **Remember that transitions can be useful**—Using some sort of effect to transition from one slide to the next is a good idea because it adds visual interest, gives the audience a short breather, and helps you control the pacing of your presentation.

- **Remember that transitions can be distracting**—A slide transition is only as useful as it is unremarkable. If everybody leaves your presentation thinking "Nice transitions!" you have a problem because they *should* be thinking about your message. Simple transitions such as fades, wipes, and dissolves add interest but do not get in the way. On the other hand, if you have objects flying in from all corners of the screen, your content will seem like a letdown.

- **When it comes to transitions and animations, variety is *not* the spice of life**—Avoid the temptation to use many different transitions and animations in a single presentation. Just as slide text looks awful if you use too many fonts, your presentations will look amateurish if you use too many animated effects.

- **Keep up the pace**—For transitions, keep the duration setting low to ensure that the transition from one slide to another never takes more than a few seconds. Also, avoid running multiple object animations at the same time because it can take an awfully long time for the effect to finish, and audiences *never* like having their time wasted on such things.

- **Match your animations to your audience**—If you are presenting to sales and marketing types, your entire presentation will be a bit on the flashy side, so you can probably get away with more elaborate animations; in a no-nonsense presentation to board members, animations and transitions should be as simple as possible.

Set Up a Slide Transition

A *slide transition* is a special effect that displays the next slide in the presentation. For example, in a *fade* transition, the next slide gradually materializes, while in a *blinds* transition the next slide appears with an effect similar to opening Venetian blinds. PowerPoint has nearly 40 different slide transitions, and for each one you can control the transition speed, the sound effect that goes along with the transition, and the trigger for the transition (a click or a time interval).

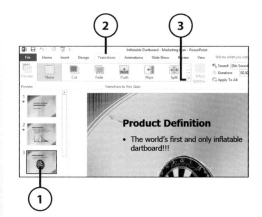

1. Select the slide you want to work with. If you want to apply the transition to multiple slides, select the slides.

2. Select the Transitions tab.

3. Select the More button in the Transition to This Slide group. PowerPoint displays a gallery of transitions.

4. Select the transition effect you want. PowerPoint previews the transition.

5. If the transition effect comes with any options, select Effect Options to see what's available.

6. In the Sound list, select the sound that you want to play during the transition. (If you are not sure which one you want, you can hover the mouse pointer over any sound effect to hear it played.)

7. Use the Duration spin box to set the time, in seconds, that it takes to play the transition.

8. If you want to move to the next slide by clicking the screen during the slide show, leave the On Mouse Click check box selected.

9. If you want to move to the next slide automatically after a set number of minutes and/or seconds, select the After check box and then specify the time interval.

10. Select Preview to try out your transition.

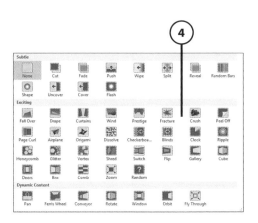

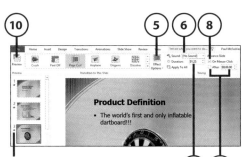

PowerPoint indicates that a slide has a transition by adding a star icon with "speed lines."

>>>Go Further
SPECIAL "SOUNDS"

The Sound list contains four special cases:

- **[No Sound]**—Select this item to run the transition without a sound effect.

- **[Stop Previous Sound]**—If the previous slide transition used a long-running sound effect, select this item to stop that sound.

- **Other Sound**—Select this item to display the Add Audio dialog box. Select the sound file you want to use and then select OK.

- **Loop Until Next Sound**—Select this command to repeat the chosen sound effect until the next effect begins.

The Loop Until Next Sound option is appropriate in few circumstances, so exercise some caution with this command. Unless your looped sound is a pleasant snippet of music (that loops smoothly) or an effect that requires some time—such as a ticking clock—the constant noise will just distract or annoy your audience.

Animate Slide Objects

A dynamic presentation is one where the slide text, graphics, and other objects are not static and lifeless on the screen. Instead, such a presentation takes advantage of PowerPoint's four types of animation effects:

- **Entrance**—These effects control how the object comes onto the slide.

- **Emphasis**—These effects add emphasis to an object by altering various text properties, including the typeface, size, boldface, italic, and color.

- **Exit**—These effects control how the object goes off the slide when you move to the next slide.

- **Motion Paths**—These effects control the path that the object follows when it comes onto and goes off the slide.

Again, you don't want to overdo any of these effects, but neither should you ignore them.

Add an Animation

PowerPoint's Ribbon offers the Animations tab, which makes it easy to select an animation for any object on a slide.

1. Select the slide you want to work with.

2. Select the slide object you want to animate.

Applying Animation

You can apply animation to any object, including the title and text placeholders, individual bullets or paragraphs (select the bullet or paragraph text), and drawing layer objects such as text boxes, shapes, clip art, pictures, SmartArt, charts, and tables.

3. Select the Animations tab.

4. Select the More button in the Animation group. PowerPoint displays the Animation gallery.

5. Select the animation you want to apply to the object. PowerPoint previews the animation.

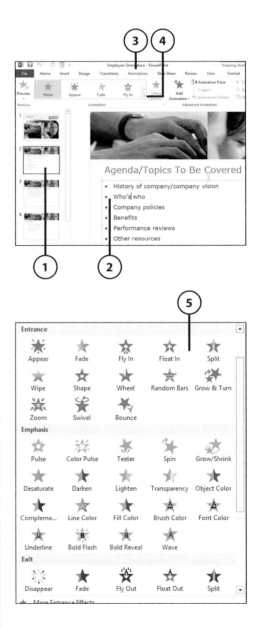

6. If the animation effect comes with any options, select Effect Options to see what's available.

7. Use the Start list to determine when the animation begins. On Click means it begins when you click the screen, which is usually what you want. You can also select With Previous to have the animation run at the same time as the previous animation, or After Previous to have the animation run immediately after the previous animation is complete.

8. Use the Duration spin box to set the time, in seconds, that it takes to play the transition.

9. Use the Delay spin box to set the time, in seconds, that PowerPoint waits before starting the transition.

10. To change the order in which the animations occur, click the object and then use the Move Earlier and Move Later commands to move the object up or down in the animation order.

11. Select Preview to try out your animation.

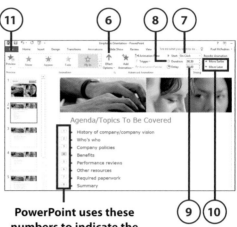

PowerPoint uses these numbers to indicate the order in which the slide animations occur.

>>>Go Further

MAKING BULLETS APPEAR ONE AT A TIME

One of the most popular animation effects is making bullets appear individually, usually in response to a mouse click. This useful presentation trick gives you full control over the display of your bullets. By animating bullets individually, you can prevent your audience from being distracted by bullets beyond the one you're currently discussing; you can hide bullets that contain "surprise" results until you're ready to present them; you can place extra emphasis on the individual bullets because they don't enter the slide individually as a group; and you add pizzazz by giving each bullet a different animation effect. (Although, of course, you want to be careful here that you don't induce animation overload on your audience.) If you've applied an animation to a text placeholder that contains bullets, you can make the bullets appear one at a time by selecting Effect Options and then selecting By Paragraph.

Preparing a Slide Show

Once you have your slides set up with content, transitions, and animations, you're ready to start thinking about the slide show that you'll be presenting. There isn't a ton that you have to do to prepare for the slide show, but there are a few tasks you should consider. These include rehearsing the timings of each slide, adding narration to individual slides or even the entire presentation, and putting together a custom slide show. The next few sections provide the details.

PowerPoint has a feature that can greatly improve your presentations. The feature is called Rehearse Timings and the idea behind it is simple: You run through ("rehearse") your presentation, and while you do this, PowerPoint keeps track of the amount of time you spend on each slide. This is useful for two reasons:

- If you have only so much time to present the slide show, Rehearse Timings lets you know whether your overall presentation runs too long or too short.

- After the rehearsal, you can examine the time spent on each slide. If you have consecutive slides where you spend a short amount of time on each, consider consolidating two or more of the slides into a single slide. Conversely, if you have some slides where you spend a great deal of time, consider splitting each one into two or more slides to avoid overwhelming (or boring) your audience.

PowerPoint also gives you a third reason to use Rehearse Timings: You can save the resulting timings and use them to run a slide show automatically. You find out how to do this later in this chapter (see "Set Up an Automatic Slide Show").

Rehearse Slide Timings

Before getting started, open the presentation you want to rehearse and collect any notes or props you'll use during the presentation.

1. Select the Slide Show tab.

2. Select Rehearse Timings. PowerPoint starts the slide show and displays the Rehearsal toolbar.

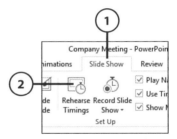

3. Present the slide exactly as you would during the actual presentation.

Resetting and Pausing

If you mess up a slide, you can start the timing of that slide over again by selecting the Repeat button. If you just need a second or two to gather your thoughts, select Pause, instead.

Next
Pause
Slide Time
The Rehearsal toolbar

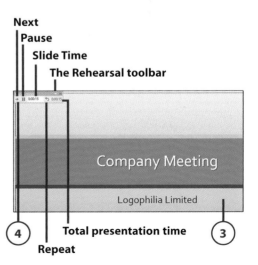

4. Select Next to move on to the next slide.

Total presentation time
Repeat

5. Repeat steps 3 and 4 for the entire presentation. When the presentation is done, PowerPoint displays the total presentation time and asks whether you want to save the slide timings.

6. To save the timings, select Yes; otherwise, select No.

With each new slide, PowerPoint resets the Slide Time value to 0:00:00.

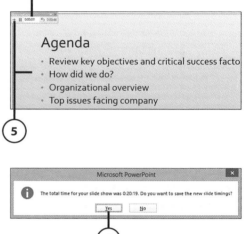

Recording Narration

Part of the appeal of a good presentation is that it feels like we are being told a story. Some words or images appear on a screen, but a person presents the underlying narrative for those words and images. There is something about a live human voice explicating some idea or process that is appealing on a deep level.

However, times may occur when you require a recorded voice for some or all of a presentation:

- You might have a slide that consists of a recorded greeting from the CEO or someone else at your company.

- You might have several slides where an expert does the presenting. If that person cannot be at your presentation, you need to record his or her material.

- You might be setting up an automatic presentation and so require recorded narration for the entire show.

PowerPoint can handle all these situations by enabling you to record narration from one or more slides or for the entire presentation.

Record Narration for a Slide

If needed, you can record narration for just a single slide.

1. Select the slide you want to narrate.

2. Select the Slide Show tab.

3. Select the bottom half of the Record Slide Show button.

4. Select Start Recording from Current Slide. PowerPoint displays the Record Slide Show dialog box.

5. If you have already rehearsed the slide timings, you can deselect the Slide and Animation Timings check box.

6. Make sure the Narrations and Laser Pointer check box is selected.

7. Select the Start Recording button. PowerPoint displays the slide and the Rehearsal toolbar.

8. Run through your narration.

9. When you're done, select More.

10. Select End Show. PowerPoint adds a sound icon to the slide.

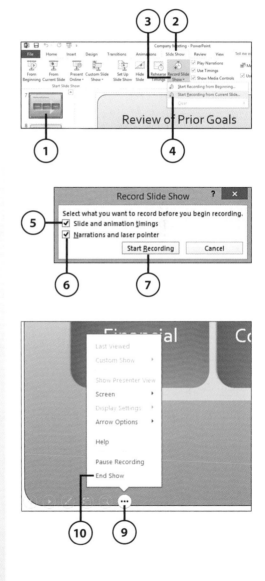

11. Select the sound icon.

12. Select the Playback tab.

13. Use the Start list to select when the narration starts: Automatically (the narration begins when you display the slide) or On Click (the narration begins when you click the slide).

Clearing the Narration

If you're not happy with your narration, you can remove it from the slide. Select the slide you used for the narration, select the Slide Show tab, select the bottom half of the Record Slide Show button, select Clear, and then select Clear Narration on Current Slide.

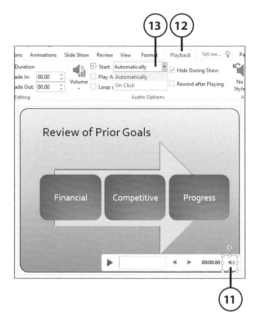

Record Narration for an Entire Presentation

If you need to record narration for the entire presentation, collect your notes, pull up your microphone, and then follow these steps.

1. Select the Slide Show tab.

2. Select the bottom half of the Record Slide Show button.

3. Select Start Recording from Beginning. PowerPoint displays the Record Slide Show dialog box.

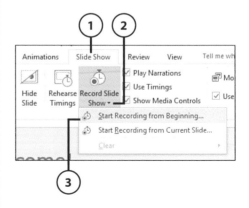

4. If you have already rehearsed the slide timings, you can deselect the Slide and Animation Timings check box.

5. Make sure the Narrations and Laser Pointer check box is selected.

6. Select the Start Recording button. PowerPoint opens the first slide and displays the Rehearsal toolbar.

7. Present the slide exactly as you would during the actual presentation, including your narration.

8. Select Next to display the next slide.

9. Repeat steps 7 and 8 until the presentation is done. PowerPoint adds a sound icon to each slide in the presentation.

10. For each slide, select the sound icon.

11. Select the Playback tab.

12. Use the Start list to select when the narration starts: Automatically (the narration begins when you display the slide) or On Click (the narration begins when you click the slide).

Running the Show Without Narration

If you need to run the slide show without narration, select the Slide Show tab and then select Set Up Slide Show to display the Set Up Show dialog box. Select the Show Without Narration check box and then select OK.

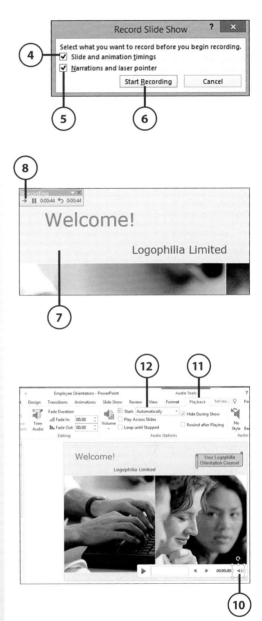

Clearing the Entire Narration

If you're not happy with any of your narration, you can remove it from the presentation. Select the slide you used for the narration, select the Slide Show tab, select the bottom half of the Record Slide Show button, select Clear, and then select Clear Narration on All Slides.

Setting Up Multiple Versions of a Slide Show

Having two or more versions of a presentation is common. Here are some examples:

- You might have a short version and a long version of a presentation.

- You might want to omit certain slides depending on whether you are presenting to managers, salespeople, or engineers.

- You might have "internal" and "external" versions; that is, you might have one version for people who work at your company and a different version for people from outside the company.

You could accommodate these different scenarios by creating copies of the presentation and then removing or reordering the slides as appropriate. However, this process takes a great deal of work, wastes disk space, and is inefficient when one slide changes and you have to make the same change in every version of the presentation that includes the slide.

A much better solution is to define one or more custom slide shows, which is a customized list of slides and the order in which you want them to appear.

Create a Custom Slide Show

You create a custom slide show by deciding which slides you want to appear in the presentation and then positioning those slides in the order you prefer.

1. Select the Slide Show tab.

2. Select Custom Slide Show.

3. Select Custom Shows. PowerPoint displays the Custom Shows dialog box.

4. Select New. PowerPoint displays the Define Custom Show dialog box.

5. Type a name for the custom slide show.

6. Select the check box beside each slide you want to include in the custom show.

7. Select Add. PowerPoint adds the selected slides to the Slides in Custom Show list.

8. Select a slide.

9. Select Up or Down to reposition the slide within the custom show.

10. Select Remove to delete the slide from the custom show.

11. Select OK to return to the Custom Shows dialog box. PowerPoint displays the name of your custom slide show in the Custom Shows list.

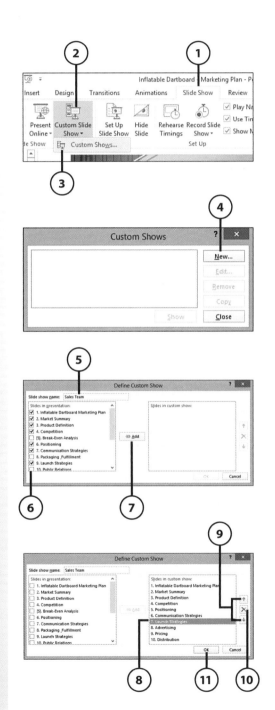

12. Select Close.

Editing a Custom Slide Show

To make changes to your custom slide show, select Slide Show, Custom Slide Show, Custom Shows; select the custom slide show and then select Edit.

Running a Slide Show

With your slides laid out, the text perfected, and the formatting just right, you are now ready to present your slide show. The next few sections show you how to start and navigate a slide show, as well as how to set up an automatic slide show.

Start the Slide Show

You can start a slide show from the beginning or from a particular slide.

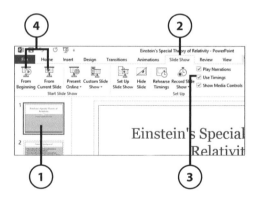

1. If you want to start the slide show from a particular slide, select that slide.

2. Select the Slide Show tab.

3. If you rehearsed the slide show timings, as described earlier in this chapter, and you want the slides to advance automatically, select the Use Timings check box.

4. To start the slide show from the current slide, select From Current Slide; otherwise, select From Beginning. PowerPoint starts the slide show.

Keyboard Shortcut
You can start your slide show from the beginning by pressing F5. To start the slide show from the selected slide instead, press Shift+F5.

>>>Go Further
STARTING A CUSTOM SLIDE SHOW

If you configured a custom slide show, as described earlier in the "Create a Custom Slide Show" section, you can also launch that custom show. To start a custom slide show, select the Slide Show tab, select Custom Slide Show, and then select Custom Shows to open the Custom Shows dialog box. Select the show you want in the list that appears and then select Show.

Navigate Slides

With your slide show running, you now need to navigate from one slide to the next.

1. Click the screen. PowerPoint displays either the next slide or the next animation in the current slide.

2. Move the mouse pointer. PowerPoint displays the slide show controls in the lower-left corner of the screen.

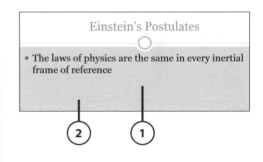

Displaying the Controls
If you have trouble getting PowerPoint to display the slide show controls, press A to make the mouse pointer visible, then move the pointer until the controls appear.

3. Click Previous to return to the previous slide or undo the most recent animation.

4. Click Next to move to the next slide or play the next animation.

5. Click Pointer Options.

6. Select the type of pointer you want to use.

7. Select a pointer color.

8. Select More. PowerPoint displays a menu of slide show controls.

9. Select End Show to stop the slide show before you reach the last slide.

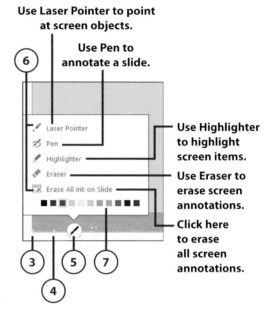

Use Laser Pointer to point at screen objects.

Use Pen to annotate a slide.

Use Highlighter to highlight screen items.

Use Eraser to erase screen annotations.

Click here to erase all screen annotations.

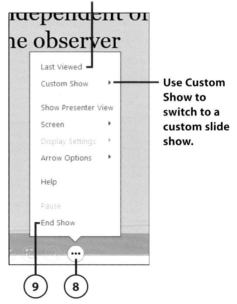

Use Last Viewed to return to the most recently viewed slide.

Use Custom Show to switch to a custom slide show.

>>>*Go Further*

NAVIGATING THE SLIDE SHOW FROM THE KEYBOARD

PowerPoint gives you quite a few keyboard alternatives for navigating and controlling the slide show. These are useful alternatives because displaying the shortcut menu can look unprofessional, and pressing a key or key combination is also usually faster.

Press	To
N	Advance to the next slide or animation (You can also press the spacebar, Enter, right arrow, down arrow, or Page Down keys.)
P	Return to the previous slide or animation (You can also press Backspace, left arrow, up arrow, or Page Up keys.)
n, Enter	Navigate to slide number *n*
S	Pause/resume an automatic slide show (You can also press plus [+].)
B	Toggle black screen on and off (You can also press period [.].)
W	Toggle white screen on and off (You can also press comma [,].)
Ctrl+T	Display the Windows taskbar
Esc	End the slide show

Set Up an Automatic Slide Show

What do you do if you want to show a presentation at a trade show, fair, or other public event, but you cannot have a person presenting the slide show? Similarly, what do you do if you want to send a presentation to a customer or prospect and you cannot be there to go through the slide show yourself? In these and similar situations, you can configure the presentation to run automatically.

1. Select the Slide Show tab.

2. Rehearse the slide show timings and save the timings when you are done.

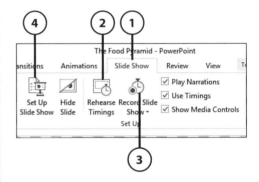

Advancing Slides Automatically

As an alternative to rehearsing the slide show timings, for each slide in the show, select the slide, select the Transitions tab, select the After check box in the Timing group, and then use the After text box to specify the number of seconds after which you want each slide to advance.

3. Add narration to the presentation.

4. Select Set Up Slide Show to display the Set Up Show dialog box.

5. Select the Browsed at a Kiosk option.

6. Select OK.

PowerPoint activates (and disables) the Using Timings, If Present option.

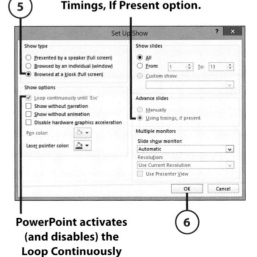

PowerPoint activates (and disables) the Loop Continuously Until 'Esc' check box.

Create a new
message.

Reply to a
message.

Forward a
message.

Move a
message.

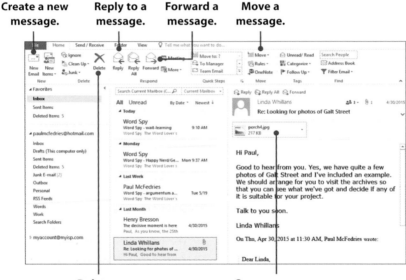

Delete a
message.

Save a message
attachment.

In this chapter, you learn about Outlook email, including setting up an account, sending and receiving mail, and working with incoming messages. Topics include the following:

→ Configuring Outlook with your email account

→ Creating and sending new messages

→ Retrieving and reading incoming messages

→ Replying to and forwarding messages

→ Working with the messages you have received

Sending and Receiving Outlook Email

Twenty-five years ago, email was more or less unheard of. Today, email is more or less indispensable. That's a huge shift in such a short time, but it's not surprising because email is fast, easy, convenient, and nearly universal. Email is the main reason why Outlook may get the most "screen time" of any Office application, because most of us leave it running all day to catch incoming messages as they arrive and to send our own messages at will.

Microsoft Outlook is an outstanding email program, in part because, as you see in this chapter, the basic email tasks of receiving, composing, and sending messages are all quick and easy.

Setting Up Your Email Account

When you launch Outlook for the first time, you are asked to run through a few configuration chores, the most important of which is setting up your email account. To get through these dialog boxes, you need at a minimum your email address and your email account password. This is enough to configure most accounts because Outlook uses Auto Account Setup to glean the rest of the account details automatically.

If this automatic route doesn't work, or if your email account requires special setup, you need to set up the account manually by entering some or all of the following settings:

- The account type: POP3 (Post Office Protocol 3) or IMAP (Internet Message Access Protocol)

- The domain names of your email provider's incoming and outgoing mail servers

- Your email account user name (This is often the same as your email address.)

Add an Account Automatically

For many account types, including Hotmail, Outlook.com, and Gmail, Outlook can configure the account automatically given just your email address and password.

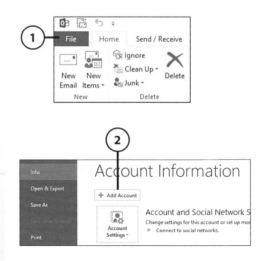

1. Click File. Outlook displays the Account Information screen.

2. Click Add Account. Outlook opens the Auto Account Setup dialog box.

Account Setup at Startup

If you're starting Outlook for the first time, click Next, select Yes, and then click Next to get to the Auto Account Setup dialog box.

---

3. Type your name.

4. Type your email address.

5. Type your password twice.

6. Click Next. For most account types, you are asked to confirm that you want to connect to the account.

7. Type your password, if it isn't filled in for you already.

8. Click to activate the Remember My Credentials check box. For some account types, this reads Save This Password in Your Password List.

9. Click OK. Outlook connects to your account.

10. Click Finish. Outlook adds the account.

Add an Account Manually

If Outlook fails to set up your account automatically, or if your email account requires a specialized configuration, you need to add the account by hand.

1. Click File. Outlook displays the Account Information screen.

2. Click Add Account. Outlook opens the Auto Account Setup dialog box.

Account Setup at Startup

If you're starting Outlook for the first time, click Next, select Yes, and then click Next to get to the Auto Account Setup dialog box.

---

3. Click Manual Setup or Additional Server Types.

4. Click Next.

5. Select the type of account you are setting up.

6. Click Next. For most account types, you are asked to confirm that you want to connect to the account.

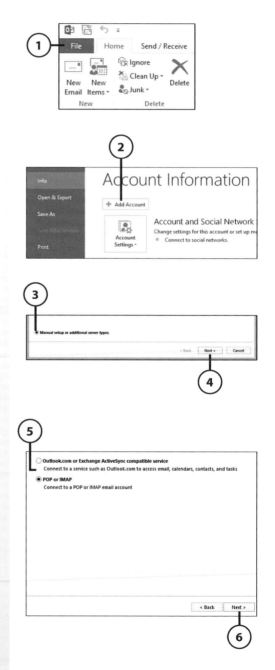

7. Type your name.

8. Type your email address.

9. Select the account type.

10. Type the address of your email provider's incoming mail server.

11. Type the address of your email provider's outgoing mail server.

12. Type your account user name.

13. Type your password.

14. Click Next. Outlook tests your account settings.

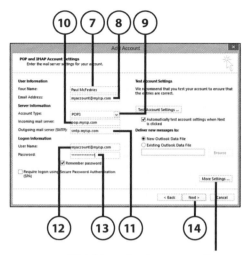

Click More Settings to configure advanced account settings.

>>>Go Further

ADVANCED ACCOUNT SETTINGS

If you're adding a POP or IMAP account, click More Settings to open the Internet E-mail Settings dialog box. You can use this dialog box to specify advanced or specialized account settings. For example, if your email provider says that its outgoing email server requires authentication, click the Outgoing Server tab and then click to activate the My Outgoing Server (SMTP) Requires Authentication check box. In most cases, you leave the Use Same Settings as My Incoming Server option selected, but if your provider requires separate authorization, click Log On Using and then enter the credentials you were given for the outgoing server.

If your provider has given you special ports to use, click the Advanced tab and then use the Incoming Server and Outgoing Server text boxes to type the port numbers. Finally, if your provider requires a secure connection to the server, click to activate the This Server Requires an Encrypted Connection (SSL) check box. Click OK to put the new settings into effect.

15. Click Close.

16. Click Finish. Outlook adds the account.

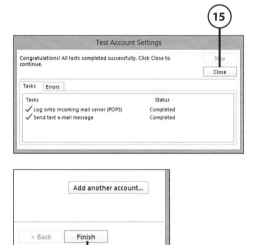

Composing and Sending a New Message

Outlook offers many features and options for sending messages to other people, but you really need to know how to do only three things: send a message to any email address, send a message to someone in your Outlook Contacts list, and attach a file to a message.

Compose a Message

Composing a message in Outlook is not all that different from composing a letter or memo in Word. You just need to add a few extra bits of information, such as your recipient's email address and a description of your message.

1. Click the Home tab.

2. Click New Email.

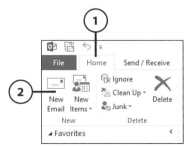

Keyboard Shortcut

You can also start a new email message by pressing Ctrl+N.

3. If you have multiple accounts, use the From list to select the account you want to use to send the message.

4. Type the email address of the message recipient. If you want to specify multiple recipients, separate each address with a semicolon (;).

5. If you want to send a copy of the message to someone, use the Cc (courtesy copy) field to type that person's email address. Again, if you want to specify multiple Cc recipients, separate each address with a semicolon (;).

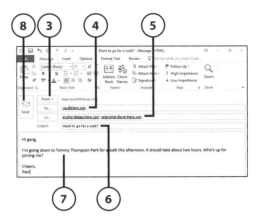

Blind Courtesy Copy

Each recipient can see the addresses of the main and Cc recipients. If you want someone to receive a copy of the message, but you don't want everyone else to see that person's address, send that person a Bcc (blind courtesy copy). To display the Bcc field, click the Options tab and then click Bcc.

6. Type a brief description of your message.

7. Type your message.

8. Click Send. Outlook sends your message to each recipient.

Use the Contacts List to Specify Recipients

When you're composing a message, you can use Outlook's Contacts list (see Chapter 13, "Keeping in Touch with Outlook Contacts") to add recipients without having to type their addresses.

1. Click the Home tab.

2. Click New Email.

Keyboard Shortcut

You can also start a new email message by pressing Ctrl+N.

3. Click To. Outlook displays the Select Names dialog box.

4. Click a contact and then click To. Outlook adds the contact to the message's To field.

5. If you want to send a courtesy copy of the message to someone, click the contact and then click Cc.

6. If you want to send a blind courtesy copy of the message to someone, click the contact and then click Bcc.

7. Click OK.

8. Fill in the rest of the message.

9. Click Send. Outlook sends your message to each contact you selected.

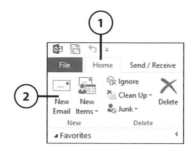

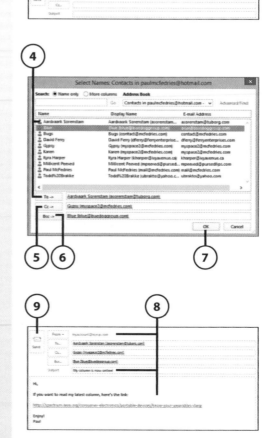

Attach a File to a Message

The information you want to send to the recipient might exist in a Word document, Excel spreadsheet, or some other file. In that case, you can attach the file to your message and Outlook sends along a copy of the file when you send the message.

1. Click the Home tab.

2. Click New Email.

3. Click the Message tab.

4. Click Attach File.

5. Click Browse This PC. Outlook displays the Insert File dialog box.

6. Select the folder that contains the file.

7. Click the file.

8. Click Insert.

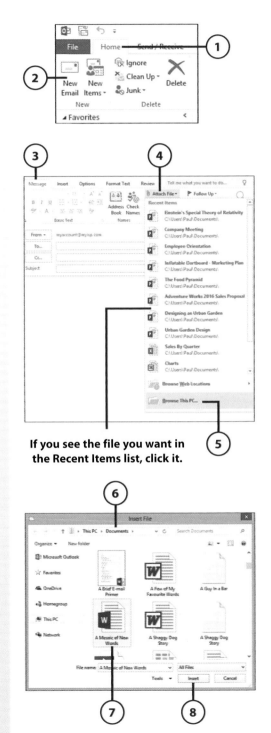

If you see the file you want in the Recent Items list, click it. 5

9. Fill in the rest of the message.

10. Click Send. Outlook sends your message to each contact you selected.

The attached file appears in the message.

Reading and Working with Incoming Mail

You won't spend all your Outlook time firing off notes to friends and colleagues. Those people will eventually start sending messages back, and you might start getting regular correspondence from mailing lists, administrators, and other members of the email community. This section shows you how to retrieve messages, read them, and use Outlook's tools for dealing with your messages.

Retrieve and Read Messages

By default, Outlook checks for incoming messages every half hour, but you can retrieve your waiting messages manually at any time.

1. Click the Send/Receive tab.

2. Click Send/Receive All Folders. Outlook retrieves any waiting messages from the server.

3. Click the message you want to read.

4. Read the message in the Preview pane.

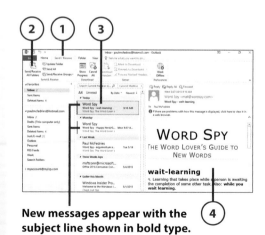

New messages appear with the subject line shown in bold type.

Changing the Message Checking Frequency

To change the frequency with which Outlook checks for new messages, click File and then click Options to open the Outlook Options dialog box. Click the Advanced tab and then click Send/Receive. In the Setting for Group "All Accounts" section, use the Schedule an Automatic Send/Receive Every *X* Minutes spin box to set the interval you prefer.

> >>>*Go Further*
> # CONTROLLING MESSAGE NOTIFICATIONS
>
> Outlook makes sure you know a message has arrived by giving you up to four notifications:
>
> - It plays a brief sound.
>
> - It briefly changes the mouse pointer to a letter icon.
>
> - It displays an envelope icon in the notification area.
>
> - It displays a Desktop Alert, a pop-up message just above the notification area that shows you the sender's name, the message subject, and the first two lines of the message.
>
> If you think this is overkill, you can turn off one or more of the notifications. Click File, Options to display the Outlook Options dialog box. Click the Mail tab and scroll down to the Message Arrival section. Click to deactivate or activate one or more of the following check boxes:
>
> - Play a Sound
>
> - Briefly Change the Mouse Cursor
>
> - Show an Envelope Icon in the Taskbar
>
> - Display a Desktop Alert

Reply to a Message

If you receive a message asking for information or requiring some other response from you, don't respond by creating a new message. Instead, use Outlook's Reply feature, which is faster and easier than crafting a new message.

1. Click the message to which you want to reply.

2. Click the Home tab.

3. Click Reply to send the response only to the person who sent the original message (any names in the Cc line are ignored). To reply not only to the original author, but also to anyone else mentioned in the Cc line, click Reply All instead. Outlook creates the reply.

Keyboard Shortcut

You can also run the Reply command by pressing Ctrl+R. For Reply All, press Ctrl+Shift+R.

---

4. In the message window, type your reply.

5. Click Send.

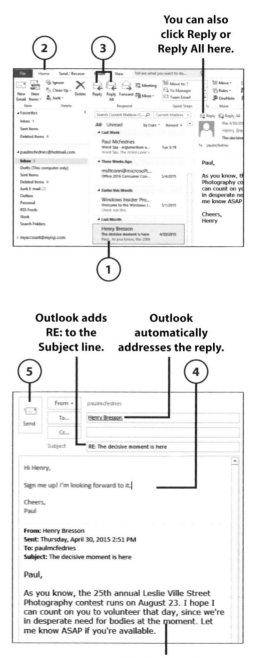

You can also click Reply or Reply All here.

Outlook adds RE: to the Subject line.

Outlook automatically addresses the reply.

Outlook quotes the original text.

Forward a Message

Instead of replying to a message, you might prefer to forward it to another person. For example, you might receive a message in error, or you might think that a friend or colleague might receive some benefit from reading a message you received.

1. Click the message you want to forward.

2. Click the Home tab.

3. Click Forward. Outlook creates the forward.

Keyboard Shortcut

You can also run the Forward command by pressing Ctrl+F.

---

4. Specify the recipient of the forward.

5. In the message window, type a brief introduction or explanation of the forward.

6. Click Send.

You can also click Forward here.

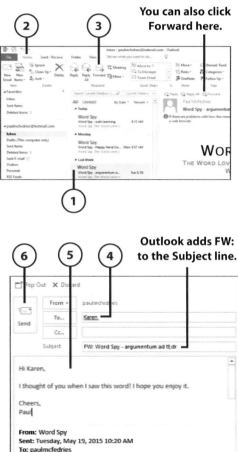

Outlook adds FW: to the Subject line.

Outlook quotes the original text.

Save an Attachment

If you receive a message with a file attachment, the message list displays a paperclip icon to let you know, and an icon for the file appears in the preview pane. You can then save the attachment to your PC.

1. Click the message that contains the attachment.

2. In the preview pane, click the attachment icon.

3. Click Save As. Outlook displays the Save Attachment dialog box.

If you only want to view the attachment, click Open.   ②

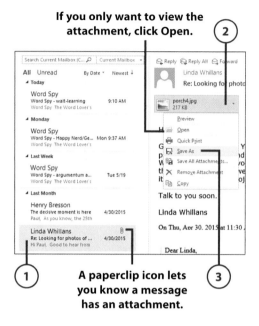

① ③

A paperclip icon lets you know a message has an attachment.

It's Not All Good

Be Careful with Attachments

Many viruses and other malware are transmitted via files attached to email messages. Before you save or even open a file attachment, make sure it comes from someone you trust. Even if you trust the sender, it's possible the person's account has been compromised, so if the attachment is unexpected, contact the sender and confirm that she sent you the attachment. In any case, it's always a good idea to have an antivirus program running on your PC. Here are some good ones to check out:

- Microsoft Security Essentials (http://windows.microsoft.com/en-us/windows/security-essentials-download)

- Norton Internet Security (www.symantec.com)

- McAfee Internet Security Suite (www.mcafee.com)

- Avast! Antivirus (www.avast.com)

- AVG Internet Security (http://free.avg.com/)

4. Select a location for the file.

5. Type the filename you want to use.

6. Click Save. Outlook saves the file to the location you specified.

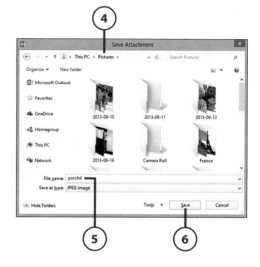

Move a Message

Instead of letting messages pile up in your Inbox folder, you should keep Outlook organized by moving each message to the appropriate folder when you are done with it.

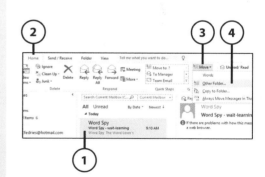

1. Click the message you want to move.

2. Click the Home tab.

3. Click Move.

4. Click Other Folder.

Drag and Drop

An often easier way to move a message is to click and drag the message from the message list and then drop it on the destination folder.

---

5. Click the destination folder.

6. Click OK. Outlook moves the message to the selected folder.

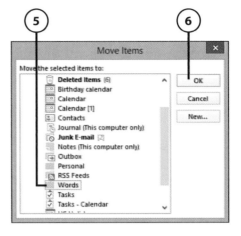

>>>Go Further

CREATING NEW FOLDERS

Although Outlook comes with a few predefined folders, you will likely want to create your own folders to suit your needs. For example, at work you might want to create a folder for each of your projects or teams, while at home you might need a folder for each of your hobbies or interests. To create a new folder, click the Folder tab and then click New Folder to open the Create New Folder dialog box. Type a name for the new folder and then click the location in which you want Outlook to store the folder. Click OK.

Delete a Message

To prevent your Inbox from become cluttered and difficult to navigate, you should delete any messages you no longer need.

1. Move the mouse pointer over the message you want to delete.

2. Click Delete. Outlook moves the message to the Deleted Items folder.

Keyboard Shortcut

You can also remove a message by clicking it and pressing Ctrl+D.

Recovering a Deleted Message

If you change your mind and decide to keep the message, click the Deleted Items folder, click the message, and then follow the steps in the "Move a Message" section earlier in the chapter to move the message back to the original folder (such as the Inbox). If instead you prefer to permanently remove the message, click the Deleted Items folder, move the mouse pointer over the message, and then click the Delete icon.

It's Not All Good

Handling Junk Email

Unsolicited commercial messages—also known as junk email or spam—are by far the biggest email annoyance. The good news is that Outlook comes with a Junk E-mail feature that can help you cope. Junk E-mail is a *spam filter*, which means that it examines each incoming message and applies sophisticated tests to determine whether the message is spam. If the tests determine that the message is probably junk, the email is exiled to the Junk E-mail folder.

Note that filtering spam is always a tradeoff between protection and convenience; that is, the stronger the protection you use, the less convenient the filter becomes because it increases the chance that it will mark legitimate messages as spam. You can set the Junk E-mail protection level to a level that works for you. Click the Home tab, click Junk, and then click Junk E-mail Options. The Junk E-mail Options dialog box appears. In the Options tab, select a setting: Start with Low, and if you find that Outlook misses too many spam messages, switch to the High setting.

Set up a meeting.

Change the view.

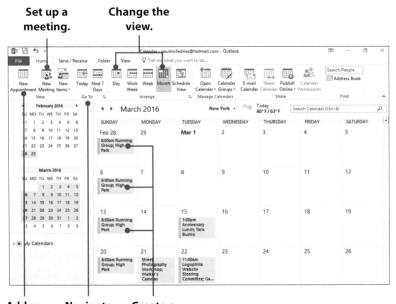

Add an appointment.

Navigate dates.

Create a recurring appointment.

In this chapter, you learn about Outlook's Calendar folder and how to use it to schedule appointments, all-day events, and meetings. Topics include the following:

→ Navigating Outlook's Calendar folder

→ Adding appointments

→ Setting up recurring appointments

→ Scheduling all-day events

→ Sending out meeting requests

Scheduling with the Outlook Calendar

Economists tell us that business productivity, after having been stagnant for several decades, began to rise in the mid-1990s. I am sure there are many reasons behind this improved productivity, but I would venture that at least part of the increase can be attributed to Microsoft Outlook, which debuted in 1997. For one thing, Outlook combined a number of functions—especially email, appointments, and contacts—into a single program. For another, Outlook's Calendar feature not only made it easy to enter and keep track of appointments and meetings electronically, but it also could be set up to *remind* us of our appointments and meetings.

Of course, Calendar can only boost your productivity if you know how to use it and that's what this chapter is designed to show you.

Using the Calendar Folder

When you display the Calendar folder, Outlook displays a window laid out more or less like a day planner or desk calendar. Here are two items to note right up front:

- **Calendar grid**—This takes up the bulk of the Calendar window and it shows one month at a time, where each row of the grid is a week. The appointments and meetings you schedule appear in this area.

- **Folder pane**—This area appears on the left side of the Calendar window and usually shows two months of dates, including the current month, the last few days from the previous month, and possibly the first few days from the next month. You use the Folder pane to change the date shown in the Calendar grid. Dates for which you have already scheduled appointments or meetings are shown in bold type. Note that today's date always has a blue square around it.

Switch to the Calendar Folder

When you launch Outlook, it displays the Inbox folder for your email, so you need to know how to switch to the Calendar folder.

1. Launch Outlook.

2. Click Calendar. Outlook switches to the Calendar folder.

Keyboard Shortcut

You can also switch to the Calendar folder by pressing Ctrl+2. To switch back to the Inbox folder, press Ctrl+1.

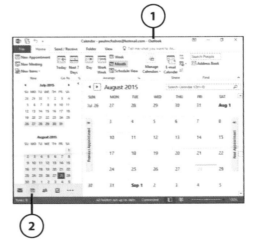

>>>Go Further
DISPLAYING THE CALENDAR FOLDER AT STARTUP

Outlook automatically opens the Inbox folder at startup, but you might find that you spend more time in the Calendar folder. Similarly, you might find that you always switch right away to the Calendar folder to check your upcoming appointments. In either scenario, you might prefer to have Outlook display the Calendar folder automatically at startup instead of the Inbox folder.

To set that up, click File and then click Options to display the Outlook Options dialog box. Click the Advanced tab. Beside the Start Outlook in this Folder box, click Browse to open the Select Folder dialog box. Click the Calendar folder and then click OK to return to the Outlook Options dialog box. Click OK.

Navigate to a Date

Calendar always opens with today's date displayed. However, if you want to work with a different day, Outlook makes it easy to navigate to that date.

1. Click the Home tab.

2. Click the Go To Date dialog box launcher. Outlook displays the Go To Date dialog box.

Click here to navigate to today's date.

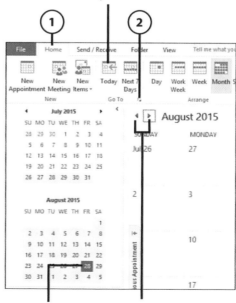

If you see the date in the Folder pane, click it.

Use these arrows to display the previous or next month.

Keyboard Shortcut

You can open the Go To Date dialog box from the keyboard by pressing Ctrl+G.

3. Type the date you want.

4. Click OK. Outlook displays the date in the Calendar folder.

Click this arrow to select the date using a calendar control.

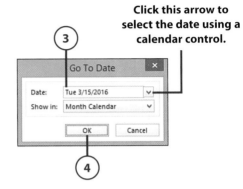

Switch the Calendar's View

Calendar's default view is the Month calendar, which shows a single month's worth of appointments and meetings. However, Calendar is flexible, and you can configure it to show just a single day, a week, or even just the work week.

1. Click the Home tab. The options that follow are also available on the View tab.

2. In the Arrange section, click the view you want to use.

Displays just the selected date

Displays the month of the selected date

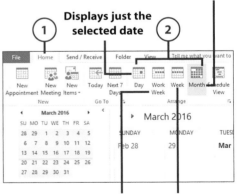

Displays the work week of the selected date

Displays the week of the selected date

Keyboard Shortcuts

From the keyboard, switch to the Day view by pressing Ctrl+Alt+1; switch to the Work Week view by pressing Ctrl+Alt+2; switch to the Week view by pressing Ctrl+Alt+3; and switch to the Month view by pressing Ctrl+Alt+4.

>>>Go Further

CONFIGURING THE WORK WEEK

Outlook assumes the work week consists of the five days from Monday to Friday. If your work week is shorter or uses different days (for example, Tuesday through Saturday, or even any number of nonconsecutive days), you can configure the Work Week view that the Calendar displays. Click File and then click Options to display the Outlook Options dialog box. Click the Calendar tab. In the Work Time section, click to activate the Work Week check boxes for the days you want to include in the Work Week view. Also, use the First Day of Week list to select the day you want Calendar to display at the beginning of the week. Click OK to put the new settings into effect.

Setting Up Appointments

Calendar differentiates between three kinds of items you can schedule:

- **Appointments**—An appointment is the most general Calendar item. It refers to any activity for which you set aside a block of time. Typical appointments include a lunch date, a trip to the dentist or doctor, or a social engagement. You can also create recurring appointments that are scheduled at regular intervals (such as weekly or monthly).

- **All-day events**—An all-day event is any activity that consumes one or more entire days. Examples include conferences, trade shows, vacations, and birthdays. In Calendar, events do not occupy blocks of time. Instead, they appear as banners above the affected days. You can also schedule recurring all-day events.

- **Meetings**—A meeting is a special kind of appointment to which two or more people are invited. Outlook has a Meeting Planner that lets you set up a meeting and send email messages inviting people to the meeting. Outlook can then track the responses so that you know who is coming to the meeting and who isn't.

The next few sections show you how to create appointments, all-day events, and meetings.

Create a New Appointment

When you create an appointment, you specify the date, the start and end times, and a subject (a short description or title). You can also optionally specify the location and notes related to the appointment.

1. Navigate to the day on which the appointment occurs.

2. Click the Home tab.

3. Click Day. If you prefer to see nearby appointments, click Work Week or Week instead.

4. Click New Appointment. Outlook displays the Appointment window.

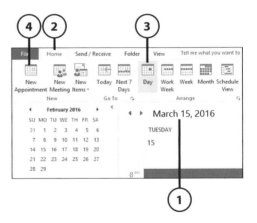

Keyboard Shortcut

You can also run the New Appointment command by pressing Ctrl+N.

5. Use the Subject text box to type a description of the appointment. This is the text that appears in the Calendar grid.

6. Use the Location text box to type the location (such as a business name, room number, or address) for the appointment.

7. Use the Start Time controls to specify the time that the appointment starts (as well as the date, if needed).

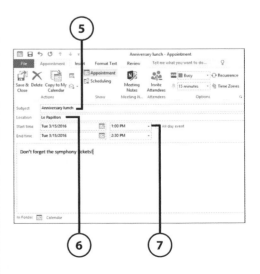

8. Use the End Time controls to specify the time (and possibly the date) the appointment ends.

9. Use the large text box to type notes about the appointment.

10. Use the Reminder list to select the number of minutes, hours, or days before the appointment that you want Outlook to remind you that your appointment is coming up. If you want Outlook to play a sound, click Sound and use the Reminder Sound dialog box to select an audio file to be played.

11. Click Save & Close to add the appointment and return to the Calendar folder.

Shortcut

You can create a basic appointment by switching to Day view, clicking the time of the appointment (or dragging the mouse over the time blocks for an appointment longer than half an hour), typing a subject for the appointment, and then pressing Enter.

Taking Advantage of AutoDate

One of Outlook's most interesting features is its capability to accept natural-language entries in date and time fields and convert those entries into real dates and times. If today is October 7, for example, typing **next week** in a date field causes Outlook to enter October 14 as the date. Similarly, you can type **noon** in a time field, and Outlook "knows" that you mean 12:00.

This useful feature is called AutoDate, and once you understand how it works, you'll find that it saves you a lot of time in certain situations. I won't give you a full description of what AutoDate understands, but a few examples should give you an idea of what it can do, and you can experiment from there.

Here are some points to keep in mind when entering dates:

- AutoDate converts *yesterday*, *today*, and *tomorrow* into their date equivalents.

- You can shorten day names to their first three letters: *sun*, *mon*, *tue*, *wed*, *thu*, *fri*, and *sat*. (Notice, too, that case isn't important.) You can also shorten month names: *jan*, *feb*, *mar*, *apr*, *may*, *jun*, *jul*, *aug*, *sep*, *oct*, *nov*, and *dec*.

- To specify a date in the current week (by default, Calendar's weeks run from Sunday through Saturday), use the keyword *this* (for example, *this fri*).

- To specify a date from last week or last month, use the keyword *last* (for example, *last aug*).

- To specify a date in the next week or month, use the keyword *next* (for example, *next sat*).

- If you want to use the first day of a week or month, use the keyword *first*. For example, *first mon in dec* gives you the first Monday in December. Similarly, use *last* to specify the last day of a week or month.

- To get a date that is a particular number of days, weeks, months, or years from some other date, use the keyword *from* (for example, *6 months from today*).

- To get a date that is a particular number of days, weeks, months, or years before some other date, use the keyword *before* (for example, *2 days before christmas*).

- AutoDate recognizes a number of holidays that fall on the same date each year, including the following: Boxing Day, Cinco de Mayo, Christmas Day, Christmas Eve, Halloween, Independence Day, Lincoln's Birthday, New Year's Day, New Year's Eve, St. Patrick's Day, Valentine's Day, Veterans Day, and Washington's Birthday.

- To get a date that is a particular number of days, weeks, months, or years in the past, use the keyword *ago* (for example, *4 weeks ago*).

- AutoDate also accepts spelled-out dates, such as *August 23rd* and *first of January*. These aren't as useful, because they probably take longer to spell out than they do to enter the date in the usual format.

For time fields, keep the following points in mind:

- AutoDate converts *noon* and *midnight* into the correct times.

- AutoDate understands military time. So if you type *9*, AutoDate converts this to 9:00 AM. However, if you type *21*, AutoDate changes it to 9:00 PM.

- Use *now* to specify the current time.

- You can specify time zones by using the following abbreviations: *CST, EST, GMT, MST,* and *PST.*

Create a Recurring Appointment

If you have an appointment that occurs at a regular interval (say, weekly or monthly), Calendar lets you schedule a recurring appointment. For example, if you create a weekly appointment, Calendar fills in that appointment auto- matically on the same day of the week at the same time for the duration you specify.

1. Navigate to the day on which the appointment occurs.

2. Click the Home tab.

3. Click New Appointment. Outlook displays the Appointment window.

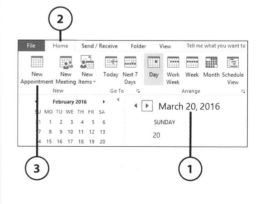

Keyboard Shortcut
You can also run the New Appointment command by pressing Ctrl+N.

4. Fill in the appointment details, as described previously in the "Create a New Appointment" section.

5. Click the Appointment tab.

6. Click Recurrence. Outlook opens the Appointment Recurrence dialog box.

7. In the Recurrence Pattern group, click the interval you want to use: Daily, Weekly, Monthly, or Yearly. The options to the right of these buttons change, depending on your selection. The Weekly option, for example, asks you to enter the length of the interval in weeks, as well as the day of the week to use.

8. In the Range of Recurrence group, use the Start box to tell Outlook when the recurring appointment should begin. If you want the appointment scheduled indefinitely, click the No End Date option. Otherwise, click End After and specify the number of appointments to schedule, or click End By and specify the date of the last appointment.

9. Click OK to return to the Appointment window.

10. Click Save & Close to add the appointment and return to the Calendar folder.

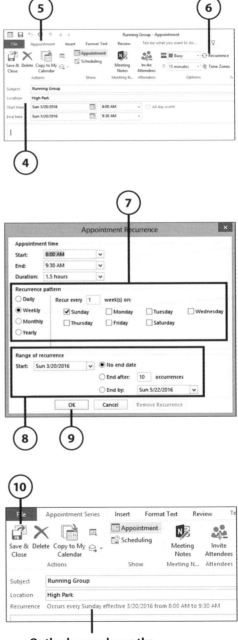

Outlook now shows the recurrence settings instead of the start and end times.

Deleting a Recurring Appointment

When you delete an appointment that is set up to repeat, you can either delete a single instance or the entire series. To delete a single instance of the recurrence, right-click that instance, click Delete, and then click Delete Occurrence. To delete the entire series of recurrences, right-click any instance, click Delete, and then click Delete Series.

Appointments Versus All-Day Events

As I mentioned earlier, an all-day event is an activity that consumes one or more days (or, at least, the working part of those days). Some activities are obvious all-day events: vacations, trade shows, sales meetings, and so on. But what about, say, a training session that lasts from 9:00 to 4:00? Is that an all-day event or just a long appointment? From Outlook's point of view, there are two main differences between an appointment and an all-day event:

- By default, an appointment is marked as "busy" time, so other people know not to schedule appointments at conflicting times. On the other hand, an all-day event is marked as "free" time.

- Appointments are entered as time blocks in the Calendar, but all-day events are displayed as a banner at the top of the calendar. This means that you can also schedule appointments on days that you have all-day events.

A good example that illustrates these differences is a trade show. Suppose the show lasts an entire day and you're a sales rep who will be attending the show. You could schedule the show as a day-long appointment. However, what if you also want to visit with customers who are attending the show? In that case, it would make more sense to schedule the show as an all-day event. This leaves the calendar open for you to schedule appointments with your customers.

Schedule an All-Day Event

Scheduling an all-day event is almost identical to scheduling an appointment.

1. Navigate to the day on which the event occurs.

2. Click the Home tab.

3. Click Day.

4. Double-click the banner that appears at the top of the Day calendar. Outlook opens the Event window.

5. Fill in the appointment details, as described previously in the "Create a New Appointment" and "Create a Recurring Appointment" sections.

6. Click Save & Close to add the appointment and return to the Calendar folder.

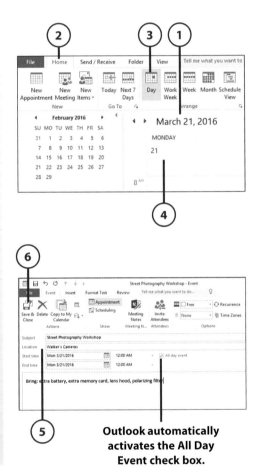

Outlook automatically activates the All Day Event check box.

Understanding Meeting Requests

The appointments and all-day events that you've worked with so far haven't required you to work directly with anyone on your network or on a remote network. Yes, you can email your calendar to other people (by clicking the Home tab's E-mail Calendar button) or even publish your calendar online (by clicking the Home tab's Publish Online button) so that others can view your appointments and all-day events. But there might be times when you need to coordinate schedules with other people to arrange a meeting.

The old-fashioned method of doing this involved a phone conversation in which each person consulted his or her day planner to try to find a mutually free time. This is not too bad if just two people are involved, but what if there are a dozen? Or a hundred? You could try sending out email messages, but you're still looking at a coordination nightmare for a large group of people.

Outlook solves this dilemma by implementing *meeting requests*, which are special messages that you use to set up small meetings. If you just need to set up a simple meeting that involves only a few people, a meeting request is all you need. A meeting request is an email message that asks the recipients to attend a meeting on a particular day at a particular time. The recipients can then check their schedules (although Outlook does this for them automatically) and either accept or reject the request by clicking buttons included in the message.

Request a Meeting

To set up a meeting with one or more people, you must create and send each potential attendee a meeting request.

1. Navigate to the day on which you want to schedule the meeting.

2. Click the Home tab.

3. Click Day. If you prefer to see nearby appointments, click Work Week or Week instead.

4. Click New Meeting. Outlook displays the Meeting window.

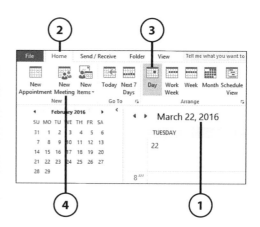

Keyboard Shortcut

You can also run the New Meeting command by pressing Ctrl+Shift+Q.

5. Enter the email address of each person you want to invite or select the addresses from your contacts.

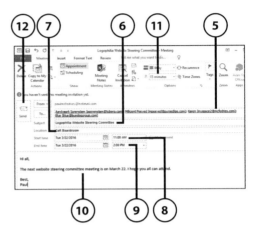

Optional Attendees

To specify attendees for whom the meeting is optional, click the To button to display your contacts. Click a contact and then click Optional. You can also add contacts to the Required field. Click OK when you're done.

6. Use the Subject text box to type a description of the meeting. This is the text that appears in the Calendar grid.

7. Use the Location text box to type the location (such as a business name, room number, or address) for the meeting.

8. Use the Start Time controls to specify the time that the meeting starts (as well as the date, if needed).

9. Use the End Time controls to specify the time (and possibly the date) the meeting ends.

10. Use the large text box to type your invitation text.

11. Use the Reminder list to select the number of minutes, hours, or days before the meeting that you want Outlook to remind you that your meeting is coming up.

12. Click Send to send the meeting requests, add the meeting to your calendar, and return to the Calendar folder.

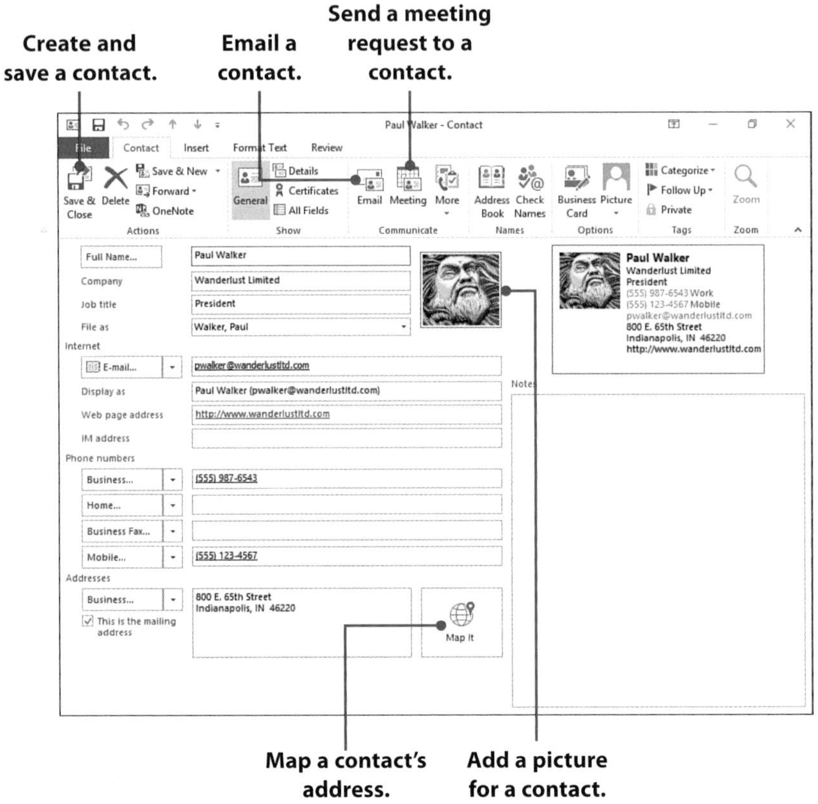

Create and save a contact.
Email a contact.
Send a meeting request to a contact.
Paul Walker - Contact
File
Contact
Insert
Format Text
Review
Save & Close
Delete
Save & New
Forward
OneNote
Actions
General
Details
Certificates
All Fields
Show
Email
Meeting
More
Communicate
Address Book
Check Names
Names
Business Card
Picture
Options
Categorize
Follow Up
Private
Tags
Zoom
Zoom
Full Name...
Paul Walker
Company
Wanderlust Limited
Job title
President
File as
Walker, Paul
Internet
E-mail...
pwalker@wanderlustltd.com
Display as
Paul Walker (pwalker@wanderlustltd.com)
Web page address
http://www.wanderlustltd.com
IM address
Phone numbers
Business...
(555) 987-6543
Home...
Business Fax...
Mobile...
(555) 123-4567
Addresses
Business...
800 E. 65th Street
Indianapolis, IN 46220
This is the mailing address
Map It
Notes
Paul Walker
Wanderlust Limited
President
(555) 987-6543 Work
(555) 123-4567 Mobile
pwalker@wanderlustltd.com
800 E. 65th Street
Indianapolis, IN 46220
http://www.wanderlustltd.com
Map a contact's address.
Add a picture for a contact.

In this chapter, you learn about Outlook's Contacts folder and how to use it to store contact information, import contact data, and work with contacts. Topics include the following:

→ Using the Contacts folder

→ Creating a new contact

→ Importing contact data from a file

→ Editing and working with contact data

→ Sending messages and meeting requests via the Contacts folder

Keeping in Touch with Outlook Contacts

Whether it's working with clients, colleagues, or suppliers, contacting others is a big part of most people's working day. It can also be time-consuming to constantly look up phone numbers, physical addresses, email addresses, web addresses, and so on. Streamlining these tasks—a process known as *contact management*—can save you a lot of time and make your work more efficient.

Outlook's contact management feature is called, appropriately enough, Contacts. This folder gives you amazing flexibility for dealing with your ever-growing network of coworkers, customers, friends, and family. Yes, you can use Contacts to store mundane information such as phone numbers and addresses, but with more than 100 predefined fields available, you can preserve the minutiae of other people's lives: their birthdays and anniversaries, the names of their spouses and children, and even their web page addresses. This chapter takes you inside the Contacts folder and shows you how to add and edit contacts, import contact data, and more.

Exploring the Contacts Folder

When you open the Contacts folder, Outlook displays a window divided into three vertical panes:

- **Folder pane**—This is the left pane and it shows just a single Contact item.

- **Contacts list**—This is the middle pane, and by default it displays a list of your contacts, sorted alphabetically by last name.

- **Reading pane**—This is the right pane, and it shows the details for the currently selected contact.

Switch to the Contacts Folder

When you launch Outlook, it displays the Inbox folder for your email, so you need to know how to switch to the Calendar folder.

1. Launch Outlook.

2. Click Contacts. Outlook switches to the Contacts folder.

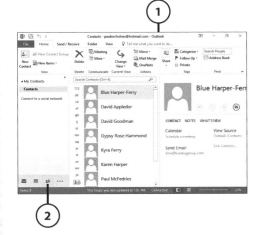

Keyboard Shortcut

You can also switch to the Contacts folder by pressing Ctrl+3. To switch back to Inbox, press Ctrl+1.

>>>Go Further
DISPLAYING THE CONTACTS FOLDER AT STARTUP

Outlook automatically opens the Inbox folder at startup, but you might find that you spend more time in the Contacts folder. Similarly, you might find that you always switch right away to the Contacts folder. In either scenario, you might prefer to have Outlook display the Contacts folder automatically at startup instead of the Inbox folder.

To set that up, click File and then click Options to display the Outlook Options dialog box. Click the Advanced tab. Beside the Start Outlook in this Folder box, click Browse to open the Select Folder dialog box. Click the Contacts folder and then click OK to return to the Outlook Options dialog box. Click OK.

Understanding the Contacts Folder Views

As with all of Outlook's folders, you can view your contacts in several ways. For example, you can set up the Contacts folder to group items by Company or Location. Outlook has eight predefined views for the Contacts folder:

- **People**—Displays the Contacts folder as a list sorted alphabetically by last name, with a reading pane to the right to show the details of the selected contact. On the Home tab, select People in the Current View gallery.

- **Business Card**—Displays each item in the Contacts folder using a rectangular format reminiscent of a business card. On the Home tab, select Business Card in the Current View gallery.

- **Card**—Displays the Contacts folder as a kind of Rolodex, with each contact given its own "card" showing basic information. On the Home tab, select Card in the Current View gallery.

- **Phone**—Displays the contacts in a table format with the fields as columns. You see the full name, company name, and phone numbers for each contact. On the Home tab, select Phone in the Current View gallery.

- **List**—Displays the Contacts folder in a format similar to the Phone view, but with contacts grouped by Company name. On the Home tab, select List in the Current View gallery.

- **Categories**—Groups the contacts on the Categories field and displays them in a table format. Within each category, contacts are sorted by the File As field. On the View tab, select Categories in the Arrangement gallery. This option requires that you also select Phone or List in the Home tab.

- **Company**—Sorts the contacts on the Company field. On the View tab, select Company in the Arrangement gallery. This option requires that you also select Phone or List in the Home tab.

- **Location**—Sorts the contacts on the Country/Region field. On the View tab, select Location in the Arrangement gallery. This option requires that you also select Phone or List in the Home tab.

Adding a New Contact

A nearly empty Contacts folder is not very useful, so you should get right down to adding some new cards. This section shows you various methods of setting up new contacts. You first learn how to add a contact by hand and then I show you several easier methods for adding contacts.

Create a New Contact from Scratch

Although Outlook can store a contact's data using dozens of separate fields, you can enter as little or as much data as you need, with the contact name being the bare minimum.

1. Click the Home tab.

2. Click New Contact. Outlook opens the Contact window.

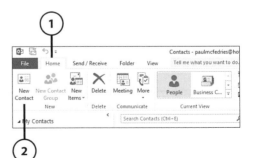

Keyboard Shortcut

In the Contacts folder, you can start a new contact by pressing Ctrl+N.

This area shows a preview of the contact's business card.

3. Fill in as many of the fields as you need.

4. Complete the contact: If you are finished adding contacts, click Save & Close; if you want to add more contacts, click Save & New and then repeat steps 2 and 3.

>>>Go Further
USING THE DETAILS AND ALL FIELDS FORMS

When you add a contact, the Contact window by default displays the General form, which represents the most commonly used contact fields. The next set of commonly used fields includes the contact's Department, Profession, Manager's Name, and Assistant's Name. On the personal side, it also includes the contact's nickname, spouse or partner's name, birthday, and anniversary. To view these and other fields, click Details in the Contact tab's Show group.

As I mentioned earlier, Outlook defines more than 100 fields for each contact. If a particular field you need to fill in is not displayed in the General form or the Details form, you can find it in the All Fields form. To display this form, click All Fields in the Contact tab's Show group. Use the Select From drop-down list to click a category of fields to work with. (If you're not sure, click All Contact Fields to see every available field.) Find the field you want and then type your data in the Value column.

Finally, if you still do not see a field to hold a particular type of data, create your own field by clicking the New button that appears at the bottom of the All Fields forms. In the New Field dialog box, type a Name, click a data Type, and then click a Format.

Understanding Outlook's Contact Data Fields

Most of the data fields provided by Contacts are straightforward; you just type in the appropriate data. However, the following list gives you some details about certain fields in the General form.

- **Full Name**—Use the Full Name text box to type the name of the contact. To type more detailed information, click the Full Name button to display the Check Full Name dialog box, which lets you type not only separate first, middle, and last names, but also the appropriate title (Mr., Ms., and so on) and suffix (Jr., II, and so on).

- **File As**—Outlook uses the File As field to determine where the contact appears alphabetically. In most cases, Outlook uses the format *Last, First*, where *Last* is the person's last name and *First* is the person's first name. For example, if you type Paul Walker in the Full Name box, Outlook adds Walker, Paul to the File As field. However, this format is not what you want if the Full Name field contains an organization name. In this case, you can either edit the File As field directly, or you can drop down the list and click the *First Last* format (for example, Paul Walker).

- **Phone Number**—Outlook can record up to 19 phone numbers for each contact. The default Contact window just shows fields for the four most common numbers: Business, Home, Business Fax, and Mobile. Other phone number possibilities include Assistant, Callback, Home Fax, and Pager. To add a different number, use the drop-down lists provided to click the type of number you want to add. (If you want to add phone numbers in addition to the ones displayed, you need to switch to the All Fields form.)

  If you want to specify phone number extras such as the country/region code or the extension, use the following format:

  +Country (Area) Local x Ext

  Here, *Country* is the country/region code, *Area* is the area code, *Local* is the local number, and *Ext* is the extension. Alternatively, click the button beside the phone number field you are using to display the Check Phone Number dialog box.

- **Address**—You use the Addresses section field to type the contact's street address, city, state or province, ZIP or postal code, and country. Use the drop-down list to specify whether this is a Business, Home, or

Other address. If this is the contact's mailing address, click the This is the Mailing Address check box to activate it. As with the name and phone number, you can also use a dialog box to type specific address information. Click the button beside the address field to display the Check Address dialog box.

- **E-mail**—Use the E-mail field to type the contact's email address. Note that Outlook can hold up to three email addresses for each contact (E-mail, E-mail 2, and E-mail 3). In each case, use the Display As field to set how Outlook displays the email address when you add this contact to the To, Cc, or Bcc field of an email message. The default format is *Name* (*Address*), where *Name* is the text in the Full Name field and *Address* is the text in the E-mail field. If you want to display just the name, just the address, or some other text, edit the Display As field accordingly.

Create a Contact from the Same Company

Having multiple contacts from the same company is common. In most cases, these people have a number of fields in common, including the Company, the Business Address, the Web Page Address, and possibly the Business Phone and Business Fax numbers. Rather than typing these common field values for each contact, you can save time by asking Outlook to create a new contact using the company data of an existing contact.

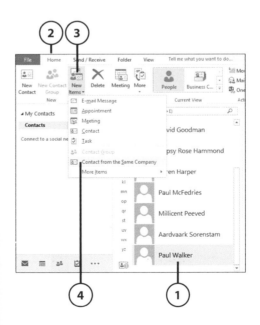

1. Click the contact that has the company data you want to use for the new contact.

2. Click the Home tab.

3. Click New Items.

4. Click Contact from the Same Company. Outlook creates a new contact, adds the company data, and displays the Contact window.

Using the Contact Window

If you just created a new contact and you still have the Contact window open, you can create another contact using the same company data by clicking the lower half of the Save & New button and then clicking Contact from the Same Company.

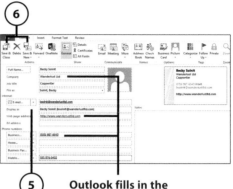

6

5. Fill in the rest of the fields, as needed.

6. Complete the contact: If you are finished adding contacts, click Save & Close; if you want to add more contacts, click Save & New and then repeat steps 1 to 5.

5 **Outlook fills in the company fields from the original contact.**

Create a Contact from an Email Message

Another quick way to add someone to your Contacts list is to create the new contact item from an existing email message.

1. Click the Inbox folder.

2. Click a message from the person you want to add as a contact.

3. Right-click the sender's address.

4. Click Add to Outlook Contacts. Outlook displays a scaled-down version of the new contact window and fills in the person's Name and Email address.

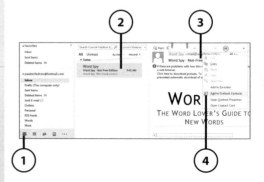

5. Fill in the rest of the fields, as needed.

6. Click Save. Outlook creates the new contact.

⑤

⑥

×

Name
Word Spy <mail@wordspy.com>

CONTACT   NOTES

⊕ Email   ⊕ Work
Email
mail@wordspy.com   ⊕ Address

⊕ Phone   ⊕ Birthday

⊕ IM

Save   Cancel

Importing Contact Data

If you have your contact data in some other application, chances are you will be able to import that data into Outlook and save yourself the hassle of retyping all that information. Outlook comes with an Import and Export Wizard that makes the task easy.

Import Contact Data

This task assumes that you have used another program to save the data you want to import using the comma separated values (.csv) format.

1. Click File.

①

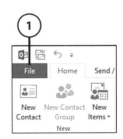

2. Click Open & Export.

3. Click Import/Export. The Import and Export Wizard appears.

4. Select Import from Another Program or File.

5. Click Next.

6. Click Comma Separated Values.

7. Click Next.

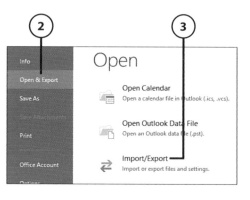

8. Click Browse. The Browse dialog box appears.

9. Select the location of the file you want to import.

10. Click the file.

11. Click OK.

12. Select whether you want to allow Outlook to create duplicate contacts.

13. Click Next.

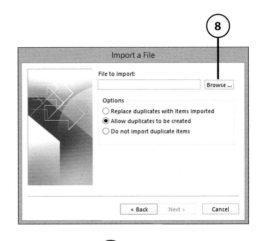

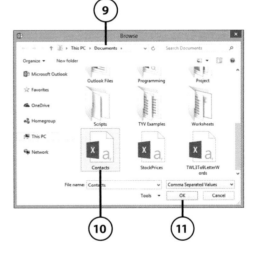

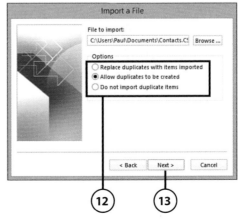

14. Make sure Contacts is selected as the destination folder.

15. Click Next.

16. Click Finish. Outlook imports the contacts.

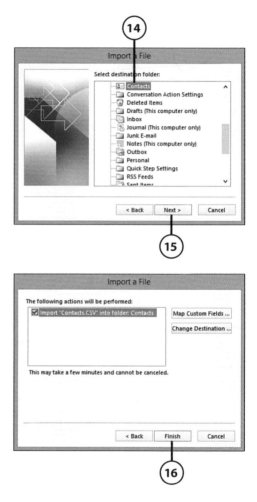

>>>Go Further
MAPPING CUSTOM FIELDS

To ensure that the data is imported into the correct fields in your Contacts folder, you can click Map Custom Fields to display the Map Custom Fields dialog box. To map a field, click and drag it from the From list and drop it on the appropriate field in the To list. When you are done, click OK to return to the wizard.

Working with Your Contacts

You did not go to all the trouble of entering or importing contact data just to look up someone's birthday or spouse's name. No, with all that information at your fingertips, you will want to do some more substantial things. Like what? Well, Outlook gives you many choices. For example, you can send an email message to a contact, request a meeting, set up a new task, and map that person's physical address, just to name a few. The following sections give you a quick tour of the methods you use to accomplish these and many other tasks from within the Contacts folder.

Edit Contact Data

Your Contacts list is only as useful as it is accurate and up-to-date, so it's worthwhile to spend a bit of time maintaining your contacts by correcting erroneous entries, updating changed data, and adding any new information that comes your way.

1. From the People view, click the contact you want to edit.

2. Click Edit. Outlook opens the contact for editing. You can also double-click the contact to open it for editing in a separate window.

3. Edit the contact data, as needed.

4. Click Save. Outlook updates the contact with the edited data.

To edit the full contact data, click the link under View Source.

>>>Go Further

EDITING DATA FOR MULTIPLE CONTACTS

If you work with a large Contacts list, having many contacts with the same data in a particular field is common. For example, you might have a number of contacts from the same company, in which case they will all have the same value in the Company field. Similarly, you might have a number of contacts from a particular department, in which case the contacts all have the same value in the Department field. This is fine until this common data changes. For example, if the name of the company or department changes, you need to edit the appropriate field for all the affected contacts.

You can avoid this tedious procedure by taking advantage of grouping. First, group the contacts according to the field you want to change. To do this, select a view that supports grouping (such as Phone or List), right-click the header of the field you want to group, and then click Group By this Field. (If you don't see the field, click the View tab and then click Add Columns to add the field to the view.) Find the group that corresponds to the contacts you want to edit. Use the group's first contact to edit the field you want to change. Outlook immediately adds a new group for the edited data and moves the first contact into that group. Now drag the group header for the rest of the contacts with the old data and drop it on the group header for the new data. Outlook updates all the contacts with the new field data.

Add a Picture for a Contact

You can make the Contacts list more useful and more interesting visually by adding a picture for some or all of your contacts.

1. From the People view, click the contact.

2. Click the link under the View Source heading. Outlook opens the full contact data for editing.

3. Click the Contact tab.

4. Click Picture.

5. Click Add Picture. The Add Contact Picture dialog box appears.

6. Select the location of the picture you want to use.

7. Click the picture.

8. Click OK. Outlook replaces the picture placeholder with the image you selected.

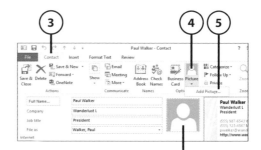

You can also click the picture placeholder.

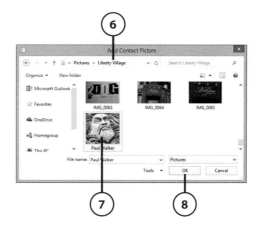

Send an Email to a Contact

If you have defined at least one email address for a contact, you can send that person a message directly from the Contacts folder.

1. From the People view, click the contact.

2. Under Send Email, click the address to which you want to send the message. Outlook creates a new message addressed to the contact.

3. Fill in the message details.

4. Click Send. Outlook sends the message to the contact.

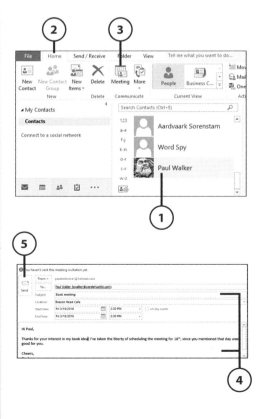

Request a Meeting with a Contact

If you have defined at least one email address for a contact, you can send that person a meeting request directly from the Contacts folder.

1. From the People view, click the contact.

2. Click the Home tab.

3. Click Meeting. Outlook creates a new meeting request addressed to the contact.

4. Fill in the meeting request details.

5. Click Send. Outlook sends the meeting request to the contact.

View a Map of a Contact's Address

If you plan on visiting a contact and you are not sure where the person is located, you would normally call or email the person to ask for directions. These days, however, doing so is a waste of time for both people because plenty of online resources are available that can show you where a particular address is located and how to get there. One of the best of these is the Bing Maps service from Microsoft. Even better, this service is integrated with Outlook 2016, so you can bring up a Bing map of a contact's address right from the Contacts folder.

1. From the People view, click the contact.

2. Click the link under the View Source heading. Outlook opens the full contact data for editing.

3. Beside the address you want to view, click Map It. Outlook loads your web browser and displays a map showing the location of the contact address.

4. Click Directions to learn how to navigate to the address from your location.

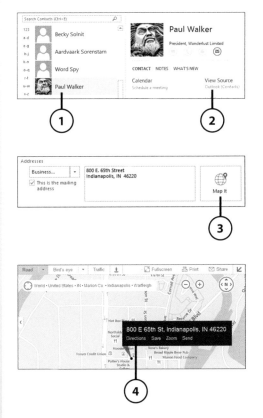

Print a Contact Address on an Envelope or Label

If you want to send an envelope to one of your contacts, you can use Word and Outlook together to place the contact's address directly on the envelope or on a label.

1. In Word, click the Mailings tab.

2. Click Envelopes. If you are creating a label, click Labels instead. Word displays the Envelopes tab (or the Labels tab) of the Envelopes and Labels dialog box.

3. Above the delivery address box, click the address book icon to open the Select Name dialog box.

4. Click the contact you want to use.

5. Click OK. Word copies the contact's address and pastes it into the Delivery Address text box.

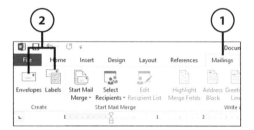

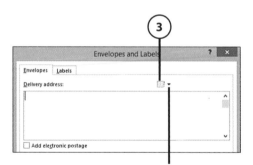

You can also click this arrow to select a contact you have used recently.

6. Fill in the rest of the envelope or label details. For example, if you're printing an envelope, type your return address.

7. Click Print. Word prints the envelope (or label).

Tag items.　　**Add sections.**　　**Add pages.**

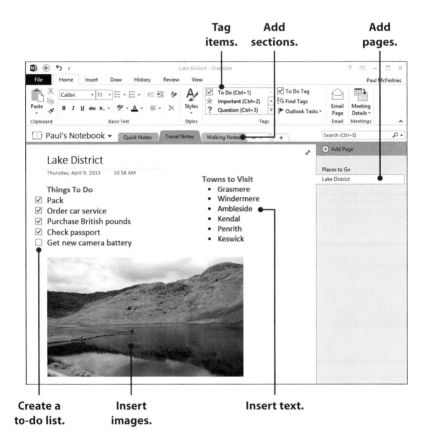

Create a to-do list.　　**Insert images.**　　**Insert text.**

In this chapter, you learn about building a OneNote notebook, working with sections and pages, entering text and lists, and tagging items. Topics include the following:

→ Building a notebook by adding sections and pages

→ Color-coding sections and pages

→ Entering text and working with page containers

→ Tagging items on a page

→ Building a OneNote to-do list

14

Building a OneNote Notebook

The Office 2016 applications that you've learned about so far in the book—Word, Excel, PowerPoint, and Outlook—enable you to enter data in a relatively structured format: Word with its sequential sentences and paragraphs; Excel with its rows, columns, and cells; PowerPoint with its sequential slides and slide placeholders, and Outlook with emails, calendars, and contact lists. However, the data we deal with in our lives isn't always so structured: thoughts, ideas, inspirations, to-do lists, phone numbers, names of books to read and movies to see, website and email addresses, and on and on.

Many of us keep notebooks handy for jotting down these random bits of data. But we live in an electronic age, so wouldn't it be great to be able to jot down stray bits of information in a digital format?

I'm happy to report that the answer to that question is, "You can!" The electronic version of your paper notebook is OneNote, which enables you to quickly and easily record just about anything that you would normally scribble on a piece of paper (even doodles, as you see in Chapter 15, "Getting More Out of OneNote"). With OneNote, you can do all that and much more:

- Paste pictures, clip art, and text.

- Insert links to websites.

- Organize data into tables.

- Share your notes with other people.

In this chapter, you learn how to use OneNote to build a notebook and add some basic items such as text and bulleted lists. See Chapter 15 to learn how to augment your notebooks with links, files, digital ink, and more.

Working with Sections

In the real world, a notebook might come with (or you might add) several tabs that divide the notebook into separate sections, each with its own collection of pages. This is the metaphor that OneNote uses. OneNote files are called *notebooks*. Each notebook consists of a series of *sections*, and each section consists of one or more *pages*. You use these pages to enter your free-form notes and other data, such as links and images.

A notebook is a collection of different types of data scraps from a variety of sources. It's important to impose some kind of order on all those scraps so that the notebook doesn't devolve into an unruly mess where it takes too long to find what you need.

Within each notebook, the main level of organization is the section, which is represented by a tab in the left pane of the notebook. You use the sections to break down the notebook's overall topic or theme into smaller subjects. You can create as many sections as you need because there's no practical limit on the number of sections you can add to a notebook.

OneNote is a hierarchical storage system, with notebooks at the top level, sections at the second level, and pages at the third level. You can fine-tune this hierarchy by taking advantage of OneNote's color-coding features, which enable you to link similar items visually by applying the same color to those items.

Insert a New Section

When you create a new notebook using OneNote, the resulting file has a single section that contains a single page. However, you are free to add more sections as needed.

1. Open the notebook you want to work with.

2. Select the Create a New Section icon. OneNote creates the new section and displays the section name in a text box.

Keyboard Shortcut

You can also create a new section by pressing Ctrl+T.

---

3. Type the section name.

4. Click an empty part of the new section, or press Enter. OneNote closes the text box.

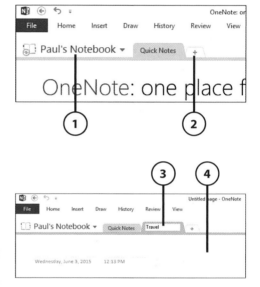

Rename a Section

If you made an error when you originally named a section, or if the section's current name no longer reflects the section's content, you can rename the section.

1. Right-click the section tab. OneNote displays a short-cut menu of section-related commands.

2. Click Rename. OneNote opens the section name for editing.

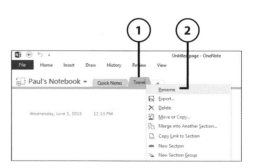

Mouse Shortcut

You can also open the section name for editing by double-clicking the section tab.

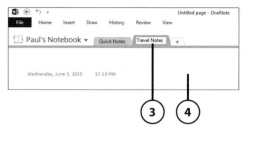

3. Type the section name.

4. Click an empty part of the new section, or press Enter. OneNote closes the text box.

Moving a Section

OneNote adds each new section to the right of the existing section tabs. To move a section, click and drag the section's tab left or right until the section is in the position you want; then release the tab.

Color-Code a Section

Color-coding a section means that you apply a specified color that appears in the section's tab (as well as the area surrounding the section when you select the section). So if a notebook contains two or more similar sections similar, you can informally relate them to one another by applying the same color.

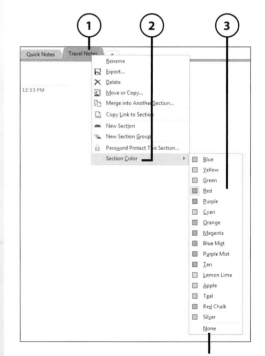

1. Right-click the tab of the section you want to color. OneNote displays a shortcut menu of section-related commands.

2. Select Section Color.

3. Select the color you want to apply. OneNote applies the color to the section.

You can also select None if you prefer the section to have no color.

Using Similar Colors Across Notebooks

If you use multiple notebooks, it's a good idea to apply the same color to the same kinds of pages in each notebook. For example, if all your notebooks have a To-Do List section, it makes navigating the notebooks easier if those sections all use the same color.

Working with Pages

After sections, the second level in the notebook organizational hierarchy is the *page*, which is more or less a blank slate into which you insert your OneNote data. Each section can have an unlimited number of pages, and the idea is that you use separate pages to break down each section into separate subtopics. Each page appears in the right pane of the notebook window.

Insert a New Page

Each new section you create comes with a new page, but you can add more pages whenever you need them.

1. Select the section in which you want to insert the new page.

2. Select Add Page. OneNote inserts a new page into the section.

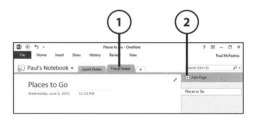

Keyboard Shortcut

You can also add a new page to the current section by pressing Ctrl+N.

3. Type the page title.

Moving a Page

OneNote adds each new page at the bottom of the existing page tabs. To move a page, click and drag the page's tab up or down until the page is in the position you want; then release the tab.

To insert a new page below an existing page, right-click the existing page and then select New Page.

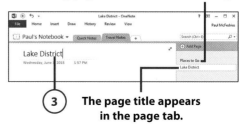

The page title appears in the page tab.

Insert a New Page from a Template

OneNote offers a collection of page templates that enable you to insert a page that comes with preset text and formatting for things like lecture notes, business meetings, and to-do lists.

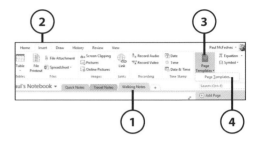

1. Select the section in which you want to insert the new page.

2. Select the Insert tab.

3. Select Page Templates.

4. Select Page Templates. OneNote displays the Templates task pane.

5. Select a category.

6. Select the page template you want to use.

You can also click Templates on Office.com to access more page templates online.

If you always want to use the same template to create a page in the current section, use this list to select that template.

>>>*Go Further*

SAVING A PAGE AS A TEMPLATE

If you find yourself using similar text and formatting for many of your pages, you can save yourself some work by saving that text and formatting as a page template that you can apply using the steps in this section. To save the current page as a template, select Insert, Page Templates, Page Templates to open the Templates task pane. At the bottom of the pane, select Save Current Page as a Template to open the Save As Template dialog box. Type a name for the template. If you always want to use this template to create a page in the current section, select the Set as Default Template… check box. Select Save.

Enter Text on a Page

Filling your pages with content is what OneNote is all about, and OneNote makes it easy to insert everything from simple typewritten or handwritten notes, dates and times, image files, screen captures, and even entire files. All OneNote content appears inside a *container*, which is essentially a box that surrounds the content. After you have some content inside a container, you can move the container around on the page, edit or format the container content, split the content into multiple containers, and more.

Most page content consists of text notes, and OneNote makes it simple to add text to a page:

- For typewritten notes, click where you want the note to appear and then start typing. OneNote immediately places a container around the text. When you're done, select outside the container.

- To create a bulleted list, click where you want the list to appear and then select Home, Bullets. You can also select Home, Numbering if you prefer a numbered list.

- To add text from a document, open the document, copy the text, return to OneNote, click inside the page where you want the text to appear, and then paste the copied text.

See Chapter 15 to learn how to add more types of content to a page.

Work with Page Containers

When you insert data on a page—whether text, a link, an image, or clip art—the data appears inside a special object called a *container*. When you have one or more containers on a page, working with the data is almost always straightforward. For example, to edit container text, you select inside the container and change the existing text or add new text. To format the text, you select it and use the buttons in the Ribbon's Home tab.

Selecting Container Text
To quickly select all the text in a container, double-click the top edge of the container.

You'll probably spend a significant amount of time in OneNote adjusting containers from one part of a page to another to get the best or most efficient layout for your data. Here are the basic techniques to use:

- **Moving a container**—Select the container to display its frame. Drag the top edge of the container and drop it on the new position.

- **Sizing a container**—Select the container to display the selection handles on the corners and sides. Drag a selection handle to get the width you want.

Building a OneNote Table

A typical notebook page, like a typical page in a paper notebook, is a jumble of text, with placeholders scattered around the page. This randomness isn't necessarily a bad thing because it's in keeping with OneNote's inherent informality and (at least on the surface) structure-free format. However, there will be times when you *want* your notes to have some structure. If it's a list of items, you can insert a bulleted list into a placeholder (on the Home tab, click Bullets); if it's an ordered sequence of items, use a numbered list instead (on the Home tab, click Numbering).

However, you might have data that consists of multiple items, each of which has the same set of details. For example, you might want to record a list of upcoming flights, each of which has an airline name, flight number, departure date and time, destination, arrival date and time, seat number, and so on.

For these kinds of data structures, you can insert a table into a container. A table is a rectangular structure with the following characteristics:

- Each item in the list gets its own horizontal rectangle called a *row*.

- Each set of details in the list gets its own vertical rectangle called a *column*.

- The rectangle formed by the intersection of a row and a column is called a *cell*, and you use the table cells to hold the data.

In other words, a OneNote table is similar to an Excel worksheet (and a Word table, which I discussed in Chapter 5, "Working with Page Layout and Design in Word").

Insert a Table

When you want to construct a table in OneNote, your first step is to create the empty table structure that specifies the number of rows and columns you want in your table. So you need to examine your data and figure out how many items there are (that value will be the number of rows you need in your table), and how many details you want to record for each item (that value will be the number of columns you need in your table). Once you've done that, you're ready to insert the table.

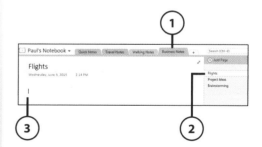

1. Select the section that contains the page you want to work with.

2. Select the page in which you want to insert the table.

3. Select where you want the table to appear.

4. Select the Insert tab.

5. Select Table. OneNote displays the Insert Table gallery.

6. Select Insert Table to display the Insert Table dialog box.

7. Specify the number of columns you want in your table.

8. Specify the number of rows you want in the table.

9. Select OK. OneNote inserts the table.

10. Type your text into the table cells.

Working with a OneNote Table

A OneNote table is similar to a Word table, so you can use the same techniques to add and delete rows and columns, select table items, and so on. See Chapter 5 for the details.

You can also click a box that represents the number of rows and columns you want.

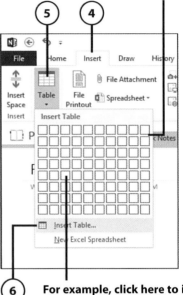

For example, click here to insert a table with three columns and five rows.

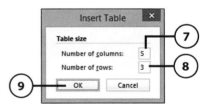

Use the tools on the Layout tab to work with your table.

Working with Tags

OneNote enables you to augment items in a page with small icons called *tags*. For example, many tags can help you prioritize page data, including the Important, Critical, and Question tags. Similarly, many tags can help you organize your data, including the Project A and Project B tags.

However, probably the most common use of tags is to set up a to-do list. One of the secrets of productivity in a fast-paced, information-overloaded world is organizing the things that require your attention and your effort in a way that minimizes stress and maximizes efficiency. If you have a long list of things to do, the worst way to handle the list is to keep it in your head. If you do this, you'll not only worry about forgetting something, but you'll always have each task rumbling around in your brain, so you'll jump from one to the other rather than concentrating on a single task at a time. Plastering sticky notes all over your monitor isn't good, either, because all the tasks are still "in your face," and you won't be much better off.

The best way to organize a list of pending and current tasks is to have a single place where you record the tasks' particulars and can augment those particulars as things change and new data becomes available. This place must be one that you check regularly so that there's never a danger of overlooking a task, and ideally it should be a place where you can prioritize your tasks. This way, you can focus on a single task, knowing that everything you need to do is safely recorded and prioritized. As you've probably guessed by now, the place I'm talking about is OneNote, which is ideally suited to recording, organizing, and prioritizing tasks and to-do lists.

Tag an Item

You can apply a tag to a single item, multiple items, or to every item within a container. You can also apply multiple tags to a single item.

1. Select the section that contains the page you want to work with.

2. Select the page that contains the data you want to tag.

3. If you want to tag a specific paragraph within a text container, select inside that paragraph. If you want to apply the same tag to multiple paragraphs, select those paragraphs. If you want to apply the same tag to every paragraph, click the top edge of the container to select all the text.

4. Select the Home tab.

5. Select More in the Tags group. OneNote displays the Tags gallery.

6. Select the tag you want to use. OneNote applies the tag to the data.

**Click here to select
everything inside the container.**

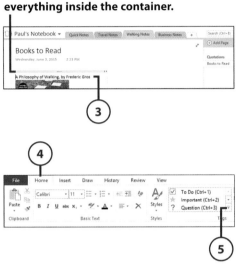

**The tag appears
to the left of the item.**

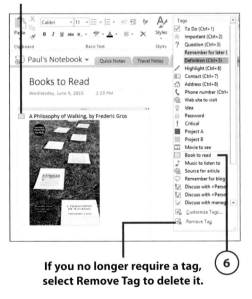

**If you no longer require a tag,
select Remove Tag to delete it.**

>>>Go Further
CREATING A CUSTOM TAG

If none of the default OneNote tags is just right for your needs, you can create a custom tag. Open the Tags gallery and select the Customize Tags command. In the Customize Tags dialog box, select New Tag to open the New Tag dialog box. Type a name for your custom tag. Use the Symbol, Font Color, and Highlight Color lists to construct your custom tag, and then click OK.

Build Lists

To-do lists are an important part of OneNote, and part of the evidence for that is the large number of check box–like tags it offers. Besides the standard To Do tag, there are eight others:

- Discuss with <Person A>

- Discuss with <Person B>

- Discuss with Manager

- Schedule Meeting

- Call Back

- To Do Priority 1

- To Do Priority 2

- Client Request

Each of these tags gives you a check box augmented with a small icon. When you complete a task, you select the check box to place a red check mark inside, which gives you a strong visual clue about which tasks are done and which are still pending.

Create a To-Do List

You create a OneNote to-do list by building a list and then tagging it using the To Do tag.

1. Select the section that contains the page you want to work with.

2. Select the page where you want your to-do list to appear.

3. Type each item in your to-do list.

4. Click the top edge of the container to select the entire to-do list.

5. Select the Home tab.

6. Select More in the Tags group. OneNote displays the Tags gallery.

7. Select the To Do tag. OneNote applies the tag to the data.

Keyboard Shortcut

You can also apply the To Do tag by pressing Ctrl+1.

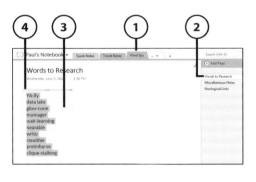

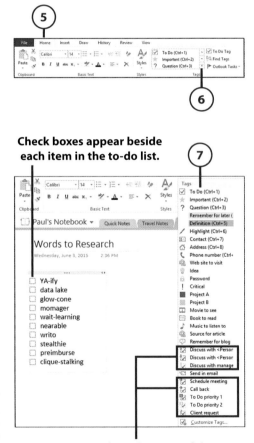

Check boxes appear beside each item in the to-do list.

You can also select one of the other check box tags.

Insert spreadsheets.

Insert the date and time.

Insert file attachments.

Work with notebooks.

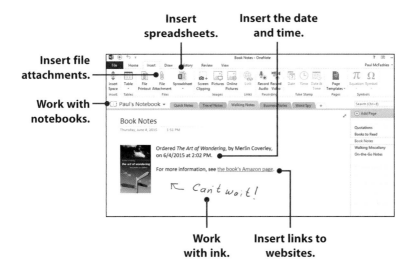

Work with ink.

Insert links to websites.

In this chapter, you learn how to get more out of OneNote notebooks, including creating new notebooks, inserting links and files, and adding ink to a page. Topics include the following:

→ Creating new notebooks

→ Inserting the date and time

→ Adding links to a page

→ Inserting spreadsheets and other files

→ Annotating a page with written text and other ink

Getting More Out of OneNote

You learned the basics of working with OneNote in Chapter 14, "Building a OneNote Notebook," but there's much more the program can do. In this chapter, you extend your OneNote education by learning a few more useful tasks, such as creating new notebooks, adding data such as the current date and time and links to other objects, and inserting files on a page. If you're running OneNote on a touch-based PC, you can also populate and annotate a page by writing directly on the screen, and you learn how to use this "ink" later in this chapter.

Working with Notebooks

The hierarchical structure of a OneNote notebook means that you can break down your data in a number of ways. That is, you can assign major topics their own sections and then subdivide each topic into multiple pages within a section. That works well for most people, and it's common to use only a single notebook. However, you might find that your notebook has so many sections that it is difficult to navigate and to find the data you need. In that case, you might consider creating a second notebook. For example, many people maintain one notebook for personal data and another for business data. Similarly, if you share your computer with other people but haven't set up separate user accounts, you'll no doubt prefer that everyone use her own notebook.

Create a New Notebook

You can create a new notebook either locally on your PC or remotely on your OneDrive. For the latter, you need to be logged in to your Microsoft account.

1. Select the File tab.

2. Select New.

3. Select your OneDrive.

4. Type a name for the notebook.

5. Select Create Notebook. OneNote creates the new notebook and then asks whether you want to share it.

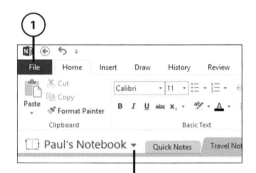

You can also click here and then click Add Notebook.

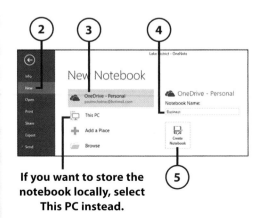

If you want to store the notebook locally, select This PC instead.

6. Select Not Now.

Sharing

To learn how to share data through OneDrive, see "Sharing a Document Online" in Chapter 18, "Collaborating with Others."

Switch Between Notebooks

When you have two or more notebooks open, OneNote gives you a quick and easy method for switching from one to another.

1. Select the name of the current notebook. OneNote displays the Notebook pane.

2. Select the notebook you want to use. OneNote switches to that workbook.

Closing a Workbook

If you no longer want a particular notebook to appear in the Notebook pane, you need to close it. Display the Notebook pane, right-click the notebook you want to close, and then select Close This Notebook.

Pin Notebook Pane to Side

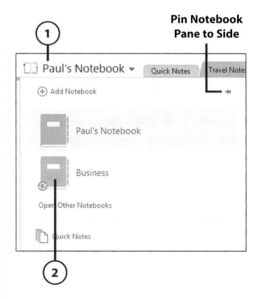

>>>Go Further

PINNING THE NOTEBOOK PANE

If you find that you often switch from one notebook to another, you can make the switching process even easier by opening the Notebook pane and then clicking Pin Notebook Pane to Side (the pin icon that appears in the upper-right corner of the pane). This tells OneNote to always display the Notebook pane on the left side of the window, so you can switch to any open notebook just by clicking it.

If you later decide that the Notebook pane is taking up too much room, you can hide it again by clicking Unpin Notebook Pane from Side (the vertical pin icon that appears in the upper-right corner of the Notebook pane).

Set Notebook Properties

A notebook's properties control the name of the notebook and the color the notebook appears in the Notebook pane. You can access the notebook's properties to change one or both of these settings.

1. Select the File tab.

2. Select Info.

3. Select Settings for the notebook you want to modify.

4. Select Properties. The Notebook Properties dialog box opens.

5. Use the Display Name text box to change the notebook's name.

6. Select the Color drop-down list and then select a notebook color.

7. Select OK. OneNote applies the new property values.

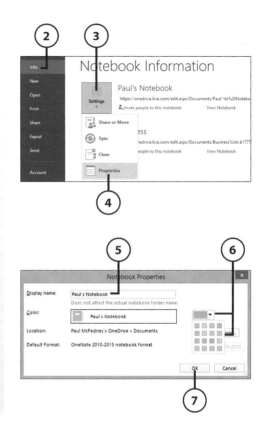

Accessing the Notebook Properties

Another way to access a notebook's properties is to display the Notebook pane, right-click the notebook, and then select Properties.

Adding Data to a Page

The straightforward click-and-type nature of a OneNote page makes it easy to add simple notes, lists, and other text snippets. And, of course, you're free to take advantage of the techniques you learned in Chapter 3, "Working with Office 2016 Graphics," to populate a page with pictures, SmartArt, WordArt, and shapes. The inherent free-form approach offered by OneNote also means that you can add plenty of other data types to a page. The most common of these are the date and time, links, Excel worksheets, and files, each of which is described in the next few sections.

Insert the Date and Time

Some of the content you add to a OneNote page will be date- and/or time-sensitive. For such content, you should date- and/or time-stamp the placeholder by inserting the current date, time, or both.

1. Select the section you want to use.

2. Select the page you want to use.

3. Position the insertion point where you want to insert the date.

4. Select the Insert tab.

5. Select Date. OneNote inserts today's date.

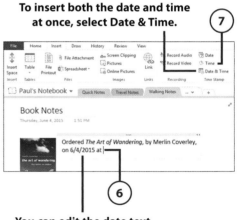

Keyboard Shortcut

You can also insert today's date by pressing Alt+Shift+D.

6. Position the insertion point where you want to insert the time.

7. Select Time. OneNote inserts the current time.

Keyboard Shortcut

You can also insert the current time by pressing Alt+Shift+T.

To insert both the date and time at once, select Date & Time.

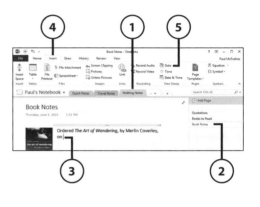

You can edit the date text if you want to display a different date.

Add a Link to a Website

OneNote comes with a Links command that enables you to insert links to websites. This is handy if you use your pages to store links to websites you visit often or want to visit in the future.

1. Select the section you want to use.

2. Select the page you want to use.

3. Position the insertion point where you want to insert the link. You can also select existing text that you want to turn into a link.

4. Select the Insert tab.

5. Select Link. OneNote displays the Link dialog box.

Keyboard Shortcut

You can also display the Link dialog box by pressing Ctrl+K.

6. If you didn't select text in advance, type the link text.

7. Type the link address, or paste it from your browser's address box.

8. Select OK. OneNote inserts the link.

Editing a Link

To make changes to a link, right-click the link and then click Edit Link.

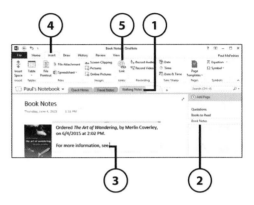

You can also click Browse the Web to select the web page using a browser.

Add a Link to a OneNote Location

Besides linking to a website, OneNote also enables you to create a link to another OneNote location: a notebook, a section within a notebook, a page within a section, or even a note within a page. This makes navigating OneNote easy because you can select a link to jump instantly to that location.

1. Select the section you want to use.

2. Select the page you want to use.

3. Select the text that you want to turn into a link. You can also position the insertion point where you want to insert the link.

4. Select the Insert tab.

5. Select Link. OneNote displays the Link dialog box.

Keyboard Shortcut

You can also display the Link dialog box by pressing Ctrl+K.

6. If you didn't select text in advance, type the link text.

7. Select the notebook you want to use.

8. If you want to link to a section, select the section.

9. If you want to link to a page, select the page.

10. Select OK. OneNote inserts the link.

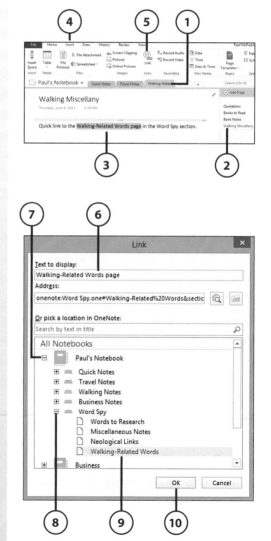

>>>Go Further

EASIER LOCATION LINKS

If you find yourself inserting many location links in your notebooks, OneNote offers several methods that make it even easier to create such links:

- To link to a notebook, right-click the notebook title and then click Copy Link to Notebook.

- To link to a section, right-click the section tab and then click Copy Link to Section.

- To link to a page, right-click the page tab and then click Copy Link to Page.

- To link to a note, right-click the note container and then click Copy Link to Paragraph.

Then position the insertion point where you want the link to appear, select the Home tab, and then select Paste.

Insert a Spreadsheet File

If you have an existing Excel workbook that you want to view within OneNote, you can insert the file on a page.

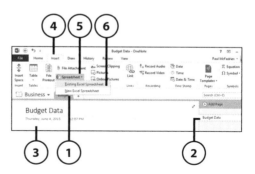

1. Select the section you want to use.

2. Select the page you want to use.

3. Position the insertion point where you want the spreadsheet file to appear.

4. Select the Insert tab.

5. Select Spreadsheet.

6. Select Existing Excel Spreadsheet. OneNote displays the Choose Document to Insert dialog box.

7. Select a location.

8. Select the spreadsheet file you want to insert.

9. Select Insert. OneNote displays the Insert File dialog box.

10. Select Insert Spreadsheet. OneNote inserts the workbook data into the page.

11. To work with the spreadsheet, select Edit to open the file in Excel.

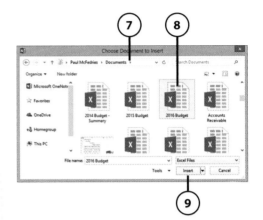

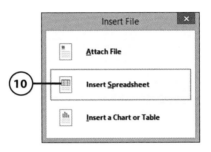

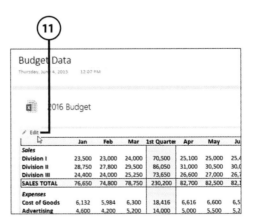

Insert a New Spreadsheet

If you don't have an existing spreadsheet you want to insert, you can instead insert a new spreadsheet.

1. Select the section you want to use.

2. Select the page you want to use.

3. Position the insertion point where you want the spreadsheet file to appear.

4. Select the Insert tab.

5. Select Spreadsheet.

6. Select New Excel Spreadsheet. OneNote inserts the new spreadsheet.

7. To work with the spreadsheet, select Edit to open the file in Excel.

Attach a File

If you want quick access to any type of file, you can attach that file to a OneNote page.

1. Select the section you want to use.

2. Select the page you want to use.

3. Select where you want the file icon to appear.

4. Select the Insert tab.

5. Select File Attachment. OneNote displays the Choose a File or a Set of Files to Insert dialog box.

6. Select a location.

7. Select the file you want to attach.

8. Select Insert. OneNote displays the Insert File dialog box.

9. Select Attach File. OneNote inserts an icon for the file into the page.

10. To work with the file, double-click it. OneNote displays a warning dialog box.

11. Select OK. The file opens in its default application.

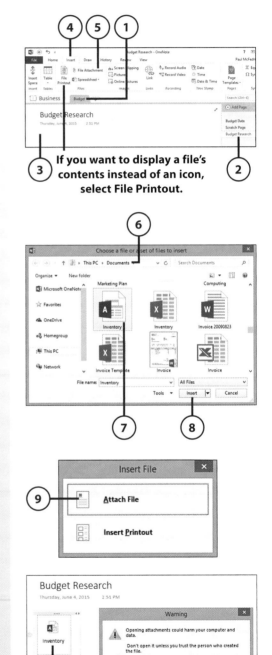

If you want to display a file's contents instead of an icon, select File Printout.

Adding Ink

Office 2016 includes *ink integration*, which means that an object type called *digital ink* or, simply, *ink* is part of the Office system, like the AutoShape and Text Box object types, for instance. In fact, ink objects are part of the Office drawing layer that holds AutoShapes, text boxes, WordArt, pictures, and so on, and you can format ink like other drawing layer objects by changing, for example, the text color and line weight.

Ink enables you to mark up OneNote pages using your finger or a digital pen or stylus. This enables you to annotate a page directly, which means either writing notes using your own handwriting or adding highlighting, diagrams, proofreader marks, or other symbols. You can even convert ink text into regular text.

Handwrite Text

For quick notes, you can use your finger or a digital pen to handwrite notes directly on a page.

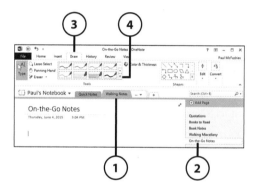

1. Tap the section you want to use.

2. Tap the page you want to use.

3. Tap the Draw tab.

4. Tap the More button in the Tools group. OneNote displays the Tools gallery.

5. Tap the pen you want to use.

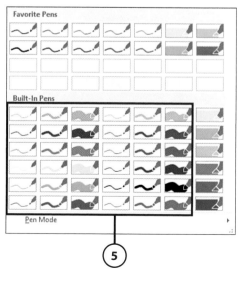

6. Use your finger or digital pen to handwrite directly on the screen.

You can tap Color & Thickness to gain more control of the color and size of the ink.

Highlight Text

To emphasize text on a page, you can use your finger or digital pen to apply a highlight to the text.

1. Tap the section you want to use.

2. Tap the page you want to use.

3. Tap the Draw tab.

4. Tap the More button in the Tools group. OneNote displays the Tools gallery.

5. Tap the highlighter you want to use.

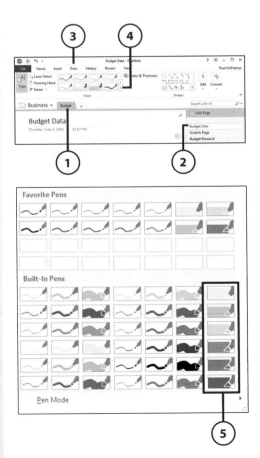

6. Use your finger or digital pen to tap and drag across the text you want highlighted.

> ## Budget Data
> Thursday, June 4, 2015   12:07 PM
>
> IMPORTANT! We need the preliminary budget numbers no later than June 15! — **6**

Convert Ink to Text

Handwriting text is quick and easy, but it suffers from some major drawbacks: It can't be searched, spell-checked, or used in any program that doesn't support ink. To work around these problems, you need to convert your handwriting to digital text.

1. Tap the section you want to use.

2. Tap the page you want to use.

3. Tap the Draw tab.

4. Tap Lasso Select.

5. Position your finger or the digital stylus above and to the left of the ink you want to convert.

6. Draw a clockwise circle around the ink.

7. When the text is completely within the lasso, release the screen. OneNote selects the ink.

8. Tap Ink to Text. OneNote converts the selected handwriting to digital text.

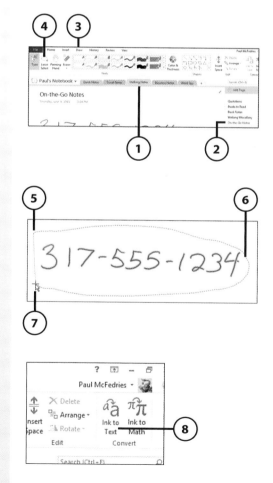

Faster Ink Conversions

In many cases, an even easier way to convert ink to text is to tap and hold the ink to display the Mini Toolbar, tap the drop-down arrow, tap Convert Ink, and then tap Ink to Text.

Erase Ink

If you have ink you no longer need, or if you've made some stray marks on the page, you can erase the ink.

1. Tap the section you want to use.

2. Tap the page you want to use.

3. Tap the Draw tab.

4. Tap Eraser.

5. Tap Stroke Eraser.

6. Tap the ink stroke you want to erase. OneNote removes the stroke. Repeat as necessary.

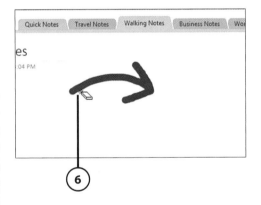

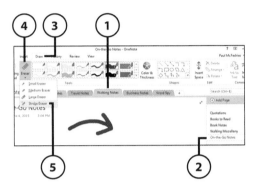

Build tables. **Construct queries.** **Design reports.**

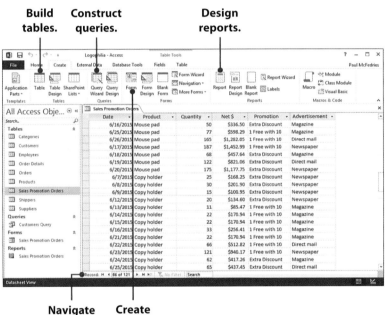

Navigate records. **Create forms.**

In this chapter, you learn about creating Access databases, building tables, querying table data, and creating forms and reports. Topics include the following:

→ Creating a database

→ Designing and building tables

→ Entering, sorting, and filtering data

→ Querying your data

→ Creating data entry forms

→ Building reports to showcase your data

Learning Access Basics

Microsoft Access is a *database management system*. This means that Access not only stores your information but also supplies you with the means to manage this information—for example, by sorting, searching, extracting, summarizing, and so on.

Access is a large, complex, and often intimidating program. However, much of the program's complexity comes from its wealth of features aimed solely at database professionals. If you are looking just to enter data, access external data, query and summarize data, and produce useful reports, you will find that a minimum of database theory combined with the right techniques can turn Access into a usable, powerful program. In other words, with the techniques you learn in this chapter, you can extract meaningful and useful information from whatever jumble of data you now have.

Understanding Access Databases

In simplest terms, a *database* is a collection of data with some sort of under-lying organization. In most systems, anything related to the data (such as a data entry screen or a report that summarizes the data) is considered a sepa-rate piece of the overall pie. Access, though, is different because its databases consist not only of the basic data but also of related items you use to work with the data.

If you like, you can think of an Access database as a kind of electronic tool shed. In this tool shed you have not only your raw materials (your data) stored in bins and containers of various shapes and sizes, but you also have a number of tools you can use to manipulate these materials, as well as a work area where all this manipulation happens.

Each Access database can store a number of different types of objects, but in this chapter you learn about four in particular: tables, queries, forms, and reports:

- **Tables**—In Access databases, you store your information in an object called a *table*. Tables are rectangular arrangements of rows and columns, where each column represents a field (a specific category of information) and each row represents a record (a single entry in the table).

- **Queries**—Queries are, literally, questions you ask of your data and they enable you to extract from one or more tables a subset of the data. For example, in a table of customer names and addresses, what if you want-ed to see a list of firms located in France? No problem. Just set up the fol-lowing query: "Which records have 'France' in the Country field?"

- **Forms**—To make entering data easier, you can create Access database objects called *forms*. Forms provide a "template" that you fill in whenever you enter a record. The form displays a blank box or list for each field in the table. Data entry becomes a simple matter of filling in the appropri-ate boxes or selecting data from the lists.

- **Reports**—To make your data more palatable for others to read, you can create a fourth type of database object: a *report*. Reports let you define how you want your data to appear on the printed page. You can decide which fields to include in the report, where they appear on the page, and which font to use. You can also add your own text and graphics.

Creating a Database

Access comes with a sample database called Northwind, which is great for experimenting and getting to know the program's features. However, you will eventually need to create and work with your own databases so that you can store, view, and manipulate your own data.

Create a Database

The most direct way to set up a database is to create a blank database container into which you can drop tables, queries, forms, and reports.

1. Click File. If you have just started the program, you can skip to step 3.

2. Click New.

3. Click Blank Desktop Database. Access prompts you for a name.

4. Type the name you want to use for your database file.

5. Click Create. Access creates the database file and then displays a new table ready to be built (see "Create a Table," later in this chapter).

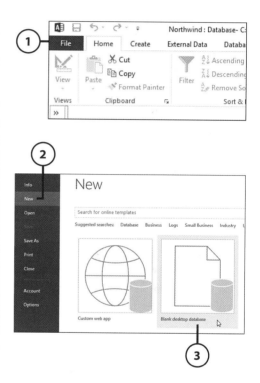

To change the save location, click here.

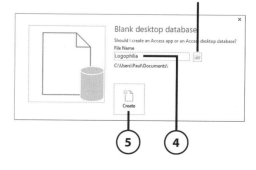

>>>*Go Further*

CREATING A TABLE FROM A TEMPLATE

Instead of a blank database, you may prefer to use a template to create a database that already has a basic structure in place. Access offers two dozen templates that cover common database uses such as asset tracking, contact management, project management, personnel, and inventory. To create a database from a template, follow the steps in this section, except at step 3, click the template you want to use instead of the Blank Desktop Database. If you don't see a template that does exactly what you need, use the Search for Online Templates text box at the top of the New tab to search the thousands of templates available via the Microsoft Office Online site.

Building and Working with Tables

Tables are the most fundamental of the Access objects because you use them to store your data, and you can't really do much of anything in Access until you have supplied the program with data. The importance of tables is made manifest by the fact that, when you create a new database, Access automatically creates a new table and displays the table design view. Before you go any further, however, you should take a few minutes to understand how to design a table.

Designing a Table

With your database created, you now need to populate it with one or more tables. Before you create a new table, however, you need to plan your table design. By asking yourself a few questions in advance, you can save yourself the trouble of redesigning your table later. For simple tables, you need to ask yourself four basic questions:

- **Does the table belong in the current database?**—Each database you create should be set up for a specific purpose. It could be home finances, business transactions, personal assets, or whatever. In any case, once you know the purpose of the database, you can then decide whether the table you want to create fits in with the database theme. For example, if the purpose of the database is to record only information related to your personal finances, it wouldn't make sense to include a table of recipes in the same database. Similarly, it would be inappropriate to include a table of office baseball pool winners in a database of accounts payable invoices.

- **What type of data should I store in the table?**—The most important step in creating a table is determining the information you want it to contain. In theory, Access tables can be large, with hundreds of fields. In practice, however, you should minimize the size of your tables. This saves memory and makes managing the data easier. Therefore, you should strive to set up all your tables with only essential information. For example, suppose you want to store your personal assets in a database. You have to decide whether you want all your assets in a single table, or whether it would be better to create separate tables for each type of asset. If you're only going to be entering basic information—such as the date purchased, a description of each item, and its current value—you can probably get away with a single table.

  More detailed data will almost certainly require individual tables for each asset. For example, a table of books might include information on the title, the author, the publisher, and so on. Clearly, such a table wouldn't work for, say, your collection of jewelry. When you have decided on the tables you want to use, you then need to think about how much data you want to store in each table. In your book collection, for example, would you want to include information on the number of pages, the publishing date, and the number of people the author thanks in the acknowledgments? This might all be crucial information for you, but you need to remember that the more data you store, the longer it takes you to enter each record.

- **What fields should I use to store the data?**—Now you are almost ready for action. The next thing you need to figure out is the specific fields to include in the table. For the most part, the fields are determined by the data itself. For example, a table of business contacts would certainly include fields for name, address, and phone number. However, should you split the name into two fields—one for the first name and one for the last name? If you think you will need to sort the table by last name, then, yes, you probably should. What about the address? You will probably need individual fields for the city, state, and postal code. There are two general rules to follow when deciding how many fields to include in your tables: First, ask yourself whether you really need the data for a particular field (or whether you might need it in the near future).

For example, if you think your table of contact names might someday be used to create form letters, a field to record titles (Ms., Mr., Dr., and so on) would come in handy. When in doubt, err on the side of too many fields rather than too few. Second, always split your data into the smallest fields that make sense. Splitting first and last names is common practice, but creating a separate field for, say, the phone number area code would probably be overkill.

- **Which field should I use for the primary key?**—When you create a table, you need to decide which field to use as the *primary key*. The primary key is a field that uses a unique number or character sequence to identify each record in the table. Keys are used constantly in the real world. Your Social Security number is a key that identifies you in government records. Most machines and appliances have unique serial numbers. This book (like most books) has a 10-digit ISBN—International Standard Book Number (which you can see on the back cover). Why are primary keys necessary? Well, for one thing, Access creates an index for the primary key field. You can perform searches on indexed data much more quickly than on regular data, so many Access operations perform faster if a primary key is present. Keys also make it easy to find records in a table, because the key entries are unique (things such as last names and addresses can have multiple spellings, which makes them hard to find). Finally, a primary key is a handy way to avoid data-entry errors. Since the entries in a primary key field must be unique, there is no chance for someone to, say, enter the same account number for two different customers.

  You can set things up so that Access sets and maintains the primary key for you, or you can do it yourself. Which one do you choose? If your data contains a number or character sequence that uniquely defines each record, you can set the key yourself. For example, invoices usually have unique numbers that are perfect for a primary key. Other fields that can serve as primary keys are employee IDs, customer account numbers, and purchase order numbers. If your data has no such unique identifier, let Access create a key for you. This means that Access sets up an AutoNumber field (see "Learning About Access Data Types") that assigns a unique number to each record (the first record is 1, the second 2, and so on).

Finally, don't worry too much about the design process right now. As you will see, it is easy to make changes down the road by, say, adding and deleting fields, so you are never stuck with a bad design.

Learning About Access Data Types

When building a table you need to assign a data type to each field, which tells Access what kind of data will appear in the field. Access supports a large number of data types, but the following are the ones used most often:

- **Short Text**—This is a catch-all type you can use for fields that contain any combination of letters, numbers, and symbols (such as parentheses and dashes). These fields usually are short entries (the maximum is 255 characters) such as names, addresses, and phone numbers. For purely numeric fields, however, you should use either the Number or Currency type (discussed in a moment).

- **Number**—Use this type for fields that contain numbers only. This is particularly true for fields you use for calculations. (Note, though, that fields containing dollar amounts should use the Currency type, described in a moment.)

- **Currency**—Use this field for dollar values.

- **Date & Time**—This type is for fields that use only dates and times. Access can handle dates from the year 100 right up to the year 9999.

- **Yes/No**—Use this type for fields that contain only Yes or No values.

- **Long Text**—Use this type for longer alphanumeric entries. Long text field entries are usually several sentences or paragraphs long, but they can contain up to 64,000 characters. These types of fields are useful for long text passages or random notes. In a table of customer names, for example, you could use a memo field to record customers' favorite colors, the names of their spouses and kids, and so on.

- **Rich Text**—This is the same as Long Text, except that Access allows you to enter character formatting, such as fonts, colors, bold, and italics.

- **Hyperlink**—This field type is used for addresses of Internet (or intranet) sites or email addresses. When you display the table in Datasheet view, Access configures the addresses as links that you can click.

- **AutoNumber**—This type creates a numeric entry that Access fills in automatically whenever you add a record. Because this type of field assigns a unique number to each record, it's ideal for setting up your own primary key.

Create a Table

You create a table by specifying one or more fields that you want to use to store your data, and for each field you assign a name and a data type.

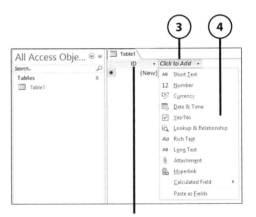

If you prefer to define your table in Design view, click Table Design instead.

1. Click Create. If you have just created a new database and Access has already created a new table for you, skip to step 3.

2. Click Table. Access creates the new table and displays it in Datasheet view.

Access Views

For tables, Access has two views: Datasheet and Design. You use Datasheet view to define the table structure, as well as to view, enter, and edit your table data. (*Datasheet* is the Access term for the row-and-column format that it uses to display table data.) You use Design view for more advanced options regarding the table structure.

Access automatically creates an AutoNumber field named ID.

3. Select Click to Add. Access displays a list of data types.

4. Click the data type you want to use for the field. Access adds the field.

5. Type the field name.

6. Repeat steps 3–5 to define all the fields in your table.

7. Click Save. Access displays the Save As dialog box.

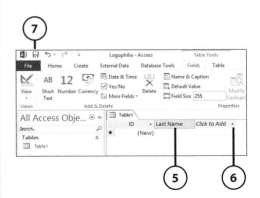

8. Type a name for the table.

9. Click OK.

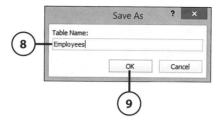

>>>Go Further

SPECIFYING A DEFAULT FIELD VALUE

In many cases, you can save yourself (or whoever does your data entry) a ton of time by setting up a field with a default value. A *default value* means that Access automatically enters the value into the field each time you add a new record to the table. To specify a default value, click anywhere in the field's column, click the Fields tab, and then click Default Value. In the Expression Builder dialog box that appears, enter the default value in the large text box after the equal sign (=) and then click OK.

Enter Data

Although you can use forms to enter data (described later in this chapter), for most databases it is easier to enter data directly using the table's datasheet.

Access fills in any AutoNumber fields as soon as you begin entering data.

1. Type the data for the current field and then press Tab. Access opens the next field for editing, and you repeat until the record is complete.

Click the Editing icon at any time to save the current record.

2. Start the next record by clicking anywhere in the bottom row of the table, which is marked with the New Record icon on the left.

Keyboard Shortcuts

If you're currently inside the last field of the table's last record, you can also start a new record by pressing Tab. Alternatively, press Ctrl+Shift+= from any field in any record.

The New Record icon

Click here to close the table when you are done.

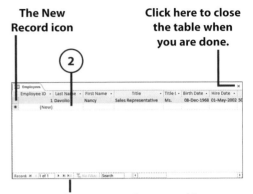

You can also start another record by clicking the New Record button.

>>>Go Further
ENTERING DATA

Entering data in Access is, for the most part, straightforward. You just select a field and start typing. Here are a few notes to keep in mind when entering table data:

- If you see a field that contains (New), this means that the field uses the AutoNumber format, so Access automatically assigns numbers to the field.

- When entering dates, use your locale's standard date format. In the U.S., for example, use the format mm/dd/yyyy, where mm is the month number (for example, 12 for December), dd is the day, and yyyy is the year.

- When entering times, use the format hh:mm:ss, where hh is the hour, mm is the minutes, and ss is the seconds. You can either use the 24-hour clock (for example, 16:30:05), or you can add a.m. or p.m. (for example, 4:30:05 p.m.).

- You can add today's date to a field by pressing Ctrl+; (semicolon). To add the current time, press Ctrl+: (colon).

- When entering a number in a Currency field, don't bother entering a currency symbol (such as $); Access adds it for you automatically.

Sort Table Data

One way to make sense out of the data in a large table is to *sort* the table. Sorting means that you place the records in order (alphabetical, numeric, or date) based on the data in a field.

1. Click anywhere inside the field on which you want to sort the table.

2. Click the Home tab.

3. Click Ascending. If you prefer to sort the data in descending order, click Descending instead.

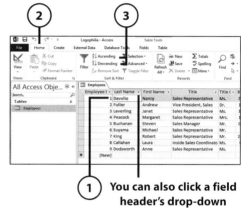

You can also click a field header's drop-down arrow and then select a sort from the menu.

Ascending Versus Descending

An ascending sort orders the field data from A to Z (for a text field), 0 to 9 (for a numeric field), or earliest to latest (for a date field). A descending sort orders the field data from Z to A (for a text field), 9 to 0 (for a numeric field), or latest to earliest (for a date field).

Filter Table Data

You can make a large table more manageable by *filtering* the table, which means that Access temporarily hides the records you specify so that you're left to work with only a subset of the records.

1. Click anywhere inside the field you want to use to filter the table.

2. Click the Home tab.

3. Click Filter. Access displays a list of the unique items in the field.

4. Deactivate the check box for each item you want to temporarily hide.

5. Click OK. Access now only shows the items you selected.

6. To view all the records, repeat steps 1 to 4 and click Select All.

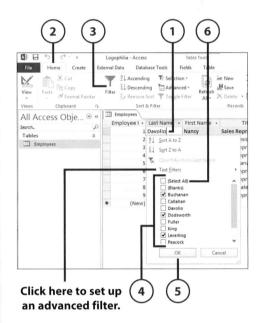

Click here to set up an advanced filter.

> ## >>>Go Further
> ## CREATING ADVANCED FILTERS
>
> Rather than filtering out individual field values, you can use advanced filters to filter records based on the value you specify. In the filter dialog box, click Text Filters, select a command such as Begins With, Contains, or Ends With, and then enter a value. For example, if you select Begins With and then enter **C**, Access filters the table to only show those records where the filtered field begins with the letter C. For numeric fields, you can click Number Filters and then select a command such as Does Not Equal, Less Than, or Greater Than. For a date field, click Date Filters and then select a command such as Before, After, or Last Year.

Querying Access Data

This section gets you up to speed with one of the most powerful concepts in all of Access: *queries*. Queries are no great mystery, really. Although the name implies that they are a kind of question, thinking of them as requests is more useful. In the simplest case, a query is a request to see a particular subset of your data. For example, showing only those records in a customer table where the country is "Sweden" and the first name is "Sven" would be a fairly simple query to build.

In this respect, queries are fancier versions of the filters you learned about in the previous section. However, unlike a filter, a query isn't simply a different view of the table data. It's a separate database object that looks and acts much like a datasheet, and many of the operations you can perform on a datasheet can also be performed on a query's results.

Design a Simple Query

Access offers the Simple Query Wizard that you can use to create a basic query step-by-step.

1. Click the table you want to use as the basis for the query.

2. Click the Create tab.

3. Click Query Wizard. Access opens the New Query dialog box.

4. Make sure that Simple Query Wizard is selected.

5. Click OK. Access launches the Simple Query Wizard.

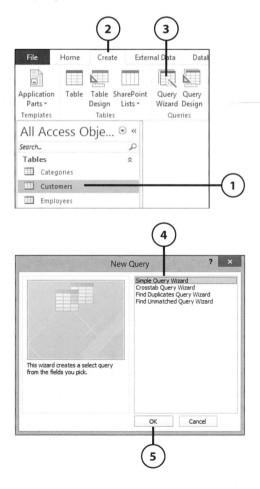

6. For each field you want to include in the query, click the field and then click Add.

7. When you are done, click Next.

8. Type a name for the query.

9. Click Finish. Access runs the query and displays the results.

You can click here to add all the fields.

Understanding Query Criteria

A query is only as useful and as accurate as the criteria that define it. For this reason, it is crucial to understand query criteria if you want to get the most out of the powerful query capabilities of Access.

A query's criteria consist of one or more expressions that manipulate the underlying table in some way. For example, if your query includes a Country field, you could specify the string "USA" as the expression. When you apply such an expression to a field for each record in the table, the result contains only those records for which the expression is true. In the example, adding the literal value "USA" to the Country field is equivalent to the following logical formula:

Country = "USA"

Access builds the dynaset by applying this formula to each record in the table and selecting only those records for which it returns True (that is, those records where the value in the Country field is equal to "USA").

More powerful queries use more complex expressions that combine not only literals, but also operators, table fields, and even built-in functions. Access evaluates the expression on the field in which it was defined and, again, the records where the expression returns a True result are the records that appear in the query dynaset.

Let's take a more detailed look at the two main components of a query criteria expression: operands and operators.

An *operand* is a data value that gets manipulated in some way in an expression. The two operand types that you use most often in your criteria expressions are

- **Literal**—This is a value that you type directly into the expression. Access recognizes four types of literals: text, numbers, dates and times, and a constant (True, False, or Null). When you use a date or a time as a literal in a criteria expression, be sure to surround the value with pound signs (#). For example, #8/23/2016# or #3:15 PM#.

- **Field name**—Also called an *identifier*, this is the name of a field from the query's underlying table, surrounded by square brackets; for example, [Country] or [Company Name].

An *operator* is a special symbol that manipulates one or more operands in some way. The most common operators in query expressions are the comparison operators. You use comparison operators to compare the values in a particular field with a literal value, a function result, the value in another field, or an expression result. Here are the comparison operators used by Access:

Operator	Matches records where
= (equal to)	The value of the criteria field is equal to a specified value.
<> (not equal to)	The value of the criteria field is not equal to a specified value.
> (greater than)	The value of the criteria field is greater than a specified value.
>= (greater than or equal to)	The value of the criteria field is greater than or equal to a specified value.
< (less than)	The value of the criteria field is less than a specified value.
<= (less than or equal to)	The value of the criteria field is less than or equal to a specified value.

For example, suppose your table has a Quantity field and you want to see just those records where the quantity is greater than 100. To do this, you would type the following expression in the Criteria cell for the Quantity field (see "Enter Query Criteria" next):

>100

When you need to build mathematical expressions, use the arithmetic operators:

Operator	Description
+ (addition)	Adds one value to another
- (subtraction)	Subtracts one value from another
- (unary)	Changes the sign of a value
* (multiplication)	Multiplies one value by another
/ (division)	Divides one value by another
\ (integer division)	Divides one value by another as integers
^ (exponentiation)	Raises one value to the power of a second value
Mod (modulus)	Divides one value by another and returns the remainder

For example, if you want to calculate the *extended total* for an invoice, you first multiply the quantity ordered by the unit price. If these values are stored in the table using fields named Quantity and UnitPrice, your criteria expression would look like this:

[Quantity]*[UnitPrice]

Finally, if you need to allow for multiple spellings in a text field, or if you are not sure how to spell a word you want to use, the wildcard characters can help. The two wildcards are the question mark (?), which substitutes for a single character, and the asterisk (*), which substitutes for a group of characters. You use them in combination with the Like operator, as shown in these examples:

Example	Description
Like "Re?d"	Matches records where the field value is Reid, Read, reed, and so on
Like "M?"	Matches records where the field value is MA, MD, ME, and so on
Like "R*"	Matches records where the field value begins with R
Like "*office*"	Matches records where the field value contains the word *office*
Like "12/*/2016"	Matches records where the field value is any date in December 2016

Enter Query Criteria

The last query design step is to specify the criteria that determine the subset of records you want to work with from the table.

1. Double-click the query, if it isn't open already.

2. Click the Home tab.

3. Click the bottom half of the View button and then click Design View. Access opens the query in Design view.

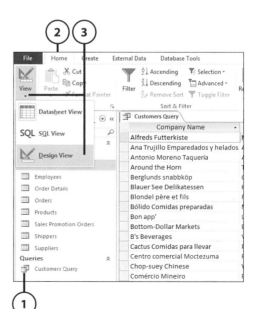

4. Click inside the Criteria row in the column that represents the field you want to use in your query expression.

5. Type the expression.

6. Click the Design tab.

7. Click Run. Access applies the criteria and displays the results.

Type multiple criteria in different rows to apply any one of the criteria.

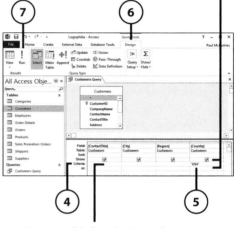

Type multiple criteria in the same row to apply all the criteria.

>>>Go Further

SPECIFYING MULTIPLE CRITERIA

Access allows you to enter more than one criteria expression. How you do this depends on whether you want Access to apply all the criteria you enter or any one of the criteria.

Applying all the criteria means that Access only matches records if they return true for every expression you enter. To apply all the criteria, enter each criteria expression in a single Criteria row. For example, if you enter **"USA"** in the Country field and **Like "S*"** in CompanyName field, Access returns all records where the Country field is USA and the CompanyName starts with S.

Applying any one of the criteria means that Access only matches records if they return true for at least one of the expressions you enter. To apply any one of the criteria, enter each criteria expression in a separate Criteria row. For example, if you enter **"USA"** in the Country field and **"Canada"** in a separate row of the Country field, Access returns all records where the Country field is either USA or Canada.

Creating Forms

After you use Access for a while, you quickly come to realize that using a datasheet to enter data into a table is not particularly efficient—you usually have to scroll to the right to get to all the fields, which means you cannot see the entire record on the screen—and the no-nonsense row-and-column format of the datasheet is serviceable but not at all attractive.

The datasheet is a reasonable tool if you are only entering one or two records, but if you are entering a dozen records or even a hundred, you need to leave the datasheet behind and use the Access data entry tool of choice: the *form*. A form is a collection of controls—usually labels and text boxes but also lists, check boxes, and option buttons—each of which represents either a field or the name of a field. As you see in this chapter, forms not only make data entry easier and more efficient, but thanks to Access's large collection of formatting tools, they can also make data entry more attractive.

Create a Basic Form

By far the easiest way to create a form is to let Access do all the work for you by creating a basic form.

1. Click the table you want to use as the basis of the form.

2. Click the Create tab.

3. Click Form. Access creates and then displays the basic form.

4. Use the controls in the Format, Arrange, and Design tabs to customize the form as needed.

5. Click Save. Access prompts you to name the new form.

6. Type a name for the form.

7. Click OK.

Switching to Form View

Right now your basic form is open in Layout view, which makes it easy to edit and format the form. When you're ready to use the form for data entry, you should switch to Form view by clicking the Home tab, clicking the lower half of the View button, and then clicking Form View.

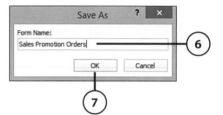

Navigating Form Fields and Records

The basic form shows one record at a time and you can see all the table's fields onscreen. This feature makes navigating the form fields and records using your mouse easy:

- To navigate to a field, click the field's control (text box, list box, or whatever).

- To navigate records, use the navigation buttons at the bottom of the form. These are the same navigation buttons that appear at the bottom of a datasheet, so you use the same techniques.

However, when entering data in a form, you're most often using the keyboard, so navigating the fields and records using keyboard techniques is usually more efficient. Here are three basic techniques you should know:

- When you have finished typing data in a field, press Enter. This action causes the field to accept the data you entered into it and then moves the focus to the next field.

- Press Tab or Shift+Tab to move from field to field.

- When the focus is on the last field in the form, press Tab to move to the next record.

Otherwise, to navigate fields and records in a form you can use the keys outlined here:

Press	To Move To
Tab or right arrow	The next field to the right or, from the last field, the first field in the next record
Shift+Tab or left arrow	The previous field to the left or, from the first field, the first field in the previous record
Home	The first field
End	The last field
Page Down	The same field in the next record
Page Up	The same field in the previous record
Ctrl+Home	The first field of the first record
Ctrl+End	The last field of the last record

Run the Form Wizard

The basic form should be fine for most of your form needs, but it is likely that in some cases the resulting form will not be exactly what you require. For a bit more control over your forms, use the Form Wizard, which takes you step-by-step through the entire form-creation process.

1. Click the table you want to use as the basis of the form.

2. Click the Create tab.

3. Click Form Wizard. Access launches the Form Wizard.

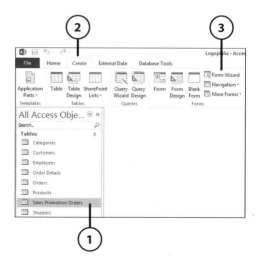

4. For each field you want to include in the form, click the field and then click Add.

5. When you are done, click Next.

6. Select a layout for the form.

Form Wizard Layouts

In the Columnar layout, the fields are arranged in columns, and only one record is shown at a time (similar to the basic form layout you learned about earlier in this chapter). In the Tabular layout, the fields are arranged in a table, with the field names at the top and the records in rows. In the Datasheet layout, the fields are arranged in a datasheet configuration (like a table or the results of a query). In the Justified layout, the fields are arranged across and down the form with the field names above their respective controls.

7. Click Next.

8. Type a name for the form.

9. Click Finish. Access creates the form and displays it.

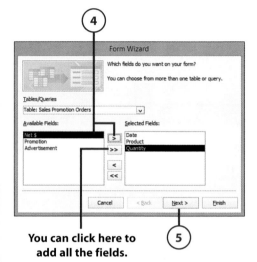

You can click here to add all the fields.

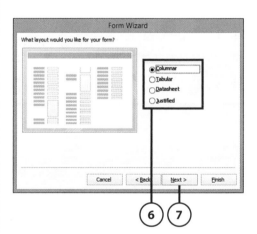

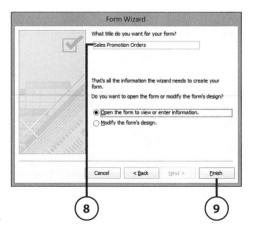

Creating Reports

The various Access database objects have different purposes. Tables store data; queries analyze data; and forms ease data entry. When it comes time to display your data in its best light, you need to turn to another Access database object: the *report*. You use reports to organize your table or query data so that it makes sense to other people, and format it so that it is easy to read.

As you see in this section, building a report is not all that different from building a form. This is good news because, as explained earlier in this chapter, Access offers many tools for easing form creation, and that applies to reports as well.

Create a Basic Report

The easiest and fastest way to create a report is to let Access do the work by creating a basic report.

1. Click the table or query you want to use as the basis of the report.

2. Click the Create tab.

3. Click Report. Access creates and then displays the basic report.

4. Use the controls in the Design, Arrange, Format, and Page Setup tabs to customize the report as needed.

5. Click Save. Access prompts you to name the new report.

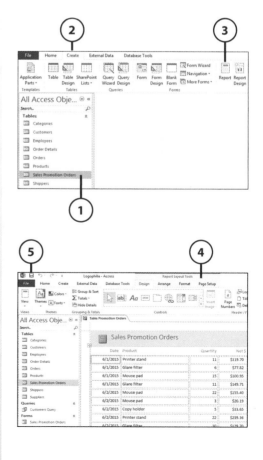

6. Type a name for the report.

7. Click OK.

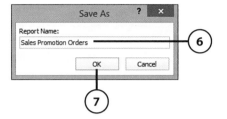

Switching to Report View

When you first create the basic report, Access opens it in Layout view, which you use to edit and format the report. When you're ready to view and print the report itself, you should switch to Report view by clicking the Home tab, clicking the lower half of the View button, and then clicking Report View.

Run the Report Wizard

For a bit more control over your reports, use the Report Wizard, which takes you step-by-step through the report-creation process.

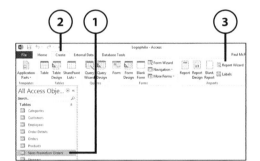

1. Click the table you want to use as the basis of the report.

2. Click the Create tab.

3. Click Report Wizard. Access launches the Report Wizard.

4. For each field you want to include in the report, click the field and then click Add.

5. When you are done, click Next.

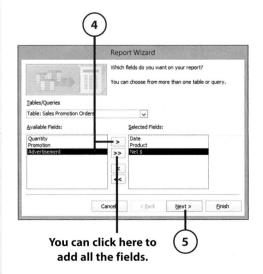

You can click here to add all the fields.

6. If you want to group the report based on the values of a field, click the field and then click Add.

Grouping Levels

A *grouping level* is a field on which the report records are grouped. In the Sales Promotion Orders table, if you choose Advertisement as the grouping level, the records are grouped according to each unique advertisement item in that field.

7. If you want to add a subgroup based on the values of a field, click the field and then click Add.

8. Click Next.

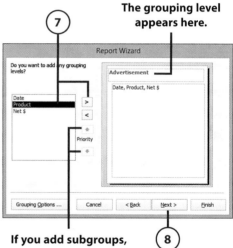

The grouping level appears here.

If you add subgroups, use the Priority arrows to set the grouping hierarchy.

>>>Go Further
CREATING CUSTOM GROUPING LEVELS

To create a custom grouping level, click the Grouping Options button; then use the Grouping intervals list to click a custom grouping level for each group-level field. For example, a text field enables you to group according to the first letter, first two letters, and so on; similarly, for a date field, you can group by week, month, quarter, and so on.

9. Use one or more of the four drop-down lists to choose a sort order for the records. For each field, you can also click the toggle button to choose Ascending or Descending.

10. Click Next.

11. Click the layout you want to use for the report.

12. Click the orientation you want to use for the report.

13. Click Next.

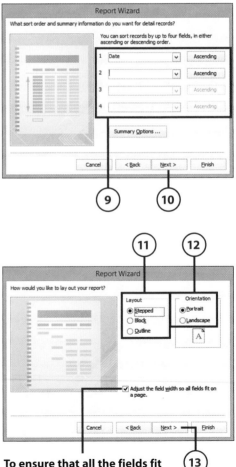

To ensure that all the fields fit the width of the page, leave this check box activated.

14. Type a name for the report.

15. Click Finish. Access creates the report and displays it.

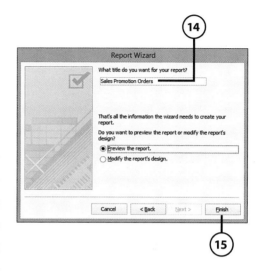

Customize the Quick Access Toolbar.

Add Ribbon commands to the Quick Access Toolbar.

Change the background.

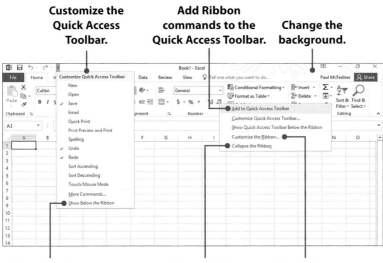

Move the Quick Access Toolbar below the Ribbon.

Pin and hide the Ribbon.

Customize the Ribbon.

In this chapter, you learn about customizing the Office 2016 applications, including working with the application options and customizing the interface. Topics include the following:

→ Accessing the Options dialog box for the Office 2016 applications

→ Changing your Office 2016 user name and initials

→ Pinning, hiding, and customizing the Ribbon

→ Positioning and customizing the Quick Access Toolbar

→ Changing the background for the Office 2016 applications

Customizing the Office 2016 Applications

This book is called *My Office 2016*, so it's time you learned how to put the "My" in Office 2016. I speak, of course, about customizing the applications in some way. After all, the interface and settings that you see when you first use Office 2016 are the "factory defaults." That is, how the program looks and how it works out of the box has been specified by Microsoft. However, this "official" version of the program is almost always designed with some mythical "average" user in mind. Nothing is wrong with this concept, but it almost certainly means that the program is not set up optimally for *you*. This chapter shows you how to get the most out of the main Office 2016 programs—Word, Excel, PowerPoint, Outlook, OneNote, and Access—by performing a few customization chores to set up the program to suit the way you work.

Working with Application Options

Customizing Office 2016 most often means tweaking a setting or two in the Options dialog box that comes with each program. Each program has a unique Options dialog box configuration, so it's beyond the scope of this book to discuss these dialog boxes in detail. Instead, I introduce them by showing you how to get them onscreen and by going through some useful settings.

Working with the Options Dialog Box

You often need to access the Options dialog box for an Office 2016 application, so let's begin by quickly reviewing the steps required to access and work with this dialog box in your current Office 2016 program.

1. **Select File.** The Office 2016 application, Excel in this example, displays the File menu.

2. **Select Options.** The Office 2016 application opens the Options dialog box.

3. **Select a tab.** The Office 2016 application displays the options related to the selected tab.

4. **Use the controls to tweak the application's settings.**

5. **Select OK.** The Office 2016 application puts the changed options into effect.

Keyboard Shortcut

You can also open the Options dialog box in any Office 2016 application by pressing Alt+F, T.

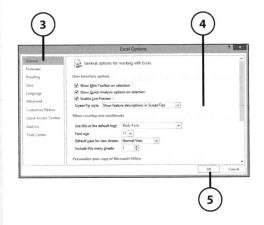

Changing Your User Name and Initials

In Chapter 18, "Collaborating with Others," you learn how to insert comments into a document and track document changes. In both cases, the underlying program keeps a record of each "reviewer" who made changes to the document. For revisions, the program identifies the reviewer by his or her Office 2016 user name; for comments, the program identifies the reviewer by his or her Office 2016 initials. You can change both your user name and your initials to whatever you prefer.

1. Select File to open the File menu.

2. Select Options to open the Options dialog box.

3. Select the General tab.

4. Use the User Name text box to type your user name.

5. In Word, PowerPoint, and OneNote, use the Initials text box to type your initials.

6. Select OK. Office 2016 puts the new user name and initials into effect.

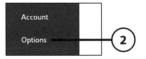

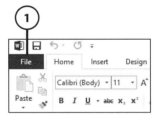

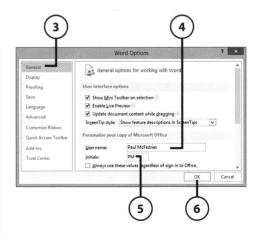

Universal User Name and Initials

Your user name and initials are universal in Office 2016. That is, changing your user name or initials in one program automatically means the new user name or initials appear in the other Office 2016 programs.

APPLYING YOUR USER NAME AND INITIALS ACROSS ACCOUNTS

If you have multiple Microsoft accounts, you might still want to use the same user name and initials no matter which account you're currently signed in with. You can configure Office 2016 to do this by opening the Options dialog box in any Office 2016 application, selecting the General tab, and then selecting the Always Use These Values Regardless of Sign In to Office check box. Select OK to put the setting into effect.

Bypassing the Start Screen at Launch

By default, Word, Excel, and PowerPoint display the Start screen when you first launch the application, which lets you choose a template for a new file or select a recently used file. If you almost always opt to open a blank document, workbook, or presentation at startup, you can make this the default behavior.

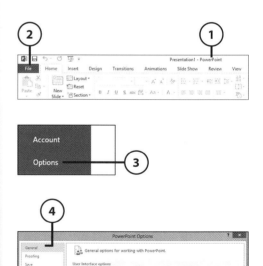

1. Launch the Office 2016 application you want to customize.

2. Select File to open the File menu.

3. Select Options to open the Options dialog box.

4. Select the General tab.

5. Deselect the Show the Start Screen When This Application Starts check box.

6. Select OK. The Office 2016 application puts the setting into effect.

Customizing the Interface

Besides the work area of any Office 2016 application window, the Office 2016 interface mostly consists of the Ribbon and its associated Quick Access Toolbar. These two elements are the royal road to all things Office 2016, so you'll be less efficient and less productive if these elements aren't set up to suit the way you work.

Pinning the Ribbon

By default, some of the Office 2016 applications hide the Ribbon to give you maximum screen real estate for your documents, and you display the Ribbon by clicking any tab. If you find that extra click to be a pain, you can avoid it by pinning the Ribbon so that it appears on screen full-time.

You can also click here and then click Show Tabs and Commands

1. Click any Ribbon tab to display the Ribbon.

2. Click Pin the Ribbon. The Ribbon appears onscreen full-time.

Shortcuts for Pinning the Ribbon

The Office 2016 applications give you two shortcut methods for pinning the Ribbon: Either double-click any Ribbon tab or press Ctrl+F1.

Hiding the Ribbon

If you followed the steps in the previous section to display the Ribbon all the time, you might later decide that you prefer the extra screen space over the convenience and want to revert to hiding the Ribbon until needed.

1. Click any Ribbon tab to display the Ribbon.

2. Click Collapse the Ribbon. The Office 2016 application hides the Ribbon.

You can also click here and then click Show Tabs

Shortcuts for Unpinning the Ribbon

As with pinning, Office 2016 gives you two shortcuts for unpinning the Ribbon: Either double-click any Ribbon tab or press Ctrl+F1.

Customizing the Ribbon

The Ribbon is handy because it enables you to run Office commands with just a few clicks. However, the Ribbon doesn't include every command for a given Office 2016 app. If there's a command that you use frequently, you should add it to the Ribbon for easy access.

1. In the Office 2016 application you want to customize, select File.

2. Select Options. The Options dialog box opens.

3. Select the Customize Ribbon tab.

Faster Access to the Customize Ribbon Tab

A quicker route to the Customize Ribbon tab is to right-click any part of the Ribbon and then select Customize the Ribbon.

4. Select the tab you want to customize.

5. Select New Group. The Office 2016 application adds the group.

6. Select Rename.

7. Type a name for the group.

8. Select OK.

The new group appears here.

Use these buttons to reorder the tabs and commands.

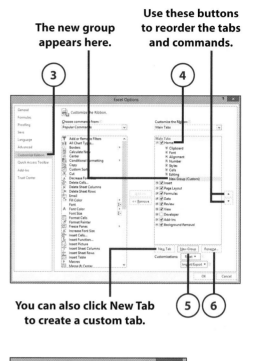

You can also click New Tab to create a custom tab.

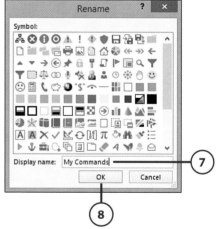

9. Use the Choose Commands From list to select the command category you want to use.

10. Select the command you want to add.

11. Select the custom group or tab to which you want to add the command.

Customizing Tool Tabs

The tabs that appear only when you select an object are called *tool tabs*, and you can add custom groups and commands to any tool tab. Drop down the Customize the Ribbon list, select Tool Tabs, and then select the tool tab you want to customize.

12. Select Add. The Office 2016 application adds the command to the custom group or tab. Repeat steps 9 to 12 as needed.

13. Select OK. The Office 2016 application adds the new groups and commands to the Ribbon.

The new command appears here.

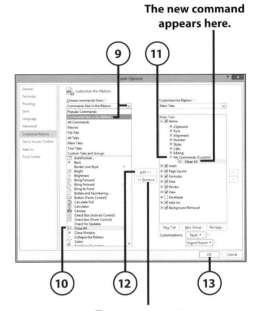

To remove a custom command, select it and then select Remove.

>>>Go Further
EXPORTING RIBBON CUSTOMIZATIONS

Customizing the Ribbon or the Quick Access Toolbar is not difficult, but it can be time consuming, particularly if you want to make a substantial number of changes. If you use the same Office 2016 application on another computer, it's likely that you want to have the same customizations on the other computer so that you are dealing with a consistent interface no matter where you do your work. Rather than wasting valuable time repeating the same customization steps on the other computer, you can export your customizations to a file. You can then import that file on the other computer, and the Office 2016 application automatically applies the customizations for you.

In the Customize Ribbon tab of the Options dialog box, select Import/Export and then select Export All Customizations. In the File Save dialog box, select a location for the customization file, type a name for the file, and then select Save. Select OK to close the Options dialog box.

To apply the Ribbon customizations on another computer running the same Office 2016 application, you need to import the customization file. Note, however, that importing a customization file replaces any existing customizations that you have created. Display the Customize Ribbon tab of the Options dialog box, select Import/Export, and then select Import Customization File. In the File Open dialog box, locate and then select the customization file, and then select Open. When the application asks you to confirm that all your existing customizations will be replaced, select Yes and then select OK.

Changing the Position of the Quick Access Toolbar

The Quick Access Toolbar offers one-click access to common commands such as Save and Undo. By default, the Quick Access Toolbar appears above the Ribbon. This spot is good if you only have a few commands on the Quick Access Toolbar because the relatively small size of the Quick Access Toolbar means that the host Office 2016 program has enough room to display the document title and application name. If you want to load up the Quick Access Toolbar with many commands, consider moving it below the Ribbon. Doing so gives the Quick Access Toolbar the full width of the window, although it does reduce the amount of space available for your document content.

1. Select Customize Quick Access Toolbar.

2. Select Show Below the Ribbon. The Office 2016 application moves the Quick Access Toolbar below the Ribbon.

The Quick Access Toolbar

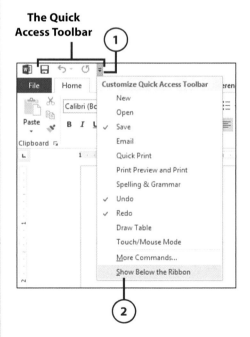

Customizing the Quick Access Toolbar

To get the most out of the Quick Access Toolbar, you need to populate it with the commands that you use most often. Note that you are not restricted to just a few commands. If you place the Quick Access Toolbar below the Ribbon, as described in the previous section, you can use the full width of the window, plus you get a More Controls button at the end of the toolbar that enables you to display a whole other row of commands.

1. If the command you want to add is on the Ribbon, right-click the command and then select Add to Quick Access Toolbar.

Adding a Gallery to the Toolbar

You can add a Ribbon gallery to the Quick Access Toolbar. Use the Ribbon to open the gallery, right-click any item in the gallery, and then select Add Gallery to Quick Access Toolbar.

Adding a Group to the Toolbar

Conveniently, you can also add entire groups to the toolbar. To add a group, right-click the group name in the Ribbon and then click Add to Quick Access Toolbar.

2. Select Customize Quick Access Toolbar.

3. Select More Commands. The Office 2016 application opens the Options dialog box with the Quick Access Toolbar tab displayed.

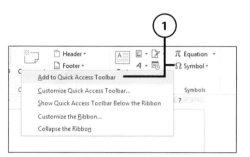

Commands already on the Quick Access Toolbar appear with check marks.

Select a command that has a check mark to remove it from the Quick Access Toolbar.

If the command you want to add appears in this list, select it to add it to the Quick Access Toolbar.

4. Use the Choose Commands From list to select the command category you want to use.

5. Select the command you want to add.

6. Select Add. The Office 2016 application adds the command to the custom group or tab.

7. Select a command and then select Move Up or Move Down to position the command within the Quick Access Toolbar. Repeat steps 4 to 7 as needed.

8. Select OK. The Office 2016 application adds the commands to the Quick Access Toolbar.

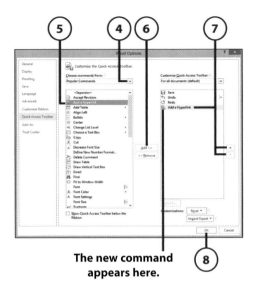

The new command appears here.

Setting the Office Background

You can add a bit of visual interest to your Office 2016 applications by applying a background pattern that appears in the title bar.

1. Select File.

2. Select the Account tab.

3. Use the Office Background list to select the pattern you want to use. Office 2016 applies the pattern to all the Office 2016 applications.

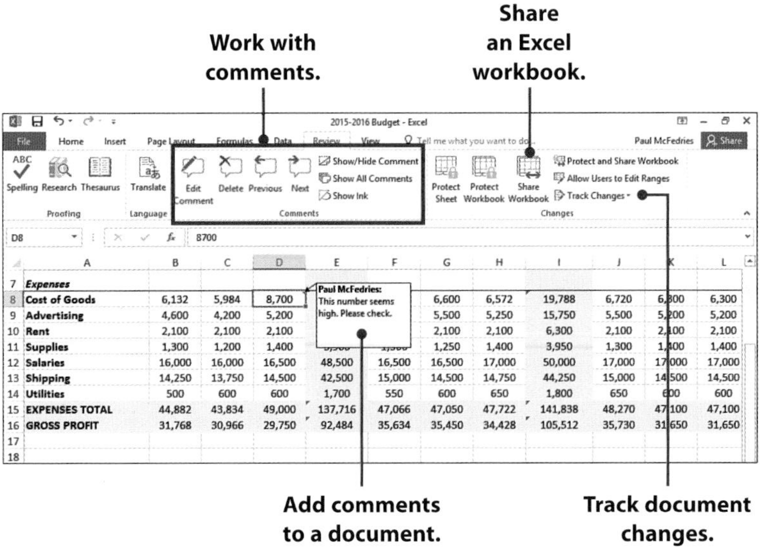

Share an Excel workbook.
Work with comments.
Add comments to a document.
Track document changes.
2015-2016 Budget - Excel
Paul McFedries:
This number seems high. Please check.

In this chapter, you learn how to collaborate with other people, particularly on Word and Excel files. Topics include the following:

→ Inserting and working with comments in Word

→ Tracking changes to Word documents

→ Inserting and working with comments in Excel

→ Tracking changes to Excel workbooks

→ Sharing an Excel workbook

→ Sharing Office documents using your OneDrive

Collaborating with Others

Whether you're a company employee, a consultant, or a freelancer, you almost certainly work with other people in one capacity or another. Most of the time, our work with others is informal and consists of ideas exchanged during meetings, phone calls, or email messages. However, we're often called upon to work with others more closely by collaborating with them on a document. This could involve commenting on another person's work, editing someone else's document, or dividing a project among multiple authors. For all these situations, Office 2016 offers a number of powerful collaborative tools. This chapter shows you how to use and get the most out of these tools.

Collaborating in Word with Comments and Changes

Microsoft Word is the collaboration champion in the Office suite because, more than any other Office program, Word boasts an impressive collection of tools that enable you to work with other people on a document. In the next few sections, you learn about the simplest and most common collaboration tools: comments and tracking changes.

Insert Comments in a Word Document

If someone asks for your feedback on a document, you could write that feedback in a separate document or in an email message. However, feedback is most useful when it appears in the proper context. That is, if you have a suggestion or critique of a particular word, sentence, or paragraph, the reader will understand that feedback more readily if it appears near the text in question. To do that in Word, you insert a *comment*, a separate section of text associated with some part of the original document.

1. Select the text you want to comment on. If you want to comment on a particular word, you can position the cursor within or immediately to the left or right of the word.

2. Select the Review tab.

3. Select New Comment. Word highlights the selected text to indicate it has an associated comment.

4. Type the comment.

5. Click outside the comment box to save it.

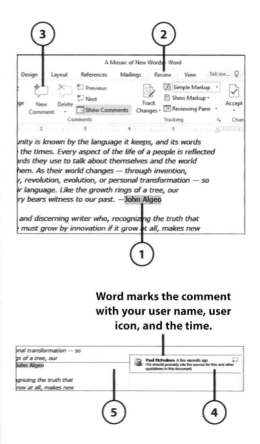

Word marks the comment with your user name, user icon, and the time.

Edit a Comment

You can edit a comment either by adding to or changing the existing comment text, or by responding to a comment made by another person.

1. Click the text of the comment you want to edit. The Comments box appears.

2. Edit the comment text as needed.

3. If you want to respond to the comment, select this icon.

4. Type your response.

5. Click outside the comment box to save it.

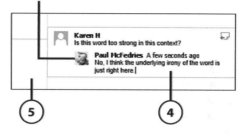

Responses appear indented from the original comment.

Delete a Comment

When you no longer need a comment, you can delete it to reduce clutter in the Word document.

1. Select the comment you want to delete.

2. Select the Review tab.

3. Select the top half of the Delete button. Word deletes the comment.

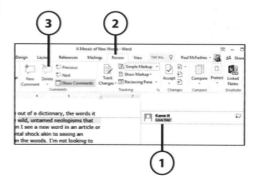

Deleting All Comments

If you want a fresh start with a Word document, you can delete all the comments. To do this quickly, select the Review tab, select the bottom half of the Delete button in the Comments group, and then select Delete All Comments in Document.

Track Changes in a Word Document

A higher level of collaboration occurs when you ask another person to make changes to a document. That is, rather than suggesting changes by using comments, the other person performs the actual changes herself with Word keeping track of all the changes made to the document. This means that any time you or another person makes changes to the original text—including adding, editing, deleting, and formatting the text—Word keeps track of the changes and shows not only what changes were made, but who made them and when.

1. Select the Review tab.

2. Select the top half of the Track Changes button. Word enables Track Changes and indicates this by leaving the Track Changes button highlighted.

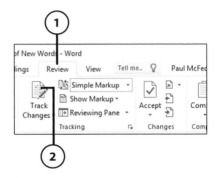

Keyboard Shortcut

You can toggle Track Changes on and off quickly by pressing Ctrl+Shift+E.

Control the Display of Comments and Changes

Depending on the document and the number of reviewers, comments and changes can make a document look messy. Fortunately, Word allows you to filter out particular types of changes and even changes made by particular reviewers.

These filters are part of Word's Show Markup list, which contains the following six commands that toggle the respective markup on and off:

Defining Markup

Markup refers to the icons, font changes, and balloons that indicate the comments and changes reviewers have made to a document.

- **Comments**—Toggles comments on and off.

- **Ink**—Toggles on and off any annotations made by a digital pen or stylus.

- **Insertions and Deletions**—Toggles the display of text that has been added to or removed from the document.

- **Formatting**—Toggles the display of changes made to formatting such as fonts and paragraphs.

- **Balloons**—This command displays a list that enables you to select which revisions appear in balloons when the reviewing pane is activated. By default, Word only shows comments and formatting changes in balloons, but you can also choose to show all revisions in balloons or all revisions inline (that is, within the text itself).

- **Specific People**—This command displays a list of reviewers so you can toggle the display of changes made by a particular reviewer.

Word also offers several options for controlling the entire markup in a document. The Display for Review list contains the following four commands:

- **Simple Markup**—This view shows the final version of the document (the version of the document if you accept all the current changes) with the markup only indicated with comment icons in the right margin and revision marks in the left margin.

- **All Markup**—This view shows the final version of the document (the version of the document if you accept all the current changes) with deletions marked as strikethrough, and comments, additions, and formatting changes shown in balloons.

- **No Markup**—This view shows the final version of the document with none of the markup showing (that is, how the document would look if all the changes had been accepted).

- **Original**—This is the original version of the document, before any changes were made (or, more precisely, either before Track Changes was turned on or since the last time all the changes were accepted).

Control the Markup Display

By default, Word shows all revisions from all reviewers using the Simple Markup display, but you can change these defaults to ones that you prefer.

1. Select the Review tab.

2. Select Show Markup.

3. Select which types of markup you want to view.

4. Pull down the Display for Review list.

5. Select how you want Word to display the document's markup.

With Simple Markup, all other revisions are indicated with vertical bars in the left margin.

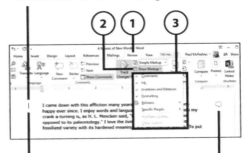

Click a bar to toggle the markup display on and off.

With Simple Markup, comments are indicated with icons in the right margin.

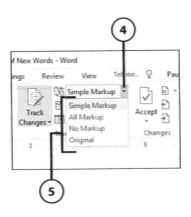

Navigate Comments and Changes

To make sure that you review every comment or change in a document, or to accept or reject comments and changes individually (see the next section), you need to use Word's reviewing navigation tools.

1. Select the Review tab.

2. In the Comments group, select Next to view the next comment in the document.

3. Select Previous to view the previous comment in the document.

4. In the Changes group, select Next to view the next revision in the document.

5. Select Previous to view the previous revision in the document.

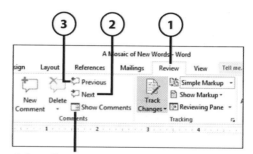

Select Show Comments to see all comments instead of just their icons.

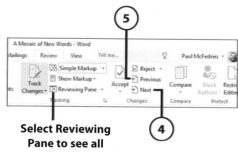

Select Reviewing Pane to see all revisions instead of just their icons.

Accept or Reject Comments and Changes

The point of marking up a document is to later review the changes and then either incorporate some or all of them into the final version or remove those that are not useful or suitable. Word gives you several tools to either accept markup (this action applies to changes only) or reject markup (this action applies to both comments and changes).

1. Select the Review tab.

2. Navigate to the comment or change you want to work with.

3. If you want to accept the change, select the top half of the Accept button.

4. If you want to reject the comment or change instead, select the Reject button.

5. Repeat steps 2 to 4 until you've gone through all the changes you want to review.

To accept all changes at once, click here and then click Accept All Changes.

To reject all changes at once, click here and then click Reject All Changes.

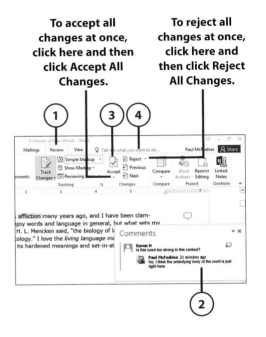

>>>Go Further
ACCEPTING SHOWN CHANGES

In many situations, you want to accept all changes of a certain type (such as formatting or insertions and deletions) and review the rest. To accept all changes of a certain type, first use the Show Markup list to turn off the display of all revisions except the type you want to accept (see "Control the Markup Display," earlier in this chapter). Then, in the Review tab, select the bottom half of the Accept button and select Accept All Changes Shown.

You can also accept only the changes made by a particular reviewer. To display the markup for a single reviewer, pull down the Show Markup list, select Specific People, and then select All Reviewers to turn off all markup. Select Show Markup, Specific People again, and this time select the reviewer whose markup you want to accept. Then, in the Review tab, select the bottom half of the Accept button and select Accept All Changes Shown.

Collaborating in Excel with Comments and Changes

As with Word, Excel enables you to collaborate with other people by adding comments and tracking changes. Although these features are implemented slightly differently in Excel, the underlying concepts are basically the same, as you see in the next few sections. Later you see that Excel also enables you to collaborate by sharing a workbook among multiple users.

Insert Comments in Cells

The simplest level of collaboration with an Excel workbook is the comment that does not change any worksheet data but offers notes, suggestions, and critiques of the worksheet content. In Excel, you associate comments with individual cells, not with ranges.

1. Select the cell in which you want to insert the comment.

2. Select the Review tab.

3. Select New Comment. Excel displays an empty comment balloon.

Turning Off the Comment Indicators

If you don't want to see the comment indicators, you can turn them off by choosing File, Options, and then clicking the Advanced tab. In the Display section, select the No Comments or Indicators option and then click OK.

4. Type the comment text.

5. When you are done, click outside the comment balloon.

Editing a Comment

If you need to make changes to a comment, select the cell, select the Review tab, and then select Edit Comment. Excel opens the comment for editing. Make your changes and then click outside the comment box. If you need to delete a comment, click the cell, click Review, and then click Delete.

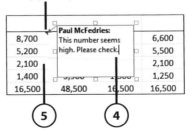

③ ②

ayout	Formulas	Data	Review	View	Tell

New Comment   Delete   Previous   Next   ☑ Show/Hide Comment   📋 Show All Comments   ◇ Show Ink

Comments

8700

₿	C	D	E	F
in	Feb	Mar	1st Quarter	Apr
₅00	23,000	24,000	70,500	25,100
750	27,800	29,500	86,050	31,000
400	24,000	25,250	73,650	26,600
₆50	74,800	78,750	230,200	82,700
32	5,984	8,700	20,816	6,616
₅00	4,200	5,200	14,000	5,000

①

Excel indicates the inserted comment by adding a small red triangle to the upper-right corner of the cell.

8,700	Paul McFedries:		6,600
5,200	This number seems		5,500
2,100	high. Please check.		2,100
1,400			1,250
16,500	48,500	16,500	16,500

⑤ ④

View Workbook Comments

By default, Excel indicates commented cells by placing a small, red triangle in the upper-right corner of the cell, but it doesn't display the comment itself. So to read a cell's comment, you must display it by hand.

1. Select the cell that contains the comment you want to view.

2. Select the Review tab.

3. Select Show/Hide Comment. Excel displays the comment.

Viewing with a Mouse

You can also view the comment by hovering the mouse pointer over the cell.

4. To hide the comment, select Show/Hide Comment.

5. Select Next to view the next comment in the worksheet.

6. Select Previous to view the previous comment in the worksheet.

If there are multiple comments, you can display them all by selecting Show All Comments.

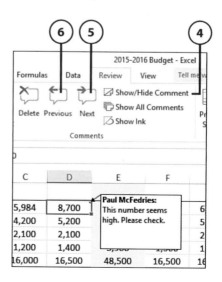

>>>Go Further
DISPLAYING COMMENTS FULL-TIME

If you find yourself constantly displaying comments in a workbook, you can configure Excel to always show them, which saves you from having to display the comments manually. Select File, Options to open the Excel Options dialog box and then select the Advanced tab. In the Display section, select the Comments and Indicators option, and then select OK.

Track Worksheet Changes

If you want other people to make changes to a workbook, keeping track of those changes is a good idea so you can either accept or reject them. Like Word, Excel has a Track Changes feature that enables you to do this. When you turn on Track Changes, Excel monitors the activity of each reviewer and stores the reviewer's cell edits, row and column additions and deletions, range moves, worksheet insertions, and worksheet renames. You can also filter the changes by date, reviewer, or worksheet location.

1. Select the Review tab.

2. Select Track Changes.

3. Select Highlight Changes. Excel displays the Highlight Changes dialog box.

4. Select the Track Changes While Editing check box. (The check box text mentions that "This also shares the workbook." You find out more details on sharing an Excel workbook later in this chapter in the "Share an Excel Workbook with Other Users" section.)

5. To filter the displayed changes by time, select the When check box and then use the list to select a time frame.

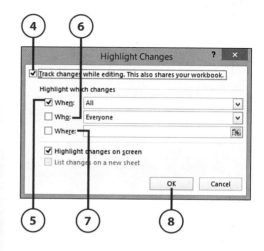

Filtering Changes by Date

To show only the changes that have occurred since a specific date, drop down the When list, select the Since Date item, and then edit the date that Excel displays (the default is the current date).

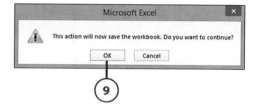

6. To filter the displayed changes by reviewer, select the Who check box and then select a reviewer or group in the list. At first, this list contains Everyone and Everyone but Me. Later, when other users have made changes, the list includes the name of each reviewer.

7. To filter the displayed changes by range, select the Where check box and then select the range in which you want changes displayed.

8. Select OK. Excel displays a dialog box letting you know that it will save your workbook.

9. Select OK.

>>>Go Further

CHANGING HOW LONG EXCEL KEEPS TRACKED CHANGES

By default, Excel keeps track of changes made for the past 30 days. To change the number of days of change history that Excel tracks, select the Review tab and then select Share Workbook to open the Share Workbook dialog box. Select the Advanced tab and then modify the value in the Keep Change History for *X* Days spin box. Select OK to put the new value into effect.

It's Not All Good

Understanding Track Changes Limitations

When you activate Track Changes, Excel does not track formatting changes. Also, Excel does not allow a number of operations, including the insertion and deletion of ranges and the deletion of worksheets. You can find a complete list of disallowed operations later in this chapter.

Accept or Reject Workbook Changes

The idea behind tracking workbook changes is so that you can review the changes and then either incorporate some or all of them into the final version of the file or remove those that are not useful or suitable.

1. Select the Review tab.

2. Select Track Changes.

3. Select Accept/Reject Changes. If your workbook has unsaved changes, Excel tells you it will save the workbook.

When a cell has changes, Excel adds a border to the cell and displays a triangle in the upper-left corner.

4. Select OK. Excel displays the Select Changes to Accept or Reject dialog box.

5. Use the When, Who, and Where controls to filter the changes, as needed (see the previous section for the details).

6. Select OK. Excel displays the Accept or Reject Changes dialog box and displays a change.

7. Click Accept or Reject. Excel moves to the next change. Repeat this step until you have reviewed all the changes.

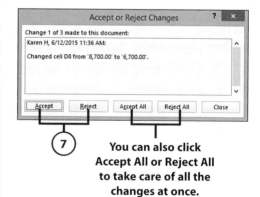

You can also click Accept All or Reject All to take care of all the changes at once.

Share an Excel Workbook with Other Users

Most Excel worksheet models are built to analyze data, but that analysis is only as good as the data is accurate. If you are building a model that brings in data from different departments or divisions, you can create a single workbook that you share with other users. This method enables those users to make changes to the workbook, and you can track those changes as described in the previous section. This is why Excel turns on workbook sharing automatically when you activate the Track Changes feature. Note, however, that the opposite is not the case. That is, you can share a workbook without also tracking changes.

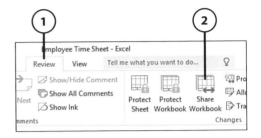

1. Select the Review tab.

2. Select Share Workbook. Excel displays the Share Workbook dialog box.

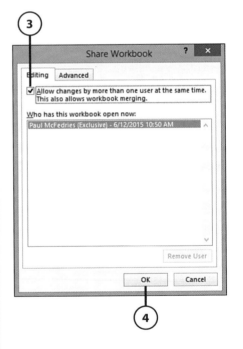

3. Select the Allow Changes by More Than One User at the Same Time check box.

4. Select OK. Excel tells you it will save the workbook.

5. Select OK. Excel shares the workbook and displays [Shared] in the title bar to remind you that the workbook is shared.

>>>*Go Further*

UPDATING A SHARED WORKBOOK ON A SCHEDULE

By default, Excel updates a shared workbook when you save the file. However, you can also configure the workbook to update its changes automatically after a specified number of minutes. Select the Review tab and then select Share Workbook to display the Share Workbook dialog box. Select the Advanced tab. In the Update changes group, select the Automatically Every *X* Minutes option to have Excel update the workbook using the interval you specify in the spin box (the minimum is 5 minutes; the maximum is 1,440 minutes). You can also elect to have Excel save your changes at the same time or just see the changes made by other users. Select OK to put the new settings into effect.

It's Not All Good

Shared Workbook Restrictions

Note that Excel doesn't allow the following operations while a workbook is shared:

- Inserting and deleting ranges (although you can insert and delete entire rows and columns)
- Inserting charts, symbols, pictures, diagrams, objects, and hyperlinks
- Creating or modifying tables or PivotTables
- Importing external data
- Deleting or moving worksheets
- Applying conditional formatting
- Working with scenarios
- Subtotaling, validating, grouping, and outlining data
- Merging cells
- Checking for formula errors

Display and Removing Reviewers

While your workbook is shared, you might also want to keep track of who is currently using it.

1. Select the Review tab.

2. Select Share Workbook. Excel displays the Share Workbook dialog box.

3. Select the Editing tab. The Who Has This Workbook Open Now list displays the current reviewers.

4. Select OK.

Excel displays [Shared] in the title bar of a shared workbook.

The workbook's current reviewers appear here.

It's Not All Good

Removing a User

Note that you can prevent a reviewer from using the workbook by clicking the user and then clicking Remove User. You should forcefully remove a user only as a last resort because doing so could easily cause the user to lose unsaved changes. Asking the person directly to save his or her changes and close the workbook is safer (and friendlier).

Handle Sharing Conflicts

If a downside exists to sharing a workbook with other users, it's that occasionally two people make changes to the same cell. For example, it could happen that another user changes a cell, saves his or her changes, and then you change the same cell before updating. This situation creates a conflict in the workbook versions that must be resolved.

1. Select Save. Before saving, Excel updates the workbook with the changes made by other users. If it detects a conflict, it displays the

2. Select which change you want to accept. Excel displays the next conflict. Repeat this step until all the conflicts have been resolved.

3. If you accepted other users' changes, select OK.

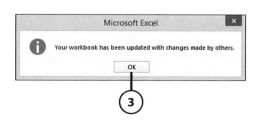

Your change appears here.

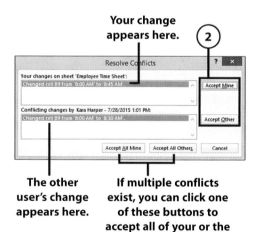

The other user's change appears here.

If multiple conflicts exist, you can click one of these buttons to accept all of your or the other user's changes.

Sharing a Document Online

If you work with a document online via OneDrive, you can share that document with other people. Office 2016 gives you two ways to share a document:

- **Using email**—In this case you send an email invitation to one or more recipients, and that message contains a link to a OneDrive location of the document you're sharing.

- **Using a link**—In this case you copy a OneDrive address (Office 2016 calls it a link) for the document you want to share. You can then distribute that address to the people you want to collaborate with (via email, text message, online post, or whatever).

In both cases, you can set up the shared document for viewing only, or to allow editing.

Save a Document to OneDrive

Before you can share a document online, you must save a copy of the document to your OneDrive.

1. Open the document you want to share.

2. Click File.

3. Click Save As.

4. Click OneDrive.

5. Click the folder you want to use.

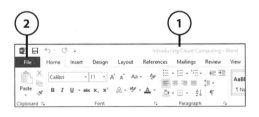

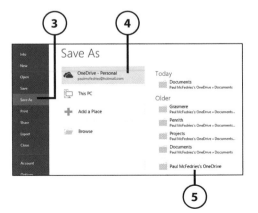

6. Select a storage folder, if needed.

7. Edit the filename.

8. Click Save.

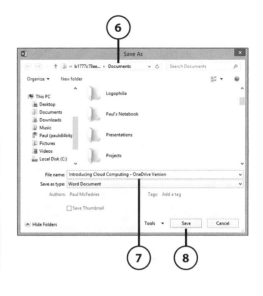

It's Not All Good

Working with the OneDrive Version

It's important to remember that after you run the Save As command, the Office 2016 application opens the OneDrive version of the document on your computer. This means that any changes you make to the document are reflected in the OneDrive version of the file, *not* the local version of the file.

Send an Invitation to Share a OneDrive Document

To allow other people to view, comment on, or even edit a document on your OneDrive, you can send an email invitation that contains a link to the document's OneDrive location.

1. Open the OneDrive version of the document you want to share.

2. Click File.

3. Click Share.

4. Click Invite People.

5. Choose your recipients.

6. Select either Can Edit (to allow the invitees to edit the document) or Can View
(to prevent editing).

7. Type a message to the invitees.

8. Activate this check box if you want the invitees to sign in to their Microsoft accounts
before they can access the document.

9. Click Share.

**Click here to open
the Address Book.**

Copy a Link to Share a OneDrive Document

If you want more flexibility when it comes to sharing a document, you can copy a link to a OneDrive address for that document, which you can then distribute to your collaborators.

1. Open the OneDrive version of the document you want to share.

2. Click File.

3. Click Share.

4. Click Get a Sharing Link.

5. If you want people to edit the document, click the Create Link button beside Edit Link. Otherwise, if you only want people to view the document, click the Create Link button beside View Link.

6. Right-click the created link and then click Copy.

7. Paste the copied link into an email message, text message, website, or whatever medium you want to use to share the link.

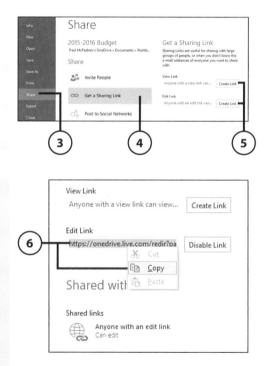

Excel Worksheet Function Reference

As you learned in Chapter 6, "Entering Excel Data," to get to the real meat of a spreadsheet model, you need to expand your formula repertoire to include Excel's worksheet functions. Several hundred of these functions exist, and they're an essential part of making your worksheet work easier and more powerfully. Excel has various function categories, including the following:

- Financial
- Logical
- Text
- Date and time
- Lookup and reference
- Math and trigonometry
- Statistical
- Engineering
- Information

- Database
- Cube
- Compatibility
- Web

(Note that this list, as well as the sections that follow, are presented in the order that the function category buttons appear in Excel's Insert Function dialog box.)

Functions are formulas that Excel has predefined. They're designed to take you beyond the basic arithmetic and text formulas you've seen so far. They do this in three ways:

- Functions make simple but cumbersome formulas easier to use. For example, suppose that you want to add a list of 100 numbers in a column starting at cell A1 and finishing at cell A100. Even if you wanted to, you couldn't enter 100 separate additions in a cell because you would run out of room. (Recall that cells are limited to 255 characters.) Luckily, there's an alternative: the SUM() function. With this function, you can simply enter =SUM(A1:A100).

- Functions enable you to include complex mathematical expressions in your worksheets that otherwise would be difficult or impossible to construct using simple arithmetic operators. For example, determining a mortgage payment given the principal, interest, and term is a complicated matter, at best, but you can do it with Excel's PMT() function just by entering a few parameters.

- Functions enable you to include data in your applications that you couldn't access otherwise. For example, the INFO() function can tell you how much memory is available on your system, what operating system you're using, what version number it is, and more. Similarly, the powerful IF() function enables you to test the contents of a cell—for example, to see whether it contains a particular value or an error—and then perform an action accordingly, depending on the result.

As you can see, functions are a powerful addition to your worksheet-building arsenal. With proper use of these tools, there is no practical limit to the kinds of models you can create.

Every function has the same basic form:

```
FUNCTION(argument1, argument2, ...)
```

The *FUNCTION* part is just the name of the function, which always appears in uppercase letters (such as SUM or PMT). Note, however, that you don't need to type in the function name using uppercase letters. Whatever case you use, Excel automatically converts the name to all uppercase. In fact, it's good practice to enter function names using only lowercase letters. That way, if Excel doesn't convert the function name to uppercase, you know that it doesn't recognize the name, which means you probably misspelled it.

The items that appear within the parentheses and separated by commas are the function *arguments*. The arguments are the function's inputs—the data it uses to perform its calculations. With respect to arguments, functions come in two flavors:

- **No arguments**—Many functions don't require any arguments. For example, the NOW() function returns the current date and time, and doesn't require arguments.

- **One or more arguments**—Most functions accept at least 1 argument, and some accept as many as 9 or 10 arguments. These arguments fall into two categories: required and optional. The required arguments must appear between the parentheses, or the formula will generate an error. You use the optional arguments only if your formula needs them.

Let's look at an example. The FV() function determines the future value of a regular investment based on three required arguments and two optional ones:

FV(**rate**, **nper**, **pmt**, *pv*, *type*)

rate	The fixed rate of interest over the term of the investment.
nper	The number of deposits over the term of the investment.
pmt	The amount deposited each period.
pv	The present value of the investment. The default value is 0.
type	When the deposits are due (0 for the beginning of the period; 1 for the end of the period, which is the default).

This is called the function *syntax*. Three conventions are at work here and in Excel:

- *Italic type* indicates a placeholder—when you use the function, you replace the placeholder with an actual value.

- Arguments shown in bold type are required.

- Arguments shown in regular type are optional.

For each required argument placeholder (and whatever optional argument you want to include), you substitute an appropriate value. For example, in the FV() function, you substitute `rate` with a decimal value between 0 and 1, `nper` with an integer, and `pmt` with a dollar amount. Arguments can take any of the following forms:

- Literal alphanumeric values

- Expressions

- Cell or range references

- Range names

- Arrays

- The result of another function

The function operates by processing the inputs and then returning a result. For example, the FV() function returns the total value of the investment at the end of the term.

Financial Functions

Excel is loaded with financial features that give you powerful tools for building models that manage both business and personal finances. You can use these functions to calculate such things as the monthly payment on a loan, the future value of an annuity, the internal rate of return of an investment, or the yearly depreciation of an asset.

Most of the formulas you'll work with involve three factors—the *present value* (the amount something is worth now), the *future value* (the amount something is worth in the future), and the interest rate (or the discount rate)—plus two related factors: the *periods*, the number of payments or deposits over the term of the loan or investment, and the *payment*, the amount of money paid out or invested in each period.

When building your financial formulas, you need to ask yourself the following questions:

- Who or what is the subject of the formula? On a mortgage analysis, for example, are you performing the analysis on behalf of yourself or the bank?

- Which way is the money flowing with respect to the subject? For the present value, future value, and payment, enter money that the subject receives as a positive quantity, and enter money that the subject pays out as a negative quantity. For example, if you're the subject of a mortgage analysis, the loan principal (the present value) is a positive number because it's money that you receive from the bank; the payment and the remaining principal (the future value) are negative because they're amounts that you pay to the bank.

- What is the time unit? The underlying unit of both the interest rate and the period must be the same. For example, if you're working with the annual interest rate, you must express the period in years. Similarly, if you're working with monthly periods, you must use a monthly interest rate.

- When are the payments made? Excel differentiates between payments made at the end of each period and those made at the beginning.

Table A.1 gives you a list of all Excel's worksheet functions in the Financial category.

Table A.1 Excel's Financial Functions

Function	What It Does
ACCRINT	Calculates the accrued interest for a security that pays periodic interest
ACCRINTM	Calculates the accrued interest for a security that pays interest at maturity
AMORDEGRC	Calculates the depreciation for each accounting period by using a depreciation coefficient
AMORLINC	Calculates the depreciation for each accounting period
COUPDAYBS	Calculates the number of days from the beginning of the coupon period to the settlement date
COUPDAYS	Calculates the number of days in the coupon period that contains the settlement date
COUPDAYSNC	Calculates the number of days from the settlement date to the next coupon date
COUPNCD	Calculates the next coupon date after the settlement date
COUPNUM	Calculates the number of coupons payable between the settlement date and maturity date
COUPPCD	Calculates the previous coupon date before the settlement date

Function	What It Does
CUMIPMT	Calculates the cumulative interest paid between two periods
CUMPRINC	Calculates the cumulative principal paid on a loan between two periods
DB	Calculates the depreciation of an asset for a specified period by using the fixed-declining balance method
DDB	Calculates the depreciation of an asset for a specified period by using the double-declining balance method or some other method that you specify
DISC	Calculates the discount rate for a security
DOLLARDE	Converts a dollar price from a fractional value to a decimal value
DOLLARFR	Converts a dollar price from a decimal value to a fractional value
DURATION	Calculates the annual duration of a security with periodic interest payments
EFFECT	Calculates the effective annual interest rate
FV	Calculates the future value of an investment
FVSCHEDULE	Calculates the future value of an initial principal after applying a series of compound interest rates
INTRATE	Calculates the interest rate for a fully invested security
IPMT	Calculates the interest portion of a loan payment for a given loan period
IRR	Calculates the internal rate of return for a series of cash flows
ISPMT	Calculates the interest paid during a specific period of an investment
MDURATION	Calculates the Macauley modified duration for a security with an assumed par value of $100
MIRR	Calculates the internal rate of return where positive and negative cash flows are financed at different rates
NOMINAL	Calculates the annual nominal interest rate
NPER	Calculates the number of periods for a loan or investment
NPV	Calculates the net present value of an investment based on a series of periodic cash flows and a discount rate
ODDFPRICE	Calculates the price per $100 face value of a security with an odd first period
ODDFYIELD	Calculates the yield of a security with an odd first period
ODDLPRICE	Calculates the price per $100 face value of a security with an odd last period

Function	What It Does
ODDLYIELD	Calculates the yield of a security with an odd last period
PDURATION	Calculates the number of periods required by an investment to reach a specified value
PMT	Calculates the periodic payment for a loan or annuity
PPMT	Calculates the principle portion of a loan payment for a given loan period
PRICE	Calculates the price per $100 face value of a security that pays periodic interest
PRICEDISC	Calculates the price per $100 face value of a discounted security
PRICEMAT	Calculates the price per $100 face value of a security that pays interest at maturity
PV	Calculates the present value of an investment
RATE	Calculates the interest rate per period of a loan or annuity
RECEIVED	Calculates the amount received at maturity for a fully invested security
RRI	Calculates an equivalent interest rate for the growth of an investment
SLN	Calculates the straight-line depreciation of an asset for one period
SYD	Calculates the sum-of-years' digits depreciation of an asset for a specified period
TBILLEQ	Calculates the bond-equivalent yield for a Treasury bill
TBILLPRICE	Calculates the price per $100 face value for a Treasury bill
TBILLYIELD	Calculates the yield for a Treasury bill
VDB	Calculates the depreciation of an asset for a specified or partial period by using a declining balance method
XIRR	Calculates the internal rate of return for a schedule of cash flows that is not necessarily periodic
XNPV	Calculates the net present value for a schedule of cash flows that is not necessarily periodic
YIELD	Calculates the yield on a security that pays periodic interest
YIELDDISC	Calculates the annual yield for a discounted security; for example, a Treasury bill
YIELDMAT	Calculates the annual yield of a security that pays interest at maturity

Date and Time Functions

The date and time functions enable you to convert dates and times to serial numbers and perform operations on those numbers. This capability is useful for such things as accounts receivable aging, project scheduling, time-management applications, and much more.

Table A.2 gives you a list of all Excel's worksheet functions in the Date and Time category.

Table A.2   Excel's Date and Time Functions

Function	What It Does
DATE	Calculates the serial number of a particular date
DATEVALUE	Converts a date in the form of text to a serial number
DAY	Converts a serial number to a day of the month
DAYS	Calculates the number of days between two dates
DAYS360	Calculates the number of days between two dates based on a 360-day year
EDATE	Calculates the serial number of the date that is the indicated number of months before or after the start date
EOMONTH	Calculates the serial number of the last day of the month before or after a specified number of months
HOUR	Converts a serial number to an hour
ISOWEEKNUM	Calculates the number of the ISO week number of the year for a given date
MINUTE	Converts a serial number to a minute
MONTH	Converts a serial number to a month
NETWORKDAYS	Calculates the number of whole workdays between two dates
NETWORKDAYS.INTL	Calculates the number of whole workdays between two dates using parameters to indicate which and how many days are weekend days
NOW	Calculates the serial number of the current date and time
SECOND	Converts a serial number to a second
TIME	Calculates the serial number of a particular time
TIMEVALUE	Converts a time in the form of text to a serial number
TODAY	Calculates the serial number of today's date

Function	What It Does
WEEKDAY	Converts a serial number to a day of the week
WEEKNUM	Converts a serial number to a number representing where the week falls numerically with a year
WORKDAY	Calculates the serial number of the date before or after a specified number of workdays
WORKDAY.INTL	Calculates the serial number of the date before or after a specified number of workdays using parameters to indicate which and how many days are weekend days
YEAR	Converts a serial number to a year
YEARFRAC	Calculates the year fraction representing the number of whole days between start_date and end_date

Math and Trigonometry Functions

Excel's mathematical underpinnings are revealed when you consider the long list of math-related functions that come with the program. There are functions for basic mathematical operations such as absolute values, lowest and greatest common denominators, square roots, and sums. There are also plenty of high-end operations for things like matrix multiplication, multi-nomials, and sums of squares. Table A.3 lists the Excel math and trigonometry functions.

Table A.3   Excel's Math and Trigonometry Functions

Function	What It Does
ABS	Calculates the absolute value of a number
ACOS	Calculates the arccosine of a number
ACOSH	Calculates the inverse hyperbolic cosine of a number
ACOT	Calculates the arccotangent of a number
ACOTH	Calculates the hyperbolic arccotangent of a number
AGGREGATE	Calculates an aggregate in a list or database
ARABIC	Converts a Roman number to Arabic, as a number
ASIN	Calculates the arcsine of a number
ASINH	Calculates the inverse hyperbolic sine of a number

Function	What It Does
ATAN	Calculates the arctangent of a number
ATAN2	Calculates the arctangent from x- and y-coordinates
ATANH	Calculates the inverse hyperbolic tangent of a number
BASE	Converts a number into a text representation with the given radix (base)
CEILING.MATH	Rounds a number up, to the nearest integer or to the nearest multiple of significance
COMBIN	Calculates the number of combinations for a given number of objects
COMBINA	Calculates the number of combinations with repetitions for a given number of items
COS	Calculates the cosine of a number
COSH	Calculates the hyperbolic cosine of a number
COT	Calculates the cotangent of an angle
COTH	Calculates the hyperbolic cotangent of a number
CSC	Calculates the cosecant of an angle
CSCH	Calculates the hyperbolic cosecant of an angle
DECIMAL	Converts a text representation of a number in a given base into a decimal number
DEGREES	Converts radians to degrees
EVEN	Rounds a number up to the nearest even integer
EXP	Calculates e raised to the power of a given number
FACT	Calculates the factorial of a number
FACTDOUBLE	Calculates the double factorial of a number
FLOOR.MATH	Rounds a number down, to the nearest integer or to the nearest multiple of significance
GCD	Calculates the greatest common divisor
INT	Rounds a number down to the nearest integer
LCM	Calculates the least common multiple
LN	Calculates the natural logarithm of a number
LOG	Calculates the logarithm of a number to a specified base
LOG10	Calculates the base-10 logarithm of a number
MDETERM	Calculates the matrix determinant of an array

Function	What It Does
MINVERSE	Calculates the matrix inverse of an array
MMULT	Calculates the matrix product of two arrays
MOD	Calculates the remainder from division
MROUND	Calculates a number rounded to the desired multiple
MULTINOMIAL	Calculates the multinomial of a set of numbers
MUNIT	Calculates the unit matrix or the specified dimension
ODD	Rounds a number up to the nearest odd integer
PI	Calculates the value of pi
POWER	Calculates the result of a number raised to a power
PRODUCT	Multiplies its arguments
QUOTIENT	Calculates the integer portion of a division
RADIANS	Converts degrees to radians
RAND	Calculates a random number between 0 and 1
RANDBETWEEN	Calculates a random number between the numbers you specify
ROMAN	Converts an Arabic numeral to Roman, as text
ROUND	Rounds a number to a specified number of digits
ROUNDDOWN	Rounds a number down, toward zero
ROUNDUP	Rounds a number up, away from zero
SEC	Calculates the secant of an angle
SECH	Calculates the hyperbolic secant of an angle
SERIESSUM	Calculates the sum of a power series based on the formula
SIGN	Calculates the sign of a number
SIN	Calculates the sine of the given angle
SINH	Calculates the hyperbolic sine of a number
SQRT	Calculates a positive square root
SQRTPI	Calculates the square root of (number * pi)
SUBTOTAL	Calculates a subtotal in a list or database
SUM	Adds its arguments
SUMIF	Adds the cells specified by a given criteria
SUMIFS	Adds the cells in a range that meet multiple criteria

Function	What It Does
SUMPRODUCT	Calculates the sum of the products of corresponding array components
SUMSQ	Calculates the sum of the squares of the arguments
SUMX2MY2	Calculates the sum of the difference of squares of corresponding values in two arrays
SUMX2PY2	Calculates the sum of the sum of squares of corresponding values in two arrays
SUMXMY2	Calculates the sum of squares of differences of corresponding values in two arrays
TAN	Calculates the tangent of a number
TANH	Calculates the hyperbolic tangent of a number
TRUNC	Truncates a number to an integer

Statistical Functions

Excel's statistical functions calculate all the standard statistical measures such as average, maximum, minimum, and standard deviation. For most of the statistical functions, you supply a list of values (called a *sample* or *population*). You can enter individual values or cells, or you can specify a range. Table A.4 lists all Excel's worksheet functions in the Statistical category.

Table A.4   Excel's Statistical Functions

Function	What It Does
AVEDEV	Calculates the average of the absolute deviations of data points from their mean
AVERAGE	Calculates the average of its arguments
AVERAGEA	Calculates the average of its arguments, including numbers, text, and logical values
AVERAGEIF	Calculates the average (arithmetic mean) of all the cells in a range that meet a given criteria
AVERAGEIFS	Calculates the average (arithmetic mean) of all cells that meet multiple criteria
BETA.DIST	Calculates the beta cumulative distribution
BETA.INV	Calculates the inverse of the cumulative distribution function for a specified beta distribution

Function	What It Does
BINOM.DIST	Calculates the individual term binomial distribution probability
BINOM.DIST.RANGE	Calculates the probability of a trial result using a binomial distribution
BINOM.INV	Calculates the smallest value for which the cumulative binomial distribution is less than or equal to a criterion value
CHISQ.DIST	Calculates the cumulative beta probability density
CHISQ.DIST.RT	Calculates the one-tailed probability of the chi-squared distribution
CHISQ.INV	Calculates the cumulative beta probability density
CHISQ.INV.RT	Calculates the inverse of the one-tailed probability of the chi-squared distribution
CHISQ.TEST	Calculates the test for independence
CONFIDENCE.NORM	Calculates the confidence interval for a population mean
CONFIDENCE.T	Calculates the confidence interval for a population mean, using a Student's t distribution
CORREL	Calculates the correlation coefficient between two data sets
COUNT	Counts how many numbers are in the list of arguments
COUNTA	Counts how many values are in the list of arguments
COUNTBLANK	Counts the number of blank cells within a range
COUNTIF	Counts the number of cells within a range that meet the given criteria
COUNTIFS	Counts the number of cells within a range that meet multiple criteria
COVARIANCE.P	Calculates covariance, the average of the products of paired deviations
COVARIANCE.S	Calculates the sample covariance, the average of the products deviations for each data point pair in two data sets
DEVSQ	Calculates the sum of squares of deviations
EXPON.DIST	Calculates the exponential distribution
F.DIST	Calculates the F probability distribution
F.DIST.RT	Calculates the right-tailed F probability distribution

Function	What It Does
F.INV	Calculates the inverse of the F probability distribution
F.INV.RT	Calculates the right-tailed inverse of the F probability distribution
F.TEST	Calculates the result of an F-test
FISHER	Calculates the Fisher transformation
FISHERINV	Calculates the inverse of the Fisher transformation
FORECAST.CONFINT	Calculates a confidence interval for the specified forecasted value
FORECAST.ETS	Calculates a forecasted value using exponential smoothing
FORECAST.ETS.SEASONALITY	Calculates the length of the repetitive (seasonal) pattern for a specific time series
FORECAST.ETS.STAT	Calculates a specified statistic for a forecast
FORECAST.LINEAR	Calculates a forecasted value using a linear trend
FREQUENCY	Calculates a frequency distribution as a vertical array
GAMMA	Calculates the Gamma function value
GAMMA.DIST	Calculates the gamma distribution
GAMMA.INV	Calculates the inverse of the gamma cumulative distribution
GAMMALN	Calculates the natural logarithm of the gamma function, $\gamma(x)$
GAMMALN.PRECISE	Calculates the natural logarithm of the gamma function, $\gamma(x)$ (in certain cases, this function might produce a more precise answer than GAMMALN)
GAUSS	Calculates 0.5 less than the standard normal cumulative distribution
GEOMEAN	Calculates the geometric mean
GROWTH	Calculates values along an exponential trend
HARMEAN	Calculates the harmonic mean
HYPGEOM.DIST	Calculates the hypergeometric distribution
INTERCEPT	Calculates the intercept of the linear regression line
KURT	Calculates the kurtosis of a data set
LARGE	Calculates the k-th largest value in a data set

Function	What It Does
LINEST	Calculates the parameters of a linear trend
LOGEST	Calculates the parameters of an exponential trend
LOGNORM.DIST	Calculates the cumulative lognormal distribution
LOGNORM.INV	Calculates the inverse of the lognormal cumulative distribution
MAX	Calculates the maximum value in a list of arguments
MAXA	Calculates the maximum value in a list of arguments, including numbers, text, and logical values
MEDIAN	Calculates the median of the given numbers
MIN	Calculates the minimum value in a list of arguments
MINA	Calculates the smallest value in a list of arguments, including numbers, text, and logical values
MODE.MULT	Calculates a vertical array of the most frequently occurring or repetitive values in an array or range of data
MODE.SNGL	Calculates the most common value in a data set
NEGBINOM.DIST	Calculates the negative binomial distribution
NORM.DIST	Calculates the normal cumulative distribution
NORM.INV	Calculates the inverse of the normal cumulative distribution
NORM.S.DIST	Calculates the standard normal cumulative distribution
NORM.S.INV	Calculates the inverse of the standard normal cumulative distribution
PEARSON	Calculates the Pearson product moment correlation coefficient
PERCENTILE.EXC	Calculates the k-th percentile of values in a range, where k is in the range 0..1, exclusive
PERCENTILE.INC	Calculates the k-th percentile of values in a range
PERCENTRANK.EXC	Calculates the rank of a value in a data set as a percentage (0..1, exclusive) of the data set
PERCENTRANK.INC	Calculates the percentage rank of a value in a data set
PERMUT	Calculates the number of permutations for a given number of objects
PERMUTATIONA	Calculates the number of permutations for a given number of objects (with repetitions) that can be selected from the total objects

Function	What It Does
PHI	Calculates the value of the density function for a standard normal distribution
POISSON.DIST	Calculates the Poisson distribution
PROB	Calculates the probability that values in a range are between two limits
QUARTILE.EXC	Calculates the quartile of the data set, based on percentile values from 0..1, exclusive
QUARTILE.INC	Calculates the quartile of a data set
RANK.AVG	Calculates the rank of a number in a list of numbers; for values with the same rank, the average rank is returned
RANK.EQ	Calculates the rank of a number in a list of numbers; equal numbers are given the same rank
RSQ	Calculates the square of the Pearson product moment correlation coefficient
SKEW	Calculates the skewness of a distribution
SKEW.P	Calculates the skewness of a distribution based on a population: a characterization of the degree of asymmetry of a distribution around its mean
SLOPE	Calculates the slope of the linear regression line
SMALL	Calculates the k-th smallest value in a data set
STANDARDIZE	Calculates a normalized value
STDEV.P	Calculates standard deviation based on the entire population
STDEV.S	Estimates standard deviation based on a sample
STDEVA	Estimates standard deviation based on a sample, including numbers, text, and logical values
STDEVPA	Calculates standard deviation based on the entire population, including numbers, text, and logical values
STEYX	Calculates the standard error of the predicted y-value for each x in the regression
T.DIST	Calculates the Percentage Points (probability) for the Student t-distribution
T.DIST.2T	Calculates the Percentage Points (probability) for the two-tailed Student t-distribution
T.DIST.RT	Calculates the Student's t-distribution

Function	What It Does
T.INV	Calculates the t-value of the Student's t-distribution as a function of the probability and the degrees of freedom
T.INV.2T	Calculates the inverse of the Student's t-distribution
T.TEST	Calculates the probability associated with a Student's t-test
TREND	Calculates values along a linear trend
TRIMMEAN	Calculates the mean of the interior of a data set
VAR.P	Calculates variance based on the entire population
VAR.S	Estimates variance based on a sample
VARA	Estimates variance based on a sample, including numbers, text, and logical values
VARPA	Calculates variance based on the entire population, including numbers, text, and logical values
WEIBULL.DIST	Calculates the Weibull distribution
Z.TEST	Calculates the one-tailed probability-value of a z-test

Lookup and Reference Functions

Getting the meaning of a word in the dictionary is always a two-step process: First, you look up the word and then you read its definition. This idea of looking something up to retrieve some related information is at the heart of many spreadsheet operations. For example, the value of one argument often depends on the value of another. Here are some examples:

- In a formula that calculates an invoice total, the customer's discount might depend on the number of units purchased.

- In a formula that charges interest on overdue accounts, the interest percentage might depend on the number of days each invoice is overdue.

- In a formula that calculates employee bonuses as a percentage of salary, the percentage might depend on how much the employee improved upon the given budget.

The usual way to handle these kinds of problems is to look up the appropriate value, and Excel offers a number of functions that enable you to perform lookup operations in your worksheet models. Table A.5 lists Excel's lookup functions.

Table A.5   Excel's Lookup and Reference Functions

Function	What It Does
ADDRESS	Calculates a reference as text to a single cell in a worksheet
AREAS	Calculates the number of areas in a reference
CHOOSE	Selects a value from a list of values
COLUMN	Calculates the column number of a reference
COLUMNS	Calculates the number of columns in a reference
FORMULATEXT	Calculates the formula at the given reference as text
GETPIVOTDATA	Calculates data stored in a PivotTable report
HLOOKUP	Looks in the top row of an array and returns the value of the indicated cell
HYPERLINK	Creates a shortcut that opens a document stored on a network or on the Internet
INDEX	Uses an index to choose a value from a reference or array
INDIRECT	Calculates a reference indicated by a text value
LOOKUP	Looks up values in a vector or array
MATCH	Looks up values in a reference or array
OFFSET	Calculates a reference offset from a given reference
ROW	Calculates the row number of a reference
ROWS	Calculates the number of rows in a reference
RTD	Retrieves real-time data from a program that supports COM automation
TRANSPOSE	Calculates the transpose of an array
VLOOKUP	Looks in the first column of an array and moves across the row to return the value of a cell

Database Functions

To get more control over your table analysis, you can use Excel's *database functions*. Table A.6 offers a complete list of Excel's worksheet functions in the Database category.

Table A.6 Excel's Database Functions

Function	What It Does
DAVERAGE	Calculates the average of selected database entries
DCOUNT	Counts the cells that contain numbers in a database
DCOUNTA	Counts nonblank cells in a database
DGET	Extracts from a database a single record that matches the specified criteria
DMAX	Calculates the maximum value from selected database entries
DMIN	Calculates the minimum value from selected database entries
DPRODUCT	Multiplies the values in a particular field of records that match the criteria in a database
DSTDEV	Estimates the standard deviation based on a sample of selected database entries
DSTDEVP	Calculates the standard deviation based on the entire population of selected database entries
DSUM	Adds the numbers in the field column of records in the database that match the criteria
DVAR	Estimates variance based on a sample from selected database entries
DVARP	Calculates variance based on the entire population of selected database entries

Text Functions

In Excel, *text* is any collection of alphanumeric characters that isn't a numeric value, a date or time value, or a formula. Words, names, and labels are all obviously text values, but so are cell values preceded by an apostrophe (') or formatted as Text. Text values are also called *strings*. Text formulas consist only of the concatenation operator (&) used to combine two or more strings into a larger string.

Excel's text functions enable you to take text formulas to a more useful level by giving you numerous ways to manipulate strings. With these functions, you can convert numbers to strings, change lowercase letters to uppercase (and vice versa), compare two strings, and more. Table A.7 gives you a list of all Excel's worksheet functions in the Text category.

Table A.7 Excel's Text Functions

Function	What It Does
BAHTTEXT	Converts a number to text, using the baht currency format
CHAR	Calculates the character specified by the code number
CLEAN	Removes all nonprintable characters from a text string
CODE	Calculates a numeric code for the first character in a text string
CONCATENATE	Joins several text items into one text item
DOLLAR	Converts a number to text, using the $ (dollar) currency format
EXACT	Checks to see whether two text values are identical
FIND	Finds one text value within another (case-sensitive)
FIXED	Formats a number as text with a fixed number of decimals
LEFT	Calculates the leftmost characters from a text value
LEN	Calculates the number of characters in a text string
LOWER	Converts text to lowercase
MID	Calculates a specific number of characters from a text string starting at the position you specify
NUMBERVALUE	Converts text to number in a locale-independent manner
PROPER	Capitalizes the first letter in each word of a text value
REPLACE	Replaces characters within text
REPT	Repeats text a given number of times
RIGHT	Calculates the rightmost characters from a text value
SEARCH	Finds one text value within another (not case-sensitive)
SUBSTITUTE	Substitutes new text for old text in a text string
T	Converts its arguments to text
TEXT	Formats a number and converts it to text
TRIM	Removes spaces from text
UNICHAR	Calculates the Unicode character referenced by the given numeric value
UNICODE	Calculates the number (code point) that corresponds to the first character of the text
UPPER	Converts text to uppercase
VALUE	Converts a text argument to a number

Logical Functions

You can bring some measure of "intelligence" to your worksheets, meaning your formulas can test the values in cells and ranges, and then return results based on those tests. This is all done with Excel's logical functions, which are designed to create decision-making formulas. For example, you can test cell contents to see whether they're numbers or labels, or you can test formula results for errors. Table A.8 summarizes Excel's logical functions.

Table A.8   Excel's Logical Functions

Function	What It Does
AND	Returns TRUE if all the arguments are true
FALSE	Returns FALSE
IF	Performs a logical test and returns a value based on the result
IFERROR	Calculates a value you specify if a formula evaluates to an error; otherwise, returns the result of the formula
IFNA	Calculates the value you specify if a formula evaluates to #N/A; otherwise returns the result of the formula
NOT	Reverses the logical value of the argument
OR	Returns TRUE if any argument is true
TRUE	Returns TRUE
XOR	Calculates a logical exclusive OR of all arguments

Information Functions

Excel's information functions return data concerning cells, worksheets, and formula results. Table A.9 lists all the information functions.

Table A.9   Excel's Information Functions

Function	Description
CELL	Returns information about various cell attributes, including formatting, contents, and location
ERROR.TYPE	Returns a number corresponding to an error type
INFO	Returns information about the operating system and environment

Function	Description
ISBLANK	Returns TRUE if the value is blank
ISERR	Returns TRUE if the value is any error value except #NA
ISERROR	Returns TRUE if the value is any error value
ISEVEN	Returns TRUE if the number is even
ISFORMULA	Returns TRUE if the referenced cell contains a formula
ISLOGICAL	Returns TRUE if the value is a logical value
ISNA	Returns TRUE if the value is the #NA error value
ISNONTEXT	Returns TRUE if the value is not text
ISNUMBER	Returns TRUE if the value is a number
ISODD	Returns TRUE if the number is odd
ISREF	Returns TRUE if the value is a reference
ISTEXT	Returns TRUE if the value is text
N	Returns the value converted to a number (a serial number if value is a date, 1 if value is TRUE, 0 if value is any other non-numeric; note that N() exists only for compatibility with other spreadsheets and is rarely used in Excel)
NA	Returns the error value #NA
SHEET	Calculates the sheet number of the referenced sheet
SHEETS	Calculates the number of sheets in a reference
TYPE	Returns a number that indicates the data type of the *value*: 1 for a number, 2 for text, 4 for a logical value, 8 for a formula, 16 for an error, or 64 for an array

Engineering Functions

Excel offers quite a few functions of use to engineers. Table A.10 gives you a list of all Excel's worksheet functions in the Engineering category.

Table A.10   Excel's Engineering Functions

Function	What It Does
BESSELI	Calculates the modified Bessel function $In(x)$
BESSELJ	Calculates the Bessel function $Jn(x)$
BESSELK	Calculates the modified Bessel function $Kn(x)$

Function	What It Does
BESSELY	Calculates the Bessel function $Yn(x)$
BIN2DEC	Converts a binary number to decimal
BIN2HEX	Converts a binary number to hexadecimal
BIN2OCT	Converts a binary number to octal
BITAND	Calculates a Bitwise And of two numbers
BITLSHIFT	Calculates a value number shifted left by shift_amount bits
BITOR	Calculates a bitwise OR of two numbers
BITRSHIFT	Calculates a value number shifted right by shift_amount bits
BITXOR	Calculates a bitwise Exclusive Or of two numbers
COMPLEX	Converts real and imaginary coefficients into a complex number
CONVERT	Converts a number from one measurement system to another
DEC2BIN	Converts a decimal number to binary
DEC2HEX	Converts a decimal number to hexadecimal
DEC2OCT	Converts a decimal number to octal
DELTA	Tests whether two values are equal
ERF	Calculates the error function integrated between 0 and the specified value
ERF.PRECISE	Calculates the error function integrated between 0 and the specified value (in some cases, this function returns more precise values than the ERF function)
ERFC	Calculates the complementary error function integrated between x and infinity
ERFC.PRECISE	Calculates the complementary function integrated between x and infinity (in some cases, this function returns more precise values than the ERFC function)
GESTEP	Tests whether a number is greater than a threshold value
HEX2BIN	Converts a hexadecimal number to binary
HEX2DEC	Converts a hexadecimal number to decimal
HEX2OCT	Converts a hexadecimal number to octal
IMABS	Calculates the absolute value (modulus) of a complex number
IMAGINARY	Calculates the imaginary coefficient of a complex number
IMARGUMENT	Calculates the argument theta, an angle expressed in radians

Function	What It Does
IMCONJUGATE	Calculates the complex conjugate of a complex number
IMCOS	Calculates the cosine of a complex number
IMCOSH	Calculates the hyperbolic cosine of a complex number
IMCOT	Calculates the cotangent of a complex number
IMCSC	Calculates the cosecant of a complex number
IMCSCH	Calculates the hyperbolic cosecant of a complex number
IMDIV	Calculates the quotient of two complex numbers
IMEXP	Calculates the exponential of a complex number
IMLN	Calculates the natural logarithm of a complex number
IMLOG10	Calculates the base-10 logarithm of a complex number
IMLOG2	Calculates the base-2 logarithm of a complex number
IMPOWER	Calculates a complex number raised to an integer power
IMPRODUCT	Calculates the product of 2 to 255 complex numbers
IMREAL	Calculates the real coefficient of a complex number
IMSEC	Calculates the secant of a complex number
IMSECH	Calculates the hyperbolic secant of a complex number
IMSIN	Calculates the sine of a complex number
IMSINH	Calculates the hyperbolic sine of a complex number
IMSQRT	Calculates the square root of a complex number
IMSUB	Calculates the difference between two complex numbers
IMSUM	Calculates the sum of complex numbers
IMTAN	Calculates the tangent of a complex number
OCT2BIN	Converts an octal number to binary
OCT2DEC	Converts an octal number to decimal
OCT2HEX	Converts an octal number to hexadecimal

Cube Functions

If you work with the multidimensional data structures called cubes, Excel offers a few functions that can make cube analysis easier. Table A.11 gives you a list of all Excel's worksheet functions in the Cube category.

Table A.11   Excel's Cube Functions

Function	What It Does
CUBEKPIMEMBER	Returns a key performance indicator (KPI) property, and displays the KPI name in the cell
CUBEMEMBER	Returns a member or tuple from the cube
CUBEMEMBERPROPERTY	Returns the value of a member property from the cube
CUBERANKEDMEMBER	Returns the *n*th, or ranked, member in a set
CUBESET	Defines a calculated set of members or tuples by sending a set expression to the cube on the server, which creates the set, and then returns that set to Excel
CUBESETCOUNT	Calculates the number of items in a set
CUBEVALUE	Returns an aggregated value from the cube

Compatibility Functions

Excel has many functions that have been replaced by newer versions, and you can still access those old functions if you need to create a model that work in older versions of Excel. Table A.12 gives you a list of all Excel's worksheet functions in the Compatibility category.

Table A.12   Excel's Compatibility Functions

Function	What It Does
BETADIST	Calculates the beta cumulative distribution
BETAINV	Calculates the inverse of the cumulative distribution function for a specified beta distribution
BINOMDIST	Calculates the individual term binomial distribution probability
CEILING	Rounds a number up to the nearest integer or to the nearest multiple of significance

Function	What It Does
CHIDIST	Calculates the cumulative beta probability density
CHIINV	Calculates the cumulative beta probability density
CHITEST	Calculates the test for independence
CONFIDENCE	Calculates the confidence interval for a population mean
COVAR	Calculates covariance, the average of the products of paired deviations
CRITBINOM	Calculates the smallest value for which the cumulative binomial distribution is greater than or equal to a criterion value
EXPONDIST	Calculates the exponential distribution
FDIST	Calculates the F probability distribution
FINV	Calculates the inverse of the F probability distribution
FLOOR	Rounds a number down to the nearest integer or to the nearest multiple of significance
FORECAST	Calculates a forecasted value using a linear trend
FTEST	Calculates the result of an F-test
GAMMADIST	Calculates the gamma distribution
GAMMAINV	Calculates the inverse of the gamma cumulative distribution
HYPGEOMDIST	Calculates the hypergeometric distribution
LOGINV	Calculates the inverse of the lognormal cumulative distribution
LOGNORMDIST	Calculates the cumulative lognormal distribution
MODE	Calculates the most common value in a data set
NEGBINOMDIST	Calculates the negative binomial distribution
NORMDIST	Calculates the normal cumulative distribution
NORMINV	Calculates the inverse of the normal cumulative distribution
NEGBINOM.DIST	Calculates the negative binomial distribution
NORM.DIST	Calculates the normal cumulative distribution
NORM.INV	Calculates the inverse of the normal cumulative distribution
NORMSDIST	Calculates the standard normal cumulative distribution
NORMSINV	Calculates the inverse of the standard normal cumulative distribution
PERCENTILE	Calculates the k-th percentile of values in a range, where k is in the range 0..1, exclusive

Function	What It Does
PERCENTRANK	Calculates the rank of a value in a data set as a percentage (0..1, exclusive) of the data set
POISSON	Calculates the Poisson distribution
QUARTILE	Calculates the quartile of the data set, based on percentile values from 0..1, exclusive
RANK	Calculates the rank of a number in a list of numbers
STDEV	Estimates standard deviation based on a sample
STDEVP	Calculates standard deviation based on the entire population
TDIST	Calculates the Percentage Points (probability) for the Student t-distribution
TINV	Calculates the t-value of the Student's t-distribution as a function of the probability and the degrees of freedom
TTEST	Calculates the probability associated with a Student's t-test
VAR	Estimates variance based on a sample
VARP	Calculates variance based on the entire population
WEIBULL	Calculates the Weibull distribution
ZTEST	Calculates the one-tailed probability-value of a z-test

Web Functions

Excel has a few functions that enable you to incorporate web-based data into your spreadsheets. Table A.13 lists all Excel's worksheet functions in the web category.

Table A.13   Excel's Web Functions

Function	What It Does
ENCODEURL	Returns a URL-encoded string
FILTERXML	Returns specific data from the XML content by using the specified XPath
WEBSERVICE	Returns data from a web service

Index

Symbols

F

REGISTER THIS PRODUCT
SAVE 35%*
ON YOUR NEXT PURCHASE!

How to Register Your Product

- Go to quepublishing.com/register
- Sign in or create an account
- Enter the 10- or 13-digit ISBN that appears on the back cover of your product

Benefits of Registering

- Ability to download product updates
- Access to bonus chapters and workshop files
- A 35% coupon to be used on your next purchase – valid for 30 days
  To obtain your coupon, click on "Manage Codes" in the right column of your Account page
- Receive special offers on new editions and related Que products

Please note that the benefits for registering may vary by product. Benefits will be listed on your Account page under Registered Products.

We value and respect your privacy. Your email address will not be sold to any third party company.

* 35% discount code presented after product registration is valid on most print books, eBooks, and full-course videos sold on QuePublishing.com. Discount may not be combined with any other offer and is not redeemable for cash. Discount code expires after 30 days from the time of product registration. Offer subject to change.

quepublishing.com